A
POSITIVE
LABOR MARKET
POLICY

A
POSITIVE
LABOR MARKET
POLICY

Policy Premises for the
Development, Operation, and Integration
of the
Employment and Manpower Services

E. WIGHT BAKKE

Sterling Professor of Economics
and Industrial Administration
Yale University

CHARLES E. MERRILL BOOKS, INC.   COLUMBUS, OHIO

LIBRARY OF CONGRESS CATALOG CARD NUMBER: 63-19892

PRINTED IN THE UNITED STATES OF AMERICA

Preface

This book concerns the premises that underlie decision-making on policy and program in the operation and development of the Employment and Manpower Services. It did not, however, begin as such. It began simply as an effort to outline some areas for research relative to the functioning of the Employment Service in the labor market. The criticisms of the Employment Service in recent years, brought to a resounding climax by former Secretary of Labor Mitchell's criticism of and challenge to the administrators of that service in Chicago, started a chain reaction of questions in interested circles, which in summary added up to the question, "What's wrong with the Employment Service?" The controversy renewed my interest in this field of public action, an interest that developed 30 years ago when I was engaged in the study of the unemployed in Great Britain.

The first step in research is to know what the researcher is solving for. I therefore began an exploration of the documents and visited the administrators of the Employment Service at the federal, state, and local levels. I also spoke with the "customers" and critics of the Service, in this country and abroad, with the object of working out a definition of what the problem was. I soon came to two conclusions. First, the problem was not limited to the Employment Service, but involved the whole set of Employment and Manpower Services and their adaptation to the changing character of factors in the labor market and the increasing significance of the impact of those factors on the whole range of public efforts to get an economy into high gear and moving toward full employment and maximum production. Second, the operating problems stemmed basically from the lack of even an approximation to consensus as to what the fundamental and central mission and operational field of these services had been, were, and could be.

This second conclusion suggested the desirability of convening a group of high-level policy makers for a series of conferences on the premises that governed their outlook on and approach to the operation and development of the services. The idea was enthusiastically accepted by Brookings Institution. A group of 25 people from the Senate and the House, from Congressmen to legislative assistants; the top employment and manpower officials in the Department of Labor; administrators of the state employment security offices; and leaders in labor, business, and academic circles were invited to, and agreed to attend, a series of bi-weekly conferences at Brookings during January and February 1963. I prepared the working papers for those conferences. At the end it was agreed that it would be desirable to rework for publication those papers with the benefit of the discussions which took place at Brookings so that the issues raised might have wider consideration and discussion.

It is regrettable that the number which could effectively participate in working conferences of this sort was so limited. Particularly would it have been desirable to have more representation of the state administrators. But they were all sent an outline of the issues to be discussed, and a large number of them held conferences with their staffs and sent in extensive commentaries, the content of which was most useful in developing the working papers.

Needless to say, my sincere gratitude is extended to all persons, here and abroad, who contributed to the substance of the papers. The officers of the employment and manpower services from the national, to state, and local offices in the United States, in Sweden, in Great Britain, and at the European Economic Community Headquarters in Brussels were generous with their time, information, and encouragement. Special thanks are due those conferees at the Brookings Conferences whose incisive criticisms of the papers were most welcome and valuable.

Those who are acquainted with the literature and activities in the field will recognize the debt I owe to Gösta Rehn, the economic philosopher and leading architect of Sweden's "positive labor market policy," with whom I have shared ideas on these matters since the middle 1940's, and to Bertil Ollson, the thoughtful and dynamic director of the Swedish Labor Market Board.

James Mitchell of Brookings Institution, who managed the conferences and led the discussions, and his staff members contributed to the intellectual product of, as well as to the organization arrangements for, the conferences. The entire staff at Brookings provided us with the most satisfactory services any such conferences could hope to have.

It goes without saying that none of those whose contributions were so helpful can be held responsible for the positions taken or for any errors of omission or commission in this book. These must lie entirely at my own door.

The members of the Ford Foundation, who supported the whole project with funds, with suggestions, with enthusiastic interest, and with freedom to the author to pursue his own course, are owed special thanks.

My secretary, Miss Edna Vreeland, and those who labored tirelessly through the numerous revisions and retyping of the manuscript are among the most important contributors to the publication of this book.

E. Wight Bakke

New Haven
April 1963

Table of Contents

ix

A
POSITIVE
LABOR MARKET
POLICY

SIGNIFICANCE OF POLICY PREMISES

Chapter One Employment and Manpower Services are indispensable facilities for any private or public effort to plan for and achieve full employment, stability, and growth in the economy. They are indispensable to achieving, within the limits set and opportunities provided by that economy, a just, rewarding, and satisfying distribution, among the workers of the country, of the chance to work and live by that work. The efficient and just functioning of a free economy requires that manpower of the quantity and quality needed shall be developed, that it shall be fully and efficiently utilized, and that it be available when and where needed to make its maximum contribution. These are the tasks of the Employment and Manpower Services.

The government of every industrial nation operates an Employment Service. They all have one function in common: to find jobs for workers seeking work and to fill jobs for employers seeking workers. Beyond that, however, there are wide differences in the range of their activities and in the effectiveness of their operations. In no country is the Employment Service carried on merely in the original sense of a local "labor exchange," matching job orders from employers with job applications from workers. Additional services, such as vocational and occupational testing, counseling, education and training, retraining of the unemployed, rehabilitation of handicapped workers, the gathering and distribution of labor market information, participation in community redevelopment projects, ancillary services to employers, some form of tide-over benefits for the unemployed, the payment of maintenance and moving expenses to workers, are to varying degrees and in varying patterns carried on either within the Employment Service agency or by other closely related manpower and labor market agencies.

To avoid confusion we shall use the singular term *Employment Service* to mean the set of activities associated with matching men

1

and jobs, and the plural term *Employment and Manpower Services* to mean the total range of employment related manpower and labor market activities. Countries differ greatly in the emphasis given to these several types of services and in the organizational arrangements for performing them.

Equally important are differences in the degree to which people who manage and use the Employment and Manpower Services in the several countries consider them up-to-date, effectively adapted to the realities of current and future labor market conditions, and as useful and significant contributors to the totality of efforts made by governments to encourage a just, dynamic, and expanding economy. Resulting in part from these differences are great variations in the *esprit de corps* of those who operate the services, in their enthusiasm and initiative, and in their sense of being on top of their problems.

What is the clue to these differences? After exploring the operation of the Employment and Manpower Services in the United States, England, Sweden, and the Common Market countries, both by personal visits and examination of the written evidence as to past and present operations, we should like to suggest this answer: the differences noted stem from differing concepts of the central mission, operational field, and status assigned to the Employment and Manpower Services and accepted by their operators, by government executives and legislators, and by the "customers" of the services as guides to their activity.

Back of every major decision affecting the operation and development of those services, back of every assignment or withdrawal of functions, back of every decision by potential customers to use or not to use the services, back of every favorable or unfavorable critcism, can be sensed an evident or hidden premise as to the mission, operational field, and status of those services. The concept of the mission itself is central. By reference to that mission, judgments are made as to the justification for the services, the resources it is necessary and desirable to allocate to them, the status and organizational relation they should occupy with respect to other agencies of government and to private agencies and associations, the operational field in which they are expected to function, and the kinds of emphases and programs it is important to employ in their operation. The evidence which has come to hand in the course of our study of these services in the United States reinforces the importance of the influence of the concept of central mission.

It was necessary before beginning that study to define the problem. Both academic and practical problem solvers have learned from experience that research and study are likely to be fruitless unless first they are clear about what they are solving for. The further we proceeded, the more clear it became that, in the United States, one problem stands out from many others as basic and critical: there exists no approximate consensus among those involved about the central mission and role of the Employment and related Manpower Services.

Decisions on policy and practice initiated within the government, and suggestions and pressures for change from interested parties have been and continue to be made on the basis of policy premises which are varied, shifting, and frequently conflicting. Since the operation and development of the Employment and Manpower Services must necessarily take into account the ideas, interests, and actions of many people, the result of this lack of even an approximation to consensus among them is a blurred collective concept of what these services are, what they should do and how, and what they should become.

Those responsible for decisions and actions relative to these services are concerned about this central problem. If the Employment and Manpower Services lack the sense of purpose and direction provided by clear and commonly accepted policy premises, we can expect low morale among administrators, confusion and ineffectiveness in administration, additions to the duties of the services irrelevant to their appropriate mission, and a failure to realize their potential and necessary contribution to the efficiency, justice, and growth of the nation's economy.

This state of confusion on policy premises is not surprising. Historically, since the establishment of a few municipal employment exchanges, followed by the first state employment office in Ohio in 1890, the eventual establishment in 1933 of the Federal-State Employment Service, and the numerous expansions of that service, the development of policy premises has proceeded in a more or less haphazard way. It has proceeded from the setting up of *action programs* of various sorts and with important public objectives, to the debate over practical choices among *directions and emphases,* to an inevitable *variety* of concepts as to the *central and basic mission* of the Employment and Manpower Services.

There has been great value in this pragmatic grass roots approach. That experience and the debate accompanying it have enriched our understanding of the alternatives available and the consequences which follow from the choices made. Today, however, we are faced with problems—in the development of our economy, in its relations to other economies, and in the impact of its operations on our people—which are different, not merely in degree, but in kind and intensity, from these matters during the period of development of the services to their present stage. They may be sufficiently different so that we could profit from a stock-taking and a rethinking of these premises, starting in the other direction, i.e., from premises with respect to the concept of mission and character, to operating direction and emphasis, to types and priorities in programs, and then to the consideration of organizational and administrative problems in the light of these premises. When the critical issues and alternatives at each of these levels of premises are considered, it will be clear that choices at each level will exercise constraints on the scope and kinds of choices which can be made at the next level.

The objective of this book is to bring these premises out into the open and to consider the consequences of action based on them. Chapters 2 through 4 deal with premises relative to the *central mission* and role of the services; Chaps. 5 and 6 with premises relative to their *operational field*; Chap. 7 with premises relative to their *status*; and Chaps. 8, 9, and 10 with premises related to their *co-ordination and integration*.

The attention of the next three chapters, then, is focused on policy premises with respect to the *central mission* of the Employment and Manpower Services.

Experience in the United States and abroad points to two critical questions about that central mission, the answers to which, when translated into action, have far-reaching consequences for the kind and quality of the role those services come to play in the economy and society:

1. The Employment and Manpower Services have important potential as instruments for accomplishing two very important social objectives: (a) an increase in the strength, stability, and growth rate of the nation's economy, and (b) an increase in the welfare of the nation's individual people and in their relief when this welfare is inadequate. Which of these objectives is to define the basic and central mission of the services through the accomplishment of which the other is achieved as a by-product?

2. Occupational, industrial, and geographical movement of workers is needed in order to achieve both of these objectives. That movement may be achieved through the operations of a managed or of a "free-choice" labor market. Shall it be a central mission of the Employment and Manpower Services to "manage" this movement or to facilitate freedom of choice about movement of jobs and workers by removing obstacles to a genuinely "free" choice?

We turn to a consideration of these two questions.

ECONOMIC AND SOCIAL
WELFARE OBJECTIVES

Chapter Two
The first question is what relative emphasis is to be placed on fundamentally economic objectives and on social welfare and relief objectives. Any agency, particularly a government agency, which deals with the employment of human beings must necessarily be concerned with both. Governments are expected to be, with good reason. Both objectives are comprehended in the constitutional mandate to government to promote the "general welfare." Work is not merely a producer of goods and services for the society and a source of income to workers for buying a living. It is a foundation for, and the key element in, living itself. Moreover, these emphases are in many ways interdependent. Employment and Manpower Services, shaped and governed by even purely community and national economic objectives, will have to implement their concern for such grand over-all goals as productivity of the economy, full employment, a balanced labor market, and a labor force competent to perform the tasks required. In so implementing the grand design, their efforts will inevitably focus upon the competence, employment, and maximum opportunity for utilization of the productive potential of millions of individual people, each of whom is a very particular bundle of problems and opportunities. "Our job is people" is not merely a pious and sentimental declaration of purpose by local managers of employment offices. It is a recognition that a large share of the tasks in those offices will involve dealing with and providing a service to these individual people. If that service is adequate, it will result in a better fit of jobs wanting men and men wanting jobs, and hence will contribute to a development of men's vocational poten-

5

tial and (hopefully) to a better income with which to buy a more satisfactory hiring. That, in turn, meets a very significant part of the workers' human and social needs, a result satisfying the humanitarian expectancies of workers, employers, and the community. Likewise, a focus of Employment and Manpower Services on humanitarian social welfare objectives cannot but have by-products helpful to the just and smooth operation of the economy.

There is, therefore, no ultimate incompatibility between the two concepts of essential and primary mission. But there are important consequences if the economic aspects of the "general welfare" are not provided for as a foundation and framework for efforts directed toward the economic and social welfare of individuals. And there are important consequences of the choice made as to which shall be the *primary* objective. The question can be raised, "As a guide to the development and operation of the services, is the economic strength and growth orientation or the social welfare and relief orientation more likely to contribute to the achievement of *both* objectives?" Or, to put it differently, "The achievement with respect to which of these objectives is to be considered a by-product of the achievement of the other?"

The difference in results is immediately evident to an observer of the British and the Swedish systems. In England one gains the impression of Employment and Manpower Services motivated and directed chiefly by the desire to benefit the unfortunate, a most worthy objective. Almost a social-work approach characterizes their operation. The concern of administrators is centered on doing the best possible job for individual youths and adults who do not have jobs and may lack the ability or training to get and hold them, or who may be short on opportunity, resources, knowledge, foresight, or physical or mental capacity to better their situation. The administrators are not unaware of the implications for the country's economic strength and stability of their activity, but such considerations are secondary, and appear more as the unanticipated consequences of action rather than as guide lines for action. Those who are concerned with the nation's economic stability and growth demonstrate little detailed interest in the consequences of the job done by the services for their "large" plans.* And the public image of the Employment Exchange is very closely associated with an image of a relief center.

---

* This is a current observation. It is well known that the fathers of the present system, people like the Webbs, Sir Hubert Llewellyn Smith, and Sir William Beveridge were economically oriented. The development of services has, however, from the beginning been related to the improvement of those facilities for the unfortunate, provided for in the 19th and early 20th centuries in the Poor Laws, and they have never lost the marks of that association.

The immediate impression of the Swedish system is quite different. One senses from top to bottom among the operating staff an overriding concern with the degree to which the Employment and Manpower Services are fitting the requirements for a strong, stable, and growing economy. Decisions on placement and movement of workers, the increasing of jobs, the training of youth and the retraining of adults, the rehabilitation of the handicapped, the kind of statistical studies required, the functions allocated to the services, and decisions on the amount of money needed all root back in calculations as to what these requirements for national economic strength are now and will be in the future. The managers of the employment offices in Sweden also claim that, when it comes to the carrying out of the greatest volume of tasks, "Our job is people." Humanitarianism is not absent, although it is difficult for a foreigner and a stranger to sense the heartbeats of a Swede from his facial or verbal expression. But the social and human values of the Employment and Manpower Services are looked upon as welcome by-products of a rational, active, and positive economic and labor market policy and practice. The "large" thinkers concerned with over-all economic policy and practice acknowledge and take detailed account of the contribution to their objectives of the operations of the Labor Market Board under the direction of which the several Employment and Manpower Services are integrated and operated.

The consequences for the operation and development of the Employment and Manpower Services of this difference in the concept of the basic emphasis in their central mission will 'become clearer when we discuss the variations in program emphasis which follow from it, or are suggested by it. We can note at once, however, several advantages of the primarily economic orientation characterizing the Swedish system.

ADVANTAGES OF THE ECONOMIC ORIENTATION

First, the integration of the Employment Service with other supporting manpower and labor market activities (such as vocational training and counseling, rehabilitation, provision of movement aids to workers, location of industry, setting in motion and regulation of private and public construction, labor market fact-finding, etc.) is made simpler because there is a common direction given to the efforts of each by reference to which their co-ordination can be organized. I doubt whether this integration can be achieved if the primary integrating principle is predominantly that of service to individual people.

Second, the same thing is true of the integrative relationship of the Employment and Manpower Services with the broader efforts to establish and implement economic policy and practice in the nation. Their respective functions are clarified. The reciprocal and mutually supporting role of general economic measures flowing from fiscal, monetary, investment, wage, trade, and tariff policy on the one hand, and the special and selective measures flowing from labor market and manpower policy on the other can be more easily recognized, and a co-ordinated program can be developed in which each plays the role appropriate to its part performance in an over-all program, directed to the increase in the nation's economic strength, stability, and growth.

Consider, for example, the commitment of governments to the maintenance of full employment, steady prices, and a stable and strong currency, objectives easier to realize in isolation from each other than simultaneously and in combination. The fiscal, monetary, and general wage policy measures employed are blunt instruments producing inflationary or deflationary effects on all sectors and sections of economic activity. But all sectors and sections are not equally in need of the stimulus or braking action involved. The economically oriented mission of the Employment and Manpower Services is to reduce the pressure on such broadside fiscal, monetary, and wage policy measures, since they can be applied as selective measures to increase or decrease labor development, availability, utilization, and movement in precisely those sectors or sections requiring such attention.*

Or consider the efforts to achieve a higher degree of balanced economic growth particularly through expansion and more effective use of public and private investment, increase in foreign trade, and the improvements in technological equipment and process. These, of course, have employment consequences, some good, some bad, from the point of view of particular workers. But to Employment and Manpower Services oriented toward economic strength as a central mission, the focus on economic growth suggests a co-ordinate role for them, not merely of picking up the pieces of broken individual careers,

---

* A frequently mentioned division of labor reported by Swedish experts is this. The general "demand" producing measures may be expected to keep unemployment at around the four per cent level. The Employment and Manpower Services under the direction of the Labor Market Board can then be utilized "selectively" to bring their impact at particular times, with respect to particular groups of the un- and underemployed, in particular surplus or undermanned labor market areas, and in anticipation of particular fluctuations in production and employment, to keep this unemployment figure below two per cent.

but of accepting those released from one sector as *resources* for the development of another. It suggests the concept of the *underutilized* rather than the *unemployed*. It suggests transforming the treatment of the "labor reserves," made available through unemployment, from one of relief for *idle* reserves to the development of *active* and *productive* reserves. It shifts the emphasis from *redundant workers* to *available manpower resources*. It suggests a productivity-increasing contribution of the Employment and Manpower Services equal to that of practices related to investment in plant and the technological and managerial improvement of the production process. Such an approach makes the operators of these Employment and Manpower Services contemporary partners in the *positive* efforts toward economic growth rather than merely the compensators for the distress caused by those efforts. (It should be noted that it is quite probable that the foregoing emphasis, which stems from the economic orientation, promises an increase in welfare for individuals as great as, or greater than, that which stems from a direct individual welfare approach.)

The third advantage of an economic orientation is that the responsible administrators of these several kinds of economically focused general demand-stimulating or -retarding activities and the Employment and Manpower Services people can speak a common core language whatever their "professional" dialects. The common language reflects their common experience in wrestling with different aspects of a common economic strength and growth problem. They can feel and act "at home" with each other. There are, of course, some jurisdictional disputes, but there is also a commonly accepted test of appropriateness in terms of optimal contribution to a common objective of national economic health which provides a basis for sense-making allocations of jurisdiction to each service. Such a state of affairs increases mutual respect among them and a recognition of the interdependence of the efforts which each is making in his own field with those made by others. The planners and administrators concerned with the economic use of nonpersonal resources do not carry on their decision-making in social service or relief terms. This procedure does not argue for neglect of the human elements in the utilization of manpower resources. But it does argue for the capacity of those concerned with manpower resources to think within the same framework of economic advantage, efficiency, and objective as the administrators of monetary and material resources.

An incidental value related to the above situation is that "outsiders," economists and political scientists, staff people and leaders in unions and employers' associations, and major politicians and statesmen, can also use this common language and, moreover, feel that the Employment and Manpower Services are worth their serious attention and study. These "outsiders" can and do make real contributions to the philosophy and operational details of the system. Statements on, and studies and criticisms of, labor market policy and practice by them need not merely include as an afterthought, "Of course, the Employment and Manpower Services need to be strengthened also."

A fourth consequence of an economic strength orientation is an amplified and truly rational and logical justification for the costs of Employment and Manpower Services. Briefly, this means that the economic cost of underutilization, of mis- or nonplacement, and of nonavailability of capable manpower is the most important cost, a cost measured by the difference between the goods and services which could have been produced, given efficient Employment and Manpower Services, and the amount actually produced. The net cost is realistically considered, not the total expenditures for these services, but that amount minus the value production of goods and services available because of their activities.

This concept of cost, incidentally, has a bearing on the issue of whether it is more costly to move jobs to men in areas of industrial decay or to move men to jobs in areas of expanding industry. The only issue is not, of course, economic cost. But if men who are surplus in declining industries can increase their productive value several times by being trained for and moved to jobs in expanding industries, there is a loss to the total economy in leaving them where they are or in engagement of their efforts in public works in which their actual or trainable skills are underutilized.

A fifth consequence of focusing the mission of the Employment and Manpower Services on the goal of economic health is to provide a justification for the *continuity* of their level of operation which is not dependent on the shifting winds of economic fluctuations and the varying amount of human distress resulting therefrom. If the goal and consequent direction of effort is growing economic strength, it does not make sense to curtail those operations when unemployment decreases, and to expand them only when unemployment increases. That may be appropriate for relief-oriented services, but not for those oriented toward economic stability and growth. It is natural that the potential-for-relieving-distress aspects of the services should be more highly emphasized when unemployment is high, but the potential-for-contributing-to-economic-health aspects are of *continuous* service to the economy, and, moreover, have opportunity for increased emphasis when the unemployment problem is less serious and when there are general or specific labor shortages.

Do we decrease resources for the Federal Reserve Board when the banking system appears to be in good working order? Do we decrease the amount of attention given to medical research and education when no epidemic is raging or imminent?

The issue can be focused in this way. Suppose we succeed, as many countries in Europe have done, in approximating full employment. Suppose there is no surplus of labor in the sense of men genuinely seeking jobs they can not find. Suppose we have guaranteed minimum of livelihood through a cradle-to-grave social security system regardless of what hazards occur to the citizens of the land. Suppose incomes for all families are above the minimum essential to a healthy existence. Can we then rationally curtail the efforts of the Employment and Manpower Services if they are geared to assuring the nation of the maximum development and utilization of its manpower potential? The economic orientation of the mission of the Employment and Manpower Services will drive home the fact that, even given these favorable economic conditions, the basic problem of most advanced industrial countries is to learn how to live with nearly full employment.

A sixth consequence of focusing on economic strength is that, instead of feeling left on the fringes of significant public endeavor, the Employment and Manpower Services people feel very much in the center of things of national importance. They do not have to brag about it; they can take that for granted. And they do in Sweden. The impact which that awareness makes on the morale, the enthusiasm, the amount of initiative displayed among the responsible people in the service is marked.

Finally, a further advantage of the choice of economic strength and growth as a central mission is that the Employment and Manpower Services must legitimately share with other economic efforts a demanding standard of evaluation in terms of what the economic health of the communities and nation is. When the director of these services, consolidated under the supervision of the National Labor Market Board in Sweden, assumes that the Board must bear its share of the blame if full employment is not achieved, if the supply of and the demand for labor is out of balance, if economic expansion is hampered, or if the general price level displays inflationary tendencies, it is clear that a very demanding criterion has been accepted as an ultimate test of achievement or failure. That is just the kind of test needed to stretch the abilities of the people who operate these services, and the kind that brings them under the critical and initiative-stimulating observation of leaders of thought and action in the economic and political as well as social affairs of the nation. Such an ultimate test does not, of course, reduce the need for more precise and daily-operation-centered standards of evaluation. But it points to the ultimate kinds of achievement which these operational standards must serve.

The acceptance of such an ultimate standard of excellence provides a guide to the kind of direction, control, and assistance needed by staff members. It also sets very high selection standards for the original quality of and training for personnel in order to assure effective operations. We shall find other organizational and administrative problems affected also by the choice made as to what concept of mission is to be expected primarily to govern the operation and development of the Employment and Manpower Services.

There is a danger in accepting the economic rather than social-service orientation as a primary definition of mission, a danger of impairment of freedom. That danger, however, we shall discuss in Chap. 4, which poses the issue of a free or managed labor market.

It is suggested (1) that the advantages named above are essential to the operation and development of Employment and Manpower Services capable of returning to the nation an economic value greater than their economic cost, and (2) that these advantages are unlikely to develop unless there is a close approximation to consensus among all involved that the primary mission of the Employment and Manpower Services should be oriented toward the nation's economic health, with the social welfare and relief of individuals considered to be a by-product of the activities consistent with that primary objective.

IS ECONOMIC HEALTH ENOUGH?

To seek such an economic objective is not to toss to one side the objective of serving the social welfare of individuals and relieving their distress. What is the basic welfare responsibility of government to its people, anyway? Is it not, first and foremost, the establishment of those conditions of life and work in which individuals, *through their own initiative and effort*, are enabled to maximize their own welfare, whatever else is done to meet the needs of those who for some reason are unable to do so? Is it not to work toward that end with the welfare interests of *all* citizens in mind, the able and the unable, the employed as well as the unemployed, the strong as well as the handicapped, the skilled as well as the unskilled? Is not this particularly true with respect to the conditions existing in the labor market?

The advantages just named of focusing attention of the Employment and Manpower Services on increasing the potential of the labor market as a contributor to the nation's economic health and growth *amplify* the potential of those services to contribute to the welfare of individuals; they do not subtract from it. Those workers whose low level of welfare stimulates our humanitarian interests benefit, no less than do all workers, from efforts to improve the human resources within, and the operations of, the labor market toward the end that the economic strength and growth of the nation are increased. They benefit from the specific measures employed, and they benefit from the amplified opportunities for work and the degree of economic security provided by achievement of that objective.

This may not be all they need. Nor does meeting this need define the limits of the welfare activities appropriate to or expected of government. But in a world in which men must work for a living, and most must find an employer in order to do so, the nation's health and growth and the functioning of its labor market are the foundation for, and set limits to, whatever degree of social welfare can be achieved by any individual either through his own efforts or the efforts of others, including government.

THE UNITED STATES SITUATION

So much by way of prologue. How do matters stand with respect to the central mission orientation of the Employment and Manpower Services in the United States? There is little question that, in our country, the origins of most of the complex of services we have labeled in this way were of the social work and relief variety. They were intended primarily to benefit individuals, particularly those in need of help, rather than to achieve a more rational and economically efficient organization of the labor market. We speak now only of origins. Vocational guidance, at least that provided by public agencies, was to supply help to individual young people, particularly those whose lack of economic resources, whose lack of opportunity for specific well-paying vocations, and whose lack of knowledge of vocational alternatives from family and social contacts, put them at a disadvantage. So it was with publicly sponsored vocational education and training.

Veterans' services were to provide aid and advice with respect to a wide variety of needs for individuals who had made great personal sacrifices in the service of their country. Rehabilitation of the physically and mentally handicapped was clearly motivated by sympathy for individuals who suffered such disadvantages.* Public and relief works were intended to provide a more self-respecting kind of relief to those unfortunate enough to have been swept out of their jobs by the depression. Unemployment insurance was originally urged as a substitute for unemployment relief, more dignified and respectable than that provided after a declaration of pauperism. Individuals were to receive compensation as a right, not simply because they were in need.† Job systemization for migrant workers was urged as a way of reducing the obvious poverty and distress of the wandering "Okies" and their families. Retraining for the unemployed was amplified by federal initiative through acts which had other purposes as well, and the whole was justified as a promotion of the nation's economic stability, e.g., Area Redevelopment Act, Manpower Development and Training Act, and Trade Expansion Act. But there is little question that the appeal to the sense of social responsibility provided by the suffering of the unemployed workers and their families was a strong persuasive factor in stirring legislators to action in this matter.

In each case there was "supporting" argument for the economic utility to employers and the nation of such measures. But the dominant motivation was to help individuals out of trouble and to raise the level of opportunity for people at a disadvantage. In other words, the original approach was that of human and social welfare. The value of such motivation is not to be downgraded or underestimated. It reflects a basic quality of humanity and a sensitivity to the human needs of individuals which indicates progress toward a more nearly civilized society. It is an evidence that the welfare of individuals has not been lost sight of in a business civilization. It is a reflection of what people expect of their government and of government's response to that expectancy. The nature and scope of the nation's Employment and Manpower Services would today be far less adapted to the maintenance of the nation's economic health were it not for that motivation in legislators, and for the political responsibility and opportunity for

---

* Except in the war or defense mobilization periods when there was a shortage of civilian manpower.

† While still regarded by some people as a "more respectable kind of *relief*," in the United States it is far from such. Indeed, because compensation is geared to a worker's previous length of employment and wages, it can be said that those who need it most receive the least, and those who need it least receive the most.

them involved in a positive response to the expectancies of their constituents as well as of their own conscience.

Over the years the impact of these Employment and Manpower Services on the nation's economic strength becomes clearer. At the same time the problems of economic health and growth for the nation were shaped by forces beyond those with which the unaided private enterprise of individuals could cope. It became increasingly necessary to ask whether these public manpower services of vocational guidance, vocational education and training, rehabilitation, public and relief works, unemployment insurance, retraining for the unemployed, etc., could be geared to dealing with these forces as well as with the private needs of individuals. That question *was* asked and the development of the services reflects a partially positive answer to it. The justification for these services has increasingly been based on advantages to society rather than merely to individuals. But even so, the advantage chiefly stressed was progress toward a more humane *social* policy, rather than progress toward a more rational economic policy.

How does this matter of the central mission stand specifically with the Employment Service? Among the early proponents of a public employment service were some economists who urged employment exchanges on primarily economic grounds to facilitate the movement of labor. When the idea was applied in the early days to the placement of immigrants, there was of course a goodly mixture of humanitarian interest with the economic interest. The economic justification, however, was normally on a very theoretical plane, and was concerned chiefly with a more *rapid* clearance of job openings and applicants for work. The fundamental recognition of the need for employment offices was originally generated from studies of the causes of poverty and the desire to reduce it. These studies led to the increasing awareness of the major role of unemployment in producing that condition. This, in turn, led to the conviction that a possible reduction of periods of joblessness could be achieved by a more systematic provision for bringing men and jobs together. The real steam behind the move for employment offices was the desire to provide a service to the poverty-plagued unemployed who didn't know their way around the labor market and to avoid the necessity of their falling into the clutches of exploiting fee-charging agencies, who took from ignorant people in desperate need of jobs a big toll from their pay for providing a very poor labor broker service.

When the Employment Service really grew to proportions which brought it to widespread public attention (aside from the brief period during World War I), it was indelibly stamped as a part of the relief system of the 1930's. Its chief and almost only customers were work relief applicants. The next stimulus to rapid expansion came with the setting up of the state unemployment insurance systems. It became, in reality, right up to the Second World War, an adjunct of this more dignified and less degrading form of unemployment relief. It still is so identified by many. Yet even in that period, tools of the trade were being developed whose use implied a much greater emphasis on the rational organization of the labor market as a primary mission. The *Dictionary of Occupational Titles* in 1934, introduced to the United States in 1939, for example, indicated a trend toward a systematic labor market program for all rather than a relief program for some.

The national defense training program in 1940–41 required attention to estimating manpower needs, selection of trainees, and contacts with sources of employment, and gave experience that lifted sights to serving rationally the needs of the labor market, even the national labor market. With the marshalling of all resources for the war effort in the '40's, the relieving office function all but disappeared, and at the close of the war at least the operators and administrators of the service, enthusiastic and fresh from their participation in an undeniably significant public interest enterprise, had caught a new vision of the scope and economic importance of what a national employment service could be.

The six point program outlining the function of the Employment Service announced at the close of the war was not an administrator's wishbook. It was the product of experience, not only of what could be done, but of what needed to be done in marshalling the nation's manpower resources for maximum production. It grew out of a change in occupation from running a relief service to operating an important and essential part of the nation's economic and productive machinery aimed at all-out production. In order to do that, it was not enough to match two cards, on one of which was the name and work history of a man in need of a job and, on the other, the job specifications submitted by an employer who needed a worker. Starting with a simple concept of the mission of operating a clearing house for two such individuals and particularly for the worker who most needed a job, the economic mission of the Employment Service during the war forced upon it activities that would scarcely be found in a social work agency. These activities, it was felt, must include:

1. An effective *placement service* geared to the needs of all kinds of workers in all occupational and industrial fields. This function to be supported by

2. A *counseling service* for the use of people faced with difficulties in making vocational and job choices and plans in the light of their present or potential abilities (determined in part through aptitude and performance *testing*) *and* in the light of existing labor market conditions.
3. Special and preferential *services to veterans*.
4. Personnel *management services* to assist employers and labor organizations in the use of personnel tools and techniques, including testing, selection, turnover reduction, and industrial and job analysis.
5. The gathering and analysis of *labor market information* and its distribution to workers, to employers, to training and educational authorities, and to community agencies and groups whose activities are affected by labor market and manpower considerations.
6. *Co-operation* with community organizations and government agencies in community employment planning and industrial redevelopment.

Moreover, these aspects of the Employment Service were, and still are, defended by reference to the changing needs of the nation's economy. The Full Employment Act of 1946 and the statement of the President on signing it identified a "healthy economy" with one that provides opportunities for those "able, willing, and seeking to work." The President's Council of Economic Advisors called upon the Bureau of Economic Security to furnish regular reports on employment conditions as one measure of the nation's economic health. A new stimulus was given to the conviction that the Employment Service was performing a significant economic job. In 1948 the Farm Placement Service was re-established in the Employment Service, and the migratory worker problem became the responsibility of that service, not simply as a social service to wandering laborers and their families, but as a more effective organization of the resources of labor and of the demand for their services in a series of areas of seasonal employment.

The defense period of 1950–53 once again highlighted the economic function of the Employment Service in developing lists of critical civilian occupations (utilized by the Selective Service System in determining deferments), in the mobilization of a labor supply for defense industries, in the development of community employment programs where the transition to defense production left blight spots among certain civilian industries, in training to meet the expanded needs of defense industry, and in retraining when the defense effort leveled off and was reduced. Co-operation with, and actual frontline operation of the work of, a series of "offices" and "administrations" set up to move industry toward a defense basis produced more experience in being at the heart of the nation's economic and industrial problems. The experience, as was the case in World Wars I and II, included the establishment of orderly procedures for recruiting workers in one labor market area for movement to another.

Beginning in 1946 the responsible directors of the Employment Service had been pointing out the need for special attention to areas plagued with chronic unemployment, and since that time the Service has participated in community development and training programs to meet that problem. The most recent focusing of such efforts has been co-operation in implementing the Area Redevelopment Act and the Manpower Training and Development Act.

Central not only to its own planning and operations but to these collaborative efforts has been the amplification in scope and improvement in quality of analyses of the present and future manpower needs of labor market areas, present and prospective training facilities, etc. Whatever criticism can be made of the quality of these surveys and analyses, they are a big step away from "flying blind," and are recognized by all knowledgeable people as the very heart of any program of operations of an agency proposing to exert leadership in the effective planning (whether public or private) for, and rational utilization and development of, manpower resources for economic stability, adjustment, and growth.

The clearest statement to date of Congressional intent with respect to the purpose of Employment and Manpower Services is contained in the statement of findings and purpose of Title I of the Manpower Development and Training Act of 1962 and the statement of general responsibility of the Secretary of Labor and the Secretary of Health, Education, and Welfare contained in that act. The statement of findings and purpose is liberally sprinkled with such terms as: "in order that the nation may meet the staffing requirements of the struggle for freedom;" the necessity of training "to meet shifting employment needs;" "skills which are or will be in demand in the labor market;" the inadequacy of "skills of many who are now employed . . . to enable them to make their maximum contribution to the nation's economy;" "to increase the nation's productivity and its capacity to meet the requirements of the space age." When this statement is coupled with the clear indication of purpose contained in the Full Employment Act of 1946, we have clearly revealed a Congressional intent that at least some of the Employment and Manpower services re expected to chart their course toward economic stability and growth of the nation.

If we look back on this record, it would appear plausible to conclude that the Employment and Manpower Services have moved steadily toward a conception of their mission primarily in terms of economic health for the nation. This is unquestionably true if by the "Employment and Manpower Services" is meant the top level federal and most of the top-level state administrators of the service, the employment security agencies of which it is a part, and the authors and sponsors of the two acts just named. The clarity and logic with which this concept of mission has been set forth, for instance, by the sponsors of the two acts, by the last two Secretaries of Labor, and by the present directors of the United States Employment Service and the Bureau of Employment Security gives unmistakable evidence of this. Equally convincing are the statements of central mission concept furnished us by more than half of the state employment security administrators in the course of assembling materials for this book.

The case is not so clear if the boundaries of the "organization" are defined to include all government legislators and officials at the federal and state levels whose choices, decisions, and actions affect the operation of the services. It is not so clear if the boundaries are extended to include the managers and staffs of the 1900 local offices where the services come to life. If those boundaries are extended still further (as some organizational theorists are inclined to do) to include the workers and employers who are actual or potential "customers" of the service, the case is not clear at all. And, in any realistic appraisal of the working and accepted central mission of the services, that extended concept of the organization must be used. The authors of acts and top level officials can propose, but they cannot create, the mission; for the mission, to be established, must be established by action. That action is compromised by the necessity of developing a working consensus on, and obtaining widespread understanding of, the objective, legitimization, and the amount of resources needed, among other influential decision makers. Moreover, the basic tools of action toward accomplishing the ultimate objective of all the services are applications from workers and orders from employers. If their concept of the mission of the Employment and Manpower Services is that they are relief or social service agencies, they will supply those applications and orders when and if they need that type of service. The supply resulting from such motivation is not sufficient either in quantity or quality to enable the services to perform effectively the economic mission proposed by their creators and officials. The official spokesmen for the services are in the position of the young man of whom it was said, "He is half married. The girl has his consent."

The record, we think, shows that only in three periods prior to the present has there been an approximation to consensus among all concerned that the central legitimate mission of the Employment and Manpower Services was that of contributing to the nation's economic health rather than merely to the social and economic well-being and relief of unfortunate and "disadvantaged" individuals. Those periods were the First World War, the Second World War, and the Korean crisis. In the absence of the obvious need for marshalling every ounce of our human resources to provide the economic strength required for war, the dominant conception of the Employment and Manpower Services as parts of a social work and relief agency has continuously (though, we believe, with diminishing force) reasserted itself.

Evidence of this statement will be apparent in succeeding chapters. Here it will be necessary merely to state some of the reasons.

First is the growing expectancy that the "general welfare" purposes of government shall express themselves in particular public efforts to promote the welfare of individual and specific groups of citizens, particularly those who have been caught and hurt in the fluctuations of economic developments. Side by side with opposition to the growth of "the welfare state" is to be found the increasing recognition that welfare programs are a legitimate and politically rewarding function of federal and state governments.

Second, and to some degree in conflict with the first, is the deeply embedded American belief that "normal," competent, fit, and ambitious people and enterprises do not need help from government agencies. If they do, there is something wrong with them. Consequently, the government agencies which deal with them are performing some kind of social work which has little relevance to the needs of the successful majority of individual and organizational producers.

Third is the persistency of the image of the Employment and Manpower Services as basically relief organizations, as they certainly were in the 1930's when they first became prominent and widespread government services.

Fourth is the reinforcement of that image by the concentration, after the wars, of efforts for veterans, particularly disabled veterans, on not only employment services, but all sorts of social services.

Fifth is the publicity given to special efforts and what were called "programs" for particular groups of workers in special need, the handicapped, the aged, the school dropouts, the Indians, the prison parolees. Even though efforts in these cases may have originated as attempts to relieve labor shortages, they continued to be supported and emphasized as a service to the unfortunate people involved.

Finally and most important has been the "*un*employment office" concept of the Employment Security Offices in local communities produced by the registration, certification, and work test activities associated with their function in relation to unemployment insurance. The frequent location of the Employment Security Office in areas associated with relief activities, and in quarters suggesting locations for such activity, has done nothing to alter the impression.

SUMMARY

This chapter raises the question of what the necessary and appropriate central mission of the Employment and Manpower Services is. The concept of the central mission is the basic policy premise by reference to which judgments are made as to the justification for the services, the resources it is necessary and desirable to allocate to them, the status and organizational relation they should occupy with respect to other agencies of government, the operational field within which they are expected to function, and the kinds of emphases and programs it is appropriate to employ in their operation.

The definition of the central mission is not accomplished by a listing of such programs, a report of what is being accomplished, and an evaluation of how well they are doing. The central mission of a service agency, unless it is self-perpetuation and glorification, must be defined as a *relationship* of the services provided to some object, for some *purpose* important to that object.

The alternatives for primary emphasis we have presented in this and the next chapter are, with regard to *object*, the nation and individual workers and employers; with regard to *purpose*, economic strength, stability, and growth, and social welfare and relief.

It is our belief that the most important and controversial questions concerning the central mission of the Employment and Manpower Services focus upon this issue of whether the emphasis in that mission is to contribute, first of all, to the economic strength, stability, and growth of the nation, or to provide unemployed people with certain kinds of social welfare and relief services. Both, of course, are legitimate and necessary, but the question is, "Which is to be the *principal* premise for decisions and action with respect to operation and development of the services?" Or, to put it differently, "The achievement with respect to which of these emphases is to be considered a by-product of the primary effort directed to the other?"

The significance of the issue is emphasized by a comparison of the characteristics with respect to these emphases between the Swedish and the English systems of Employment and Manpower Services. The potential advantages of the Swedish system, focused upon the economic-strength-of-the-nation emphasis, are as follows:

1. An organizing and integrating focus clearly related to the labor market field of operation is provided for all the Employment and Manpower Services, whatever their nature or specific function.
2. A similar organizing and integrating focus related to a common economic goal is provided for meaningful relationship of the Employment and Manpower Services to broader efforts to establish and implement economic policy in the nation.*
3. Those charged with responsibility for these two types of economically oriented efforts are provided with a common purpose and language which facilitates their understanding of the interdependence and reciprocity of their separate functions.
4. Those "outsiders" in the social sciences and involved organizations who concern themselves with the problem of economic and social health, and who have much to contribute to the improvement of agencies designed to achieve economic health, are stimulated to make such contributions and criticisms in terms understandable to and justified in the eyes of those responsible for the agencies.
5. An amplified and truly rational and logical justification for the costs of the Employment and Manpower Services is provided.
6. The services are provided with a justification for the continuity of their level of operations which is not dependent on the shifting winds of economic fluctuations and the varying amount of human distress resulting therefrom.
7. The morale of the operators of the Employment and Manpower Services is enhanced by the sense that, instead of being

* E.g., fiscal, monetary, tariff, and wage policy and practice.

left on the fringes of significant public endeavor, they are very much in the center of things of national importance.

8. The Employment and Manpower Services are furnished with the necessity of meeting an ultimate standard for evaluation and criticism of their work in terms of their impact on such ability-stretching goals as full employment, balanced labor market, economic growth, a stable currency.

9. The administrators of the Employment and Manpower Services are provided with a sharpened guide to the kinds of direction, control, and assistance needed by staff members and with a clue to the standards for original selection of and training for personnel which is required for effective operation.

It was suggested (1) that these advantages are essential to the operation and development of Employment and Manpower Services capable of returning to the nation a value greater than the economic resources devoted to their maintenance, (2) that these advantages are unlikely to develop unless there is a close approximation to consensus among all decision makers involved that the basic mission of the Employment and Manpower Services should be oriented primarily toward the nation's economic health and growth, and secondarily to individuals' social welfare and relief, the latter being considered a by-product of the first. A major justification for such a balance of emphasis is that the contribution of the Employment and Manpower Services to welfare and relief requirements of individuals is *amplified,* not reduced, by their effective contribution to the economic health and growth of the nation. Another justification for such a balance of emphasis is that concern for the economic aspects of the general welfare implies and makes essential effective attention to the economic and social welfare of the individuals, who together make up the human resources contributing to that general welfare. But concern for the social and economic welfare of individuals does not necessarily lead to the kind of adequate activity essential to maintaining the nation's economic health.

The present situation in the United States can be described as one of a slow and uneven growth of the concept of mission toward the objective of the nation's economic health from origins which emphasized the social welfare and relief objectives and utility of the services. The original emphasis, however, survives in the traditions, in actual administrative choices in the operation of the services, and especially in the image held of the service by those in a position to influence its operations and development. Some of the reasons for this survival of, and at times dominant, individual social welfare emphasis have been briefly described.

In the next chapter we turn to a discussion of certain operational choices which follow from the primary emphasis on one or the other of these concepts of the central mission of the Employment and Manpower Services.

OPERATIONAL
CONSEQUENCES
OF OBJECTIVES

Chapter Three If there is a lack of consensus as to the central mission of the Employment and Manpower Services, one can scarcely expect to find agreement on what choices the administrators should make as to the practical direction and emphasis of their daily operations. The best way to get down to brass tacks in considering how the choice of mission affects the practical performance of the services is to examine some of the alternative operating directions and emphases that are consistent with the two concepts of mission discussed in Chap. 2. In fact, we can say that these different practical directions and emphases provide us with an operational definition of what is meant by different concepts of central mission.

Let us state, as a point of departure for discussion, an initially uncompromising set of practical emphases which would characterize the Employment and Manpower Services whose primary and central mission is oriented toward the nation's economic health and growth.

The clientele to be served would be not merely the hard to place, but any and all workers, actual and potential, whose productive employment is the basic ingredient in the nation's economic strength. The placement of workers would be governed, not by privileged treatment for especially needy groups, but by evaluation of the best possible objectively determined fit of their productive capacities with productive needs of business, industrial, and professional enterprise. The mere removal of workers from the rolls of the unemployed would be looked upon, not as an end in itself, but as a by-product of the attempt fully to employ men at the highest level of production of which they are now capable or for which they could be trained. The consideration and analysis of the employers' needs and capacity to utilize effectively the services of the workers would receive an emphasis certainly equal to the consideration and analysis of the workers' needs and capacity to profit from the performing of those services. The relief of unemployment and the unemployed would have no greater value in the program than the prevention of unemployment now and in the future.

We shall consider each of these in turn.

CLIENTELE: THE ISSUE   26 - 30

The first choice of emphasis has to do with what clientele shall be served. We can put the issue in the form of several questions. Is service to be supplied predominantly to particular groups in the total labor force who face unusual difficulties in getting jobs: for example, the physically and mentally handicapped, the older worker, the youthful first-job seekers, the long-term unemployed, the nonwhite racial groups, parolees from prison, or clients of relief or private social welfare agencies? Or is the total labor force to be considered potential clientele? Is preferential treatment to be given in placement to certain groups: for example, those listed above, veterans, and trainees who have completed an authorized training course? Or shall referrals be made without preference and strictly by reference to qualifications for meeting job specifications? Shall the clientele include all industrial and occupational groups from casual day laborers to professionals and executives? Shall the employed as well as the unemployed be encouraged to seek more satisfactory and profitable jobs? Shall the manpower development services such as training, testing, and counseling be limited to the unemployed or opened to all workers employed and unemployed? The last three questions will be discussed further in connection with an issue to be presented later.

THE SITUATION

What is the present situation with respect to the hard-to-place and preferential treatment issues? The majority of placements made by the state employment offices are accounted for by the hard-to-place groups named above and by the veterans. The latter, in particular, are represented in placements to a greater degree than that equivalent to their representation among the job applicants. This concentration of results may or may not be due to the assignment of special staff and the provision of especially designed guides and training for services to these groups, but that assignment is made at the federal, state, and local levels, and that guidance is provided. The industrial and occupational distribution of placements reinforces the image of the Employment Office as the place to which those with the least marketable skills turn for help. Placements of farm labor, domestic work, casual work, and unskilled industrial work dominate the picture, although recent years have seen a steady increase in the number of white collar and professional and executive placements made. Estimates vary as to the proportion of claimants for unemployment insurance on the list of applicants. It is probably around 90 per cent. This leaves a possible 10 per cent of applicants who are employed at the time they enter their applications. There is, however, no policy of limiting services like counseling and testing to the unemployed. At the present time training, but not the other manpower development services, is limited to the unemployed.

WHY?

Does this situation indicate that the managers and other officials of the Employment Service have "chosen" to concentrate on that clientele which gives a social service and relief image to their operations rather than to lift their sights to organizing the labor market for the total labor force? Not at all. To a great degree they are faced with "Hobson's" choices.

First of all, the law requires that veterans receive privileged treatment. The order of preference in referrals to jobs is clearly implied: handicapped veterans, other veterans, nonveterans. Furthermore, legal obligations exist for the Employment Service not only to provide placement and counseling services for the handicapped but also to maintain co-operative relations with state rehabilitation agencies. The latter are legally instructed to make "maximum utilization of the services and facilities of the Employment Service Offices." Other legislative and executive action indirectly makes clear the responsibility of the Employment Service to give special attention to the vocational guidance and placement of older workers, youth, foreign nationals, and racial groups subject to discrimination. Whether the political pressures for the success of the Manpower Development and Training and the Trade Expansion Acts will make itself felt in extra efforts for those finishing training courses and for those displaced as a result of the implementation of the trade bill remains to be seen. The legal responsibility for claimants of unemployment insurance extends not merely to their registration for work but to utilizing registration and placement procedures as evidence of the claimants' availability for work and willingness to work.

To the compulsion from legislative sources is added the pressures from veterans', social welfare, and racial equality associations to give amplified attention to those groups among the unemployed in which these associations have particular interest. The development of the emphasis noted has, in other words, been in part the response to a growing and insistent public demand that special attention be given to the problems of such groups.

Added to these positive pressures for expansion of services to the hard-to-place unemployed clientele are the negative pressure from employers to avoid "pirating" of their workers, and, for some illogical reason, objections, from private fee-charging agencies, to public agencies' dealing with any but the unemployed. This objection seems to imply that if anyone "pirates" workers already employed it should be a fee-charging agency. A profit should be made from the process.

It is not intended here to criticize these compulsions and pressures or the objective of giving a special break to hard-to-place groups. But it is clear that such influencers of the operations of the Employment Service must bear their share of the responsibility for the emphasis made, and that their influence has been stimulated primarily by their conception of the mission of the service as a social welfare if not a relief agency.

A second reason that a public agency finds itself inevitably serving the "hard-to-place" clientele and concerned with the "hard-to-fill" jobs is that it is only one among many ways of bringing workers and jobs together, and the public Employment Service is a "Johnny-come-lately" on the scene. Workers who are looking for jobs do so in many ways: leads from friends; direct application to employers; want ads; trade union, professional group, and school-sponsored placement services; private fee-charging employment agencies; response to employer re- cruiters, etc. Those with the highest market value will naturally use and find jobs in one or more of these ways sanctioned by tradition before seeking the assistance of a public employment service. More- over, when layoffs must be made, employers desire to retain on their payrolls the most competent workers; they assume that other em- ployers do the same. Hence, those who appear as registered claimants for unemployment insurance are not likely to be the easiest to place.

The result? It is simply in the cards that the public employment service will find on its rolls the hardest to place.

Origin, history, legislative intent, public demand, and the preliminary sifting of applicants by traditional job-search methods combine to produce this present dominance of the hard-to-place among the clientele of the Employment and Manpower Services. But the economic developments of today and tomorrow call for accompanying developments in employment and manpower practice. The changing foreign trade relations, the alterations in military and economic balance of power, the speeding up of technological advance, the rapid modification of the occupational structure, the shifting of the proportions in blue-collar and white-collar occupations, the shrinking of the transportation and communication time boundaries of the nation, all of these developments have their impact on the labor market. The agencies concerned with the development, movement, and utilization of manpower resources are poorly equipped for a positively advantageous adaptation to those developments—even on behalf of individuals in need—if their reservoir of applicants for jobs is not widely representative of the skills required by a productive economy, skills possessed not merely by the unemployed but by the employed also.

But the attempt to make the applicant-for-job rolls more representative of the total labor force will have greater chance to be stimulated and to succeed if the concept of the mission of the Employment and Manpower Services is that of a contributor to a more rational labor market organization and thereby to a strengthened economy than if that concept is focused chiefly on a social welfare or relief objective.

Even with the former objective as a policy guideline, however, the Employment and Manpower Services may still find themselves necessarily concentrating on certain groups of the hard-to-place just because they are honestly and intelligently trying to gear their activities to the labor market as it realistically is and is becoming. For example, the concern for maximum productivity as well as responsibility to employers requires that workers not be referred to jobs in which they cannot adequately function. The hard-to-place groups must, therefore, have greater attention placed on more thoroughgoing analysis of their potential and on using whatever counseling, testing, training, and retraining devices are necessary in order to bring that potential to its maximum possibility for employment. They will, therefore, get more service than highly qualified workers. Moreover, a service which feels a responsibility for maximizing the utilization of our manpower resources cannot dodge the fact that some of these groups represent an underutilized and therefore wasted manpower resource because of employer preferences and prejudice. The lessons of experience teach that these resources will not be fully utilized unless a degree of special effort by public and private agencies is exerted on their behalf. Many in this hard-to-place group represent a potential resource which, within a framework of employer preferences and prejudices marking these groups as less than desirable, is a resource unlikely to be used unless a degree of concerted effort by public and private agencies is exerted on their behalf. In time of civilian labor shortages, as in the war and mobilization periods mentioned above, there was little question that the Employment Service, by its special efforts to bring such "disadvantaged" groups into the active working force, was performing a much-needed national economic service. Is there enough faith in the future to suggest that the United States may experience the approximation to full employment existing in a number of European countries? Then these efforts to enlarge the labor force at its margins must be recognized as serving not only individuals but the nation by supplying workers to amplify the nation's productive effort, to reduce human resource shortages, and to weaken the impact of labor-cost-stimulated inflationary tendencies which accompany such shortages.

Furthermore, analysis of future labor force trends, as a basis for adaptation to those trends, indicates that the proportion of workers available for work is likely to increase, particularly among youth, older workers, the technologically (and, therefore, probably long-term) unemployed. A rational attempt to make maximum use of available manpower would justify forward planning for and special attention to such populations, even though no remedial action were called for at the present on social welfare grounds.

It must be emphasized, therefore, that approaching the problem of clientele to be served from the angle of adaptation to economic developments does not preclude or eliminate attention to the problems of the hard-to-place. Indeed, it assures attention to their problems even if the wells of human sympathy for their condition were to dry up.

Impact on the Service

The potential consistency between the social welfare mission of devoting attention to the hard-to-place and the economic mission of serving best the supply needs of a total labor force and the demand needs of all employers are clear. We have also seen that the direction of emphasis is not altogether a matter of choice for administrators of the Employment and Manpower Services. Moreover, since the hard-to-place are an ever-present part of the labor force, consideration of their welfare is not inconsistent with finding a useful place for them and developing to the highest degree their capacity to render productive service to the economy, a labor market problem which becomes acute in times of civilian manpower shortages and with the increase in the labor force of certain categories of workers, such as youth and the aged.

Where, then, does any difficulty arise? It arises from the fact that in order to perform an adequate and efficient placement service, *even for the hard-to-place*, the service requires a large volume of job orders of wide variety and scope from employers and applications from a large number of people, employed as well as unemployed, with a variety of skills needed by the employers. The inclination of both employers and workers to supply the Employment Service with these two reservoirs of orders and applications respectively, is influenced by the image they hold of the basic function of the Service and the utility of that function for them. If the image is that of a welfare and relief agency, their orders and applications will come at such times and in such volume as their own needs as users are appropriate to and consistent with that perceived function. That is, practically never, as far as employers are concerned.

The second problem is that a reputation for being a social welfare and relief agency increases the tendency of other agencies primarily devoted to this useful and necessary help to the unfortunate to lay upon the Employment Service a pressure for emphasizing employment and other services to their clientele, thus adding momentum to the creation of an image of an agency only secondarily concerned with the most economically advantageous fitting of men to jobs.

A related third problem is that the appraisal of the importance of the Employment and Manpower Services and the interest in the degree and type of support of them on the part of government officials and legislators tends to wax and wane with the size and significance of the central mission they conceive it to be performing. If that conception emphasizes social welfare and relief, the concern is great during periods of great labor surpluses. Even during periods of labor shortage caused by war or threats of war, the concern is merely temporary until the emergency is passed. The constant resources for the steady, continuous, and rational development of Employment and

Manpower Services, as an essential and integral part of the nation's facilities for promoting economic stability and growth, are not, therefore, likely to be forthcoming with the dependability required.

THE RESOLUTION

The image of the services as activities of a welfare agency can be corrected positively only by performance. Yet publicity has a role to play in keeping that image from dominating the minds of interested people. Publicity about how well the Employment Service is doing with respect to the hard-to-place can emphasize positively the *productive* values in certain of these categories of workers rather than the humanitarian assistance provided to "disadvantaged" individuals. The latter accomplishment is of great political interest to men dependent upon electoral support, for some of these groups have political power, and even the general electorate inclines to understand and be more interested in economic labor market problems if they are colored by moral considerations and charitable sentiment. But the price of such popularizing of the case for the value of the Employment Service by trumpeting its accomplishments with respect to the hard-to-place is the creation of an image of the service which discourages employers and workers from using it. Without an ample supply of orders and applications, as indicated above, the service is robbed of an operational field in which both the welfare and economic interests can be implemented.

The evidence of performance is, however, of importance equal to or greater than that from publicity. A resolution of this problem in performance can be suggested. There are three aspects of the placement work of the Employment and Manpower Services which are interdependent. One is the *referral* to and *placement* in jobs of workers meeting as closely as possible the specifications of the employers who have jobs to offer. The second is the *discovery* and *development* of the capacity of workers to meet these specifications. The third is *selling* to the employer the conviction that the workers available can meet his specifications.

Providing equality of opportunity for applicants in the first aspect means equality of opportunity for workers of *equal ability* to be referred to the employer, with ability defined as consistency with the productive needs of the employer. In accordance with these needs the Employment Service should send an employer the best available qualified or most nearly qualified worker without preference or prejudice. Preference in the implementation of the referral and placement aspects of the Employment Service function is the right of the employer (within the requirements of the law), not of the service.

But the available workers in the files approximate in varying degrees to possessing the present or anticipated qualifications demanded by employers. Economically oriented Employment and Manpower Services, with the objective of having as many qualified applicants as possible, must legitimately appraise the varying degrees of need of the applicants in the files and provide them with equality of opportunity to be fully qualified. Equality of opportunity in this sense can be provided only by gearing the treatment to the removal of the varying factors which leave particular workers short of qualification. This is not preferential but *equal* treatment in the discovery and development of the applicants' present degree of employment potential in any common-sense meaning of the word "equal."

In convincing the employer of the qualifications of a worker referred to a job, there is no problem if the applicant's skills fit and his other characteristics are consistent with the cultural and traditional concepts of what constitutes a "normal worker." If his skill qualifications are not sufficiently close to make a successful and satisfactory trial possible, he should not be referred. If all is promising on this score, and only the departure from the stereotype of a "normal" worker stands in the way, the Employment Service is performing an economic service both to the man and the employer by making it clear to the employer that the man is being referred because he *fits the skill requirements*, not because he "needs" the job because of his disadvantage. If a program or specific attempt to get employers to accept applicants on any other basis than their being the most competent workers is to be instigated, it should be carried on by other agencies whose distinct character as special pleaders is fully consistent with their humanitarian and social welfare objective.

There are those who suggest that a service which helps the hard-to-place worker and the employer with the hard-to-fill job is about what we can expect now and in the future in a public Employment Service. There are those who say this is inevitable and, since that is so, why not accept it, be proud of it, and try to improve the quality of the service within this limitation? Some have pointed to clothing stores specializing in the "hard-to-fit" and hospitals specializing in the "hard-to-cure," such as cancer and tuberculosis centers. But these analogies do not fit the Employment Service. The crucial difference is that one of the users of the Employment Service, the employer, is not looking for a service oriented toward the "hard-to-place." In the examples given, the "hard-to-fit" and the "hard-to-cure" and their families are looking for precisely that kind of service. Where applicants for jobs and furnishers of jobs are interested in the best possible jobs and men, a reputation for specialization, even successful specialization, in the "hard-to-place and hard-to-fill" market will destroy the inclination of the great majority of both to use the Employment Service.

MAXIMUM UTILIZATION OR JOB FINDING: THE ISSUE

Closely related to the question of the clientele to be served is that of the objective of that service. Shall the goal of effort be to find jobs for the unemployed and get them as rapidly as possible off the rolls of unemployment insurance claimants; or to do all possible to maximize the utilization of our manpower potential of the unemployed *and* employed? The answer, of course, is both. The first emphasizes placement activities, the second, the full roster of activities comprehended by Employment and Manpower Services. But which emphasis is most consistent with the work of an agency oriented toward an economic stability and growth mission as well as a secondary social service mission?

There is, of course, a distinctly economic utility arising from the effort directed toward finding useful jobs for the unemployed, or what may be called the narrow placement function, even if the motivation is a concern for the social welfare of the unemployed and their families. This utility is amplified, however, if the objective toward which we move is the maximum development and utilization at its highest potential of our employed, unemployed, and underemployed manpower resources. For it is not the simple fact that workers are at work which adds to the greatest possible stability and growth of the economy, and incidentally to the welfare of their families, but the fact that they are at work where they are most needed and at tasks which use to the full the skills they have or are capable of gaining. It is a matter of whether, as a result of counseling, vocational guidance, testing, placement, training, and retraining, they find the work for which they are most suited and which contributes most to the national product. It is a question of whether, as a result of the possession, by those able to offer this guidance and those in charge of educational and training facilities, of adequate information about present and future labor market trends, the guidance and preparation they receive is realistic. It is a matter of whether those in the so-called "labor reserve," for whom no place at all can be found in the present state of demand for labor, can develop out of their potential the qualifications to respond to a demand for labor likely to arise tomorrow, next month, next year. Finding jobs for or placement of the unemployed is an important activity for reaching this objective of maximum development and utilization of our manpower, but it is a means and not an end, and it is only one among several means.

To be sure, all Employment and Manpower Services deemed essential, once the end is defined as maximum manpower development and utilization, contribute in the long or even short run to making successful placements and removing workers from the rolls of the unemployed. But the basis for the evaluation of their effectiveness and, indeed, for their justification is much broader than this.

The Present Situation

There is no doubt whatever that the concept of mission in the minds of the national, regional, and most of the state administrators of the Employment Service puts the emphasis on the maximum development and utilization of manpower. The job-finding and placement tasks take their place as essential *along with* what are called the other "manpower" activities, including retraining. Indeed, the comprehensive term used to express this concept of an Employment Service with a horizon broader than that marking the boundary of a labor exchange service is "manpower" service, and the term "manpower center" is used to represent the officially intended nature of the local Employment Service office. The statements made by the recent Secretary of Labor, the administrator of the U. S. Bureau of Employment Security, and the director of the U. S. Employment Service are replete with phrases describing the "new look" of the service in such terms as: "Reducing underutilization of our manpower resources;" "making the best use of the nation's manpower;" "promoting optimum utilization of the nation's manpower resources," etc. One statement of the director of the U. S. Employment Service is typical:

> The identification of nationally significant employment and unemployment problems and the development of programs and the application of resources to their resolution are inherent in the reorganization. The Employment Service is concerned not alone with the most effective utilization of the Nation's manpower resources by facilitating the employment process, but also with the *development of our manpower resources and raising the skill levels of the work force* through training and retraining.

In other statements he has added, "through testing, counseling, vocational guidance, pointing out needed adaptation by vocational education to current and future occupational, technological, and labor market trends, and through providing and distributing facts about manpower needs and resources and labor market trends as a guide for all of this."

The terminology has fixed itself upon the discussion of their jobs by state and local officers of the Service, but there is some lack of clarity in their minds about whether and how such a service will be different from preceding ones when so characterized. A frequent transition conception is that the "manpower" activities, such as testing, counseling, vocational guidance, labor market information, training, etc., "facilitate" the placement activities and are to be evaluated by the degree of their success in doing so.

There is within the government no consensus as to how the responsibilities concerned with this mission, focusing on maximum development and utilization of the nation's manpower, should be distributed among agencies. Certainly there is no agreement that they all should be directed and coordinated through the U. S. Employment Service, an issue to which we shall return in a later chapter. But that this objective points to an opportunity for, and a legitimate function of, government is well established in the minds of government officials, and that legitimacy is underscored by several pieces of legislation since World War II.

In particular, the Area Redevelopment Act, the Manpower Development and Training Act, and the Trade Expansion Act have resulted in amplified attention to Employment and Manpower Services which have potential for manpower *development* programs, contributing not merely to placement satisfactory to individuals but to employment essential to the nation's economic strength and growth.

WHY?

Back of this new focus for the concept of central mission of the Employment and Manpower Services is a growing recognition of the need for and responsibility of government to implement a full employment policy, to strengthen the nation's economy in the face of growing competition from old and new industrial nations, and to deal with the anomaly of simultaneous shortages and surpluses of manpower for achieving this purpose.

The experience of two world wars and the Korean War brought home to public and private leaders alike the crucial role in any crises putting our economic strength to the test, not just of a labor force, but of labor force adapted and adaptable to specific tasks and sufficiently mobile so that it could be brought to bear on the productive process when and where needed. The words "manpower resources" and the successful effort devoted to marshalling them made men aware that here was a source of economic power which could be wasted or underutilized to the disadvantage not only of the individual workers but of the nation. The search for ways of avoiding this waste continued after the crises were passed, and stimulated men to think of the possibilities which were presented by these ways for meeting the challenges to our economic strength arising from economic and military competition, from our failure to find ways of using our unemployed labor resources, from the accelerating changes in our occupational structure and the changes to be anticipated as a result of automation, from our need to maintain a rate of economic growth beyond what we had been able to achieve, and from the changing age distribution of our population, carrying with it implications for the possibility of employment.

It took no extraordinary vision, but only a willingness to gear foresight to facts that could be plainly seen, to come to the conclusion that concerted public effort was needed to supplement private effort in assuring the nation of a fully developed, adaptable, and utilized manpower equal to the test of our economic strength we faced and would continue to face.

To these factors must be added the need of administrators of the Employment Service to develop a framework of objectives by reference to which the several functions which were added to their role for various reasons made systematic sense and had meaning. These tasks as they became more important, had a manpower development and maximum utilization focus, and it was, therefore, natural to take that common element running through them as the central factor that gave them meaning and significance.

IMPACT ON THE EMPLOYMENT SERVICE

The impact of this pressure of circumstances on the Employment Service has been mostly but not entirely advantageous. First, consider the disadvantages. The effort to extend the basic job from placement to maximum manpower development and utilization has produced some disagreement among administrators, and indeed some confusion, as to what their basic task is. This confusion has not been completely dispelled by the verbal acceptance of the "manpower" emphasis proclaimed from headquarters, and accepted, on the whole, in the field.

It has renewed the jurisdictional dispute as to the distribution of powers and functions between the federal and state administrations, and in some cases has raised it to a fever pitch, inhibiting maximum exploitation of the opportunity offered for enlargement of the significance of the function of the Service. It has led to the initial steps in divorce proceedings between Unemployment Insurance and the Employment Service after they had passed, if not celebrated, their silver wedding. The steps have not been taken in an entirely friendly and cooperative manner. It has brought the Employment Service into conflict (but not universally) with other traditional agencies performing manpower functions like vocational education and counseling and apprenticeship training facilities and institutions. It has also raised jurisdictional problems with government officials who conceive of this maximum development and utilization of manpower function as too comprehensive and complicated for the Employment Service to handle. It placed in the hands of critics a new two-edged sword for attacking the Service. On the one hand one critic can contend that the Service is inadequately performing its "manpower" functions, and another can contend from the same evidence that the Service is wasting its time with these "manpower frills" and neglecting its "real job" of placement and demonstrating its capacity to increase its penetration of the hiring market.

In our judgment these are disadvantageous growing pains that will disappear, although many of the interests involved are powerful and persistent. The most significant advantage is that the Employment Service has found a potential *raison d'etre* which gives it a claim to first-class citizenship among the agencies focusing their attention and effort upon the nation's economic strength and growth, which justifies its claims to steady and continuous support independent of the fluctuating humanitarian interest of the public and their legislative and administrative representatives, and which provides a source of meaningful criteria for the evaluation of its activities.

THE RESOLUTION

In posing the issue as one of emphasis between the maximization of the development and utilization of manpower and the finding of jobs for the unemployed, we were not setting up a straw man. There are real differences among concerned people as to what that emphasis should be. In a sense, however, the issue is which objective, the manpower development and utilization, or finding jobs for the unemployed, shall be the servant of the other. In our judgment the maximum development and utilization of manpower is the larger, more comprehensive goal, and more likely to lead to adaptation to the needs not only of workers but the nation. The so-called "manpower" activities are kinds of things a good placement officer would like to do for the sake of fitting men better to jobs. To the extent that an Employment Service does function efficiently as a placement agency, it is, *ipso facto*, improving not only the utilization but the development of manpower, and at the least is preventing its atrophy through disuse. Finding jobs for the unemployed is one means of reducing unemployment. But the reduction of unemployment over the long pull is, if accomplished, a larger task. It involves the effective development and utilization of all resources, including human resources, and providing the latter with the capacity to adapt and take advantage of modifications in the nature and mode of utilization of the other resources. It involves the contribution of such efforts to making industry more productive, efficient, and profitable so that it is stimulated and able to provide more jobs. Removing people from the rolls of the unemployed one by one has no necessary relation to stimulating such demand, which is the clue to the reduction of unemployment.

And what happens to the reason for an Employment Service which is limited to finding jobs for the unemployed, if, as we hope, we ever approximate that degree of full employment we are committed to? It would be sheer ostentation and folly for the Employment Service to claim jurisdiction over every kind of effort to maximize the development and utilization of manpower for productive employment, because those efforts comprehend well-nigh all social and political as well as economic activities known to men who live in some place other than the Garden of Eden. No such claim is made. The appropriate field for the Employment Service, and indeed for all the Employment and Manpower Services, is the labor market and the problems that arise within it. But, with that definition of field accepted, the mere finding of jobs for the unemployed is an inadequate mission to furnish it with a stimulus, design, motivation, and test of excellence for the task required to make the operation of the labor market a contribution to the nation's economic as well as social stability and growth.

EMPLOYER ORIENTATION: The Issue

In a free labor market a placement is ultimately consummated by the necessary decisions of two parties, the applicant worker and the employer. The Employment and Manpower Services are concerned with facilitating and making possible the positive decisions of both. Whether the guiding concept of mission of the services is oriented toward welfare and relief or toward economic strength, this is the case. Most of the supporting manpower services we have discussed are, however, directed to the needs of the applicant worker. They seek to increase the possibility of positive employment decisions by giving attention to the discovery and development of qualifications of the workers. That emphasis is natural if the welfare of individual workers dominates the concept of mission. The more emphasis is given to the economic mission of the Employment and Manpower Services, the more those services will also be concerned about the needs of the employers.

Private placement agencies, realizing that their fees depend ultimately on the employers' favorable decision to hire their clients, are not likely to neglect these employer needs, and, indeed, tend to give them high priority in the time they spend, and the choice of referrals they make. But their definition of employer needs is, "What kind of a worker do you want us to refer?"

The Employment and Manpower Services operate under the same necessity just in order to attract business, whatever the central mission. If, however, that mission emphasizes an economic health objective, the services are presented with other possibilities of moving toward that objective by providing services to employers which aid them in various ways: to make fuller utilization of the available manpower resources, to stabilize their employment by reduction of turnover, and to expedite the selection and placement of workers through a systematic analysis of their job structure and of the manpower requirements for each occupation in that structure.

This attention to the employers' needs has two aspects. The first might be called the promotion of job orders by visits of Employment Service staff to employers, making known to them the facilities of the Service, exploring with them the kinds of jobs they need to fill now and will need to fill in the future, and encouraging them to use the Employment and Manpower Services as a resource in filling them. The second, and somewhat controversial, aspect is what amounts to the provision of a consultative service to management related to their employment and effective-utilization-of-manpower problems. Among the services offered are job analysis to provide current information on the employer's job requirements; job analysis institutes to train personnel in industry; surveys to assist employers in planning their training and manpower needs; preparation of staffing patterns; studies of physical demands of jobs; job relationship studies to help employers in utilizing the skills of the work force; the use of Employment Service tests (G.A.T.B.) in selecting trainees and apprentices; assistance in training problems through advice and the performance of liaison services between employers, the Bureau of Apprenticeship and Training, unions, apprenticeship councils, and vocational schools. In identifying employment problems, employer representatives review with employers any indications of underutilization of skills, labor hoarding, other malutilization of manpower, excessive absenteeism and turnover, etc. They share with them any remedial actions they have noted being taken by other employers with whom they have been in contact. They may arrange for appropriate services to aid them in the solution of their problems.

The implementation of the industrial or employer services program is accomplished by technicians in the local Employment Service offices with advice and assistance from the state, regional, and headquarters staff. The technicians normally do not actually perform the work in resolving manpower problems. Rather, they perform a consultative service instructing (and sometimes training) employers or their administrative personnel in the use of techniques and materials which have been developed by or recommended by the United States Employment Service.

THE SITUATION

The existing arrangements for carrying on the first aspect of this job vary from locality to locality. In smaller offices the visits to employers are usually made by the manager; in larger offices, one or more employer representatives are in charge of this task, and in others the placement officers are given a quota of employer contacts to make either by phone or by personal visits. In a normal year well over 2,000,000 personal and 1,000,000 phone contacts are made. To our knowledge no thoroughgoing evaluation has been made of the effectiveness of these contacts in terms of the net increase in employer orders over what would have come in without such stimulus and the degree to which employers' specific needs were better served as a result of the information gathered from the contacts. The issue normally discussed centers around whether the contacts should be directed primarily toward the larger employers, the so-called "major labor market," or also toward the smaller employers. Superficially the greatest chance for expansion of placements by the Service would seem to lie in contacts with employers employing the largest share of the community's workers, but this is not agreed to by all administrators.

The federal Employment Service in recent years has made contact with upwards of 100 large multiplant firms to encourage their use of the Service, but the effectiveness of these contacts, either from the point of view of meeting better the employers' needs or increasing the volume of job orders, has never been thoroughly evaluated. Nevertheless, there is no lack of appreciation of the need for this attempt better to learn of and meet the employers' requirements for number and type of workers. Any lack of attention to the job is due, not to choice, but to necessity created by inadequacy of appropriations and staff to perform it adequately.

More debatable as an appropriate function of the Employment and Manpower Services is the second aspect of attention to the employers' needs, namely, the management consultative services. Set forth as one part of the six-point program of the Employment Service after World War II, given guidance through instructions from the federal office, they have never become a prominent and widely recognized function of the Service. In the distribution of scarce funds and staff resources they have had low priority.

Impact on the Employment Service

To the degree that the central mission of the Employment and Manpower Services is to contribute to the maximum and most effective utilization of manpower, there is prima facie justification for such a basically advisory service to the utilizers of manpower, if—and it is a big IF—the personnel available in the services is qualified to provide such advice. Even the value of such services in encouraging employers, grateful for the help received, to place more orders for workers with the Employment Service is dependent on the quality of such services. In this respect such services can be compared with the estate-planning advice provided by the agents of some insurance companies. It would seem reasonable to suppose that high quality of this type of advisory service would require either the employment of staff already prepared through experience to render such service or the institution of thoroughgoing training in the complexities of the internal manpower problems of management and in employer-employee relations, job evaluation, etc. If the funds can be provided to hire staff at the salary levels attractive to men with such ready-made qualifications for the job or to provide those initially unprepared with the training necessary, there is here a promising contribution to more effective and maximal utilization of manpower and to a reduction of turnover with its accompanying waste of manpower potential. The reduction of turnover, of course, reduces need for replacements and hence the opportunity for the Service to build a placement record to which its appropriations are geared. But, as has been said, the service rendered could conceivably encourage employers receiving it to make more continuous use of the Employment Service when they do need workers.

It should not be forgotten that the Employment and Manpower Services as well as employers are aided by such consultative activities. Indeed, effectiveness of the services as manpower development and placement agencies is aided by having first-hand, adequate knowledge of changes in job content, of problems of adapting workers to new tasks, and of changing manpower requirements of management. There could be devised no better way for acquiring this knowledge than by the type of sharing of management problems involved in these consultative services.

The Resolution

It should be noted that the justification for this aspect of the Employment and Manpower Services' attention to the needs of the employer is grounded in a basic concept of mission that is far broader than that oriented toward individual workers' welfare and relief, and only indirectly related to that oriented toward the maximization of finding jobs for the unemployed. It rests upon a concept of mission which involves the Employment and Manpower Services in activities seeking to remove all factors contributing to an underutilization of manpower, and to promote employment conditions and relations which contribute to productive economic strength through maximum and effective utilization of that manpower.

PREVENTION OR REMEDY: The Issue

Another important issue related to the placing of primary emphasis on economic health or on social welfare and relief has to do with concern for the *prevention* of or the *remedy* for unemployment. Unemployment has causes. It is conceivable that the minimizing of unemployment at time 2 is accomplished by efforts at time 1 to deal with causes, to a degree equal to or even greater than efforts at time 2 to deal with the experienced consequences. What can be done by the Employment and Manpower Services in either case will always be marginal in comparison with the obviously dominating efforts made by the millions of employers and tens of millions of workers in the land. But marginal effort may conceivably have a greater impact through preventive than through remedial action.

The Employment and Manpower Services, we have seen, originated as a response to the fact that some of our people needed help. They were unemployed; they needed jobs. They were unsuccessful in finding jobs through normal channels; they needed an additional intermediary facility between them and a potential employer. They lacked knowledge of the way their employment potential, proved inadequate for the moment, could fit into job possibilities existing or developing in a shifting labor market situation; they needed counseling and testing. They lacked skills which were in demand; they needed training. They had disadvantages because of physical or mental handicaps, youth, age, race, or just because they were unemployed;* they needed a sponsor whose interest in them as employable was not governed by prejudice or customary appraisals of the undesirability of employing people having these disadvantages. They were lacking money from wages to buy a living; they needed a sum to tide them over. A community was the victim of substantial and persistent unemployment; it needed to have its job openings increased by public works, defense orders, or industrial redevelopment.

As long as such problems exist for individuals and communities, the need for remedies will exist. No one in his right mind would suggest any relaxation of the government's responsible efforts to meet this challenge to the "general welfare" by strengthening the remedial activities suggested above. The institution of a program of preventive medicine and public health does not lead to the abolition of remedial medicine.

This present issue is not, therefore, one of remedy *or* prevention but remedy *and* prevention, or an increasing and realistic emphasis on reducing the need for remedy.

The Present Situation and Its Causes

Since the motivation for establishing the Employment and Manpower Services in the first place was an interest in remedies, it is

---

* It is frequently forgotten that just being unemployed is one of the severest handicaps a worker has in seeking a new job. Employers, knowing their own interest in holding their best men on the job, immediately label, as less than among the best, a man who has been let go by another employer. They consequently suspect that there must be some reason he is unemployed related to the lack of qualifications of the man himself.

natural that administrators, legislators, and critics should measure its success or failure by reference to the remedial efficacy of the services. It is natural that the chief justification for increased or decreased financial and staff support for the services should be the fluctuations in the number of persons who received remedial service, the number of placements, the numbers counseled and tested, the numbers trained, etc. It is natural that the timing of remedial action in the case of distressed communities should bring help *after* the situation is so bad that there is no question that something has to be done. It is natural, that is, if the concept of central and chief mission of the Employment and Manpower Services is merely to repair punctures rather than also to build tires less apt to puncture.

Actually the services are engaged in a number of activities whose value as preventive means are underestimated. These activities are evaluated (frequently to their disadvantage), as to their need for available funds and staff, primarily in terms of their contribution to an ultimate payoff in increasing the number of remedial placements rather than in terms of reducing the numbers for whom placement becomes the obvious need as a remedy for their unemployment. Let us focus our attention upon a few of these preventive activities.

The management services mentioned above come immediately to mind. To the degree that these services help to stabilize employment and reduce turnover, the numbers needing re-employment are reduced (and, incidentally, the opportunity for the Employment Service to make those credit-giving placements is reduced). An incidental but important possible result of such services is the cost-reducing advantages to employers, making more likely their ability to continue as a source of job openings.

Most constructive is the approach of the Employment Service to anticipating and preparing to avoid the unemployment difficulties following upon automation. In ten experimental centers the Employment Service is cooperating with employers, trade unions, and community agencies to anticipate the problem by getting advance notice of changes, working over with the employer the occupational requirements likely to result and the numbers likely to be affected, learning whether there is opportunity for preseparation service to the employer and affected workers so that the manpower adjustment problems of the employer will be minimized and the lead time for employment or retraining of probably-to-be-displaced workers can be increased.

Another example of such preventive activities is the testing and counseling of youths, dropouts or graduates, from our high schools. That counseling can influence initial job choices, or the planning of additional education or job experience sequences, in the direction of those jobs most suitable to the individual's capacities and basic self-conceptions. To the degree that this happens there is likely to result a better and more productive and satisfactory fit of individual and work. Under such circumstances, the chances of random, un-employment-producing experimentation or of blind-alley employment experience is reduced.

A recent offer of assistance by Employment Service to college place-ment officers, by putting at their disposal the facts about, and the interpretation of, labor market trends and a wider scope of occupa-tional and job choices than normally results from the scheduling of student interviews with the recruiting agents for large firms, has potentially this same result. In addition, the most productive and satisfactory placement of college graduates is an important factor in creating whatever employment opportunities exist in future years. A large number of them will occupy managerial positions upon whose effectiveness in decision-making and action their firms will depend in the future for expanding and profitable (and hence employment-producing) operation. Such increase in job openings are particularly promising in firms which today are small but have growth possi-bilities. These are just the firms which make minimal use of college placement services as presently operated.

The special counseling, testing, and training provided to the "disadvantaged" and hard-to-place influences not only the chances of their immediate relief from unemployment but the chances for their steadier and more continuous (and hence unemployment-reduc-ing) employment.

The annual-worker plan for migrant workers and the systematic scheduling of tandem jobs reduces the number of times during the season that these people become job seekers and reduces the length of their periods of unemployment between jobs, to say nothing of the advantage to employers in reducing their cost of operations and hence increasing the chance that they will continue to be able to offer job opportunities.

The advice and cooperation provided by the Employment Service to vocational education and apprenticeship training agencies on the basis of information available to the Employment Service about occu-pational and labor market circumstances, requirements, and trends is another case of preventive activity. That advice and co-operation offer these agencies the opportunity to make their curricula and pro-cedures more consistent with those circumstances, requirements, and trends, and is obviously an effort of the greatest preventive value.

A much-needed contribution in this area is the gearing of vocational education not merely to the immediate requirements for occupational skill, but to the long-range and basic preparation which will ready workers to make shifts in their skills when the occupations are either abolished as such or greatly modified in their skill content by the accelerating pace of automation.

It should be obvious that the participation of Employment Service personnel in stimulating and participating in forward-looking programs for community and regional industrial development is of the highest sort of preventive effort in reducing the need for remedial effort tomorrow.

Whenever local Employment Service offices have been forewarned of large-scale displacement of workers because of plant shutdowns or sizable technological changes, they have the opportunity to perform preunemployment analysis of the workers' qualifications and match them with local or extralocal job possibilities so that, to the extent it is possible to place these displaced workers at all, the period of their unemployment can be minimized. In Sweden this is felt to be sufficiently important to make desirable the move they have taken to have a voluntary agreement among employers to notify the Employment Service several months in advance of any sizable layoffs for any reason.

Even a *good* placement based on careful analysis of both the individuals' qualifications and the job requirements is a preventative of future (and sometimes almost immediate) unemployment.

Obviously, the basis for all of these preventive services is the continuous attention being given by the Employment Service to the study and analysis of specific job requirements, of qualifications of the existing labor force, both employed and unemployed, of the impact of technological and managerial procedures on the structure and content of occupations, of shifting industrial and geographical factors in work opportunities and in labor market conditions and trends. These are the tools without which such preventive measures cannot be made effective.

These preventive efforts are being made by the Employment and Manpower Services at the present time. They are evidences of how far the actual character of the Employment Service has advanced beyond that of a remedial "labor exchange"—evidences with which, to judge from their comments, many people outside of the administration of the services are unfamiliar. The problem is that effort in these directions fits uneasily into a conception of the central role of an agency dominated by its remedial and relief functions. Emphasis on these preventive functions is more appropriate to an agency directed toward the maintenance of positive economic health than to one charged with relieving the human suffering following upon economic sickness. The strengthening and expansion of these preventive efforts would, of course, contribute to both objectives. But that achievement will be encouraged both among administrators and the suppliers of resources in government, and it will be facilitated by co-operation from related agencies, to a greater extent if the first type of mission is recognized as at least of equal significance and legitimacy with the second.

The Employment and Manpower Services comprehended in the responsibilities of the Labor Market Board in Sweden include prevention-of-unemployment measures, measures which, if carried on at all in the United States, are the responsibilities of agencies other than the Employment and Manpower Services, and which come into play when remedies are called for. These are briefly mentioned here in order to indicate some of the kinds of preventive action which are consistent with the role of Employment and Manpower Services geared to prevention as well as to remedy, to producing economic health as well as to providing social welfare and relief.

The Labor Market Board has control over the setting in motion of employment-producing funds and procedures in anticipation of the need for them. One of these is unique to Sweden, the so-called "investment reserves" built up by individual employers by placing a portion of their profits into those reserves. The proportion of their profits placed in such reserves are tax-free if they agree to use the fund for capital improvements, determined upon by the company itself, *only at such times, and within such time limits,* as the Labor Market Board determines such activity would help to prevent an increase in industrial unemployment. A second resource controlled by the Board is a "shelf" of public works, for which the plans have been made and approved, which can be released for immediate implementation under the same circumstances by the Board. A third is the power of the Board to recommend the direction of government orders, particularly defense orders, to those areas in which an increase in unemployment is anticipated.

The significant characteristic of these possible efforts of the Board is that they are set in motion before unemployment becomes a large problem, that is, when, on the basis of probable trends in employment over the next year or six months (a probability inferred from prognostic information gathered by local managers of the Employment Service), unemployment is anticipated in the not-too-distant future.

By a threatening situation, they mean one in which the rate of unemployment is likely to rise above two per cent. In Sweden in August, 1962, such a "threatening" situation was predicted for the building trades and forestry industry during the coming winter. The Board had already acted to set in motion public works and defense orders, appropriate for these sectors, which would come into employment-producing operation before that threat became a reality, and would be discontinued before it was anticipated that the probability of a resurgence of private enterprise could restore employment opportunities for at least 98 per cent of the available work force.

We also utilize such employment-producing measures, but after unemployment has reached, in the affected areas, a dangerous rate of six per cent and has remained there for some time, and that fact is certified by current statistics gathered by the Employment Service and the unemployment insurance administration. In other words, our action is more remedial than preventive. It comes into play after unemployment has got rolling and the skills of the unemployed labor force have become rusty and sometimes atrophied by disuse.

Impact on the Employment and Manpower Services

We observe, then, a situation in which, although the Employment and Manpower Services perform many important and useful tasks in the prevention of unemployment, the public and even people in government are either unaware of, or undervalue, such efforts in contrast to their awareness and evaluation of the remedial tasks performed, meeting the needs of people after they are unemployed, and the needs of communities or regions after unemployment is so severe that from a humanitarian and political-pressure point of view something has to be done. Moreover, even job-creating measures which might be used as preventive medicine are brought into operation after, rather than before, the fact of severe unemployment, and in any case are not under the direct supervision of the Employment and Manpower Services. The impact of this situation on the services is a perpetuation among administrators, congressional and state legislators, employers, workers, and the public of the social welfare emphasis in their mission. Furthermore, it leads to an underemphasis on, or inadequate understanding of, the potential in Employment and Manpower Service activities for long-run stabilization and smoother operation of the labor market and the maintenance and expansion of employment-producing facilities. The allocation of funds and staff to the services is premised on a conception of their appropriate role as remedial, and the formula for that allocation is geared to the number of remedial actions taken, with an inevitable underemphasis on the equally important preventive measures, since these do not pay off as automatically and as obviously. There is little encouragement save that which arises from a sense of responsibility among placement officers for doing the best possible job of prevention (an effort more likely to be punished than rewarded, since it takes more time) and from their emphasis upon the quality of placements as a preventive of future unemployment. And we have not even begun to think of the inclusion in the Employment and Manpower Services of the expansion of job opportunities before a community is, in essence, a "distressed area."

THE RESOLUTION

The resolution of this difficulty is implicit in what we have said above: an acceptance by all concerned of the significance, importance, and need for support of the preventive aspects of the work of the Employment and Manpower Services equal to that given to its remedial aspects.

SUMMARY

The alternatives of economic health for the nation or social welfare and relief for the unemployed and additionally disadvantaged workers are likely to appear general and abstract as policy premises, unless they are given operational definition. Or to put it in the form of a question, "What kind of operational emphases and direction would be given services which were guided by these two concepts of central mission?"

It was suggested that the following emphases would probably necessarily characterize Employment and Manpower Services whose central mission was primarily oriented toward the nation's economic health, counting on the social welfare and relief for individuals to be a resulting by-product of that primary emphasis.

1. The clientele to be served would be not merely the hard-to-place but any and all workers, actual and potential, employed

and unemployed, whose productive work is the basic ingredient in the nation's economic strength.

2. The placement of workers would be governed not by privileged treatment for special or needy groups, but by evaluation of the best possible objectively determined fit of their capacities with the productive needs of business, industrial, and professional enterprises.

3. The mere removal of workers from the rolls of the unemployed would be looked upon as a by-product of the attempt to employ workers at the highest level of production of which they are capable or for which they can be trained.

4. The consideration and analysis of the employers' needs and capacity to utilize effectively the services of the workers would receive an emphasis certainly equal to the consideration and analysis of the workers' needs and their capacity to profit from performing those services.

5. The relief of unemployment and of the unemployed would have no greater value in the program than the reduction of the necessity for such relief through attention to measures designed to prevent unemployment now and in the future.

In each case these statements were discussed by reference to:

1. A sharpening and amplification of the issue posed.

2. A statement of the present situation in the United States with respect to the issue as far as the operation of the Employment and Manpower Services is concerned.

3. Pointing out some of the major causes or problems that lead to that situation.

4. Indicating the observed or potential impact of the choice of emphasis on the Employment and Manpower Services.

5. A proposed resolution of any apparent difficulties arising from a concentration on one emphasis or the other.

In summary, the conception of the central mission of the Employment and Manpower Services proposed in the last two chapters is that they are instruments (a) for developing and improving the quality and employment of the total manpower resources required by the nation's economic health, strength, and growth, and (b) for allocating and counseling as to the employment and utilization of those resources. In both cases the objective is that those resources are not wasted but are used to the full and at their maximum potential for achieving that end. In the performance of that mission the Employment and

Manpower Services contribute to and amplify the social welfare of individuals and supply relief to them when needed. But their policy and operation is to be governed by the fact that they are fundamentally instruments for promoting the economic health and growth of communities and the nation which, if the effort is effective, also increase social welfare and reduce the need for relief, rather than by the fact that they are social service and relief instruments which, as a by-product, affect favorably the economic health of the communities and the nation.

In Chap. 4 we amplify this statement of mission to highlight the role of the Employment and Manpower Services as the promoters of the movement and mobility of manpower within a free labor market.

MANAGED AND FREE
LABOR MARKETS

Chapter Four The foregoing discussion of the difference between economic health for the nation and social welfare and relief for individuals as the controlling and guiding goal for the operation of the Employment and Manpower Services may have appeared to push to one side the consideration of one mission of the services to which everyone subscribes, namely, to make more speedy the movement of workers to jobs and of jobs to workers. Such has not been our intention. But it has been our intention to indicate that "speedy" is not the only descriptive adjective which needs to be applied to the kind of movement that characterizes a healthy economy.

The movement of workers and their mobility, i.e., their disposition to move, are, along with the movement and mobility of capital, the basic dynamic process we count on to assure us that the economy will produce for consumers what they want produced. If the choices of consumers, both domestic and foreign, are to be honored and satisfied, there has to be an expansion joint in the economic factors of production, an adaptive mechanism. That mechanism is the movement and mobility of capital and labor. The second definition of the central mission of the Employment and Manpower Services is to contribute to this movement and mobility in the labor market.

That movement, of course, must be accomplished in accord with the basic principles of relations among people and between people and government to which we attempt to hold all institutions and particularly government institutions. One of those principles operative in the labor market is that free choice by individual workers shall determine what work they do and where they do it, limited, of course, by the job opportunities available as a result of the exercise of free choice by employers as to the kinds of work they offer and whom they wish to do that work. Both workers and employers are, naturally, limited by the boundaries of "legal" work, in general and specifically appropriate to certain age and sex groups, and by rules governing the standards of wages, working conditions, and nondiscrimination imposed in the public interest. But, aside from these limitations, free choice is expected to govern, unless that free choice does not result in an amount and type of movement adequate to some pressing public need.

Emphasis on free choice, however, raises another issue beyond the regulation by government of that choice. What is needed, other than noninterference by government, to make choice realistically *free*? Are there obstacles to free choice which are faced differently by different workers and employers and which emphasize the tragic elements in the statement that "all Frenchmen are equally free (or have the right) to sleep under the bridges?"

In the discussion of this facilitating-of-labor-movement-and-mobility mission of the Employment and Manpower Services, consequently, we find no dispute about the abstract definition of that mission, but there are two approaches to policy at the operating level when we seek to implement this mission where differences in premises become apparent.

MANAGED OR FREE MOVEMENT

The first issue is whether we shall leave workers and employers absolutely free to make use of the Employment and Manpower Services or not, as they wish, and absolutely free to accept or reject any solution to their respective problems proposed by the administrators of those services.

On general grounds of principle this would áppear to be an open-and-shut case. Of course, free choice should govern. But there are situations which becloud the issue.

THE SITUATION AND ITS CAUSES

The first exception to the completely voluntary filing of applications for work and of job orders occurs when the need arises for a rational allocation of manpower in times of war and attendant civilian manpower shortages.

In 1918 the President ordered all employers engaged in war work with 100 or more workers to hire unskilled labor through the Employment Service.

During World War II the Employment Service became in fact the operating arm of the War Manpower Commission. The first duty here was to staff and stabilize employment in war and war-supporting activities through regulations governing recruitment, hiring, release of workers, length of the work week, establishment of plant employment ceilings, priority of referrals, etc. The attempt was made also to make full utilization of all local resources before going outside for "help." These programs took the form of restrictions on the hiring of new employees, based on the assumption that if all new hires could be regulated, the movement of workers from job to job could be directed to the advantage of the war effort. In order to rank establishments in the order of priority of their claims and to meet their manpower needs, a series of interagency committees was established to determine these relative urgencies. One of them, the Area Manpower Priorities Committees (eventually 131 of them), allocated manpower and determined employment ceilings for each individual establishment. The Employment Service, of course, responded to requests for workers in accordance with the priorities established by these regulations.

All of this government "interference" with the free employment of workers was done, however, with the advice, and' within policies suggested by, a National Labor-Management Policy Committee made up of representatives of labor and management groups, who, normally committed to freedom of choice, faced squarely and co-operatively the need for compulsory regulation in the national emergency.

Although the regulation was maintained within a framework of "voluntary co-operation," the War Manpower Commission and its operating arm, the Employment Service, did have a number of "persuasive" devices at their command. For example, the War Manpower Commission could recommend to the War Production Board and the procurement agencies that priorities for needed materials, equipment, etc. be withheld from "unco-operative" employers. A second method was to deny assistance in obtaining an adequate labor force.

The regulation of workers' choices was, of course, implied in, and affected by, this regulation of the hiring process. Further attempts to get workers to move to essential-industry jobs or to remain where they were, to enter the labor force, or to take training for jobs where shortages were evident were of a "persuasive" character. The only clear case of compulsion arose when the Army released a large number of soldiers to the enlisted reserve with the agreement that they be employed by mines, rubber plants, and foundries. An indirect form of self-induced compulsion was, of course, apparent in the "voluntary" choice of jobs through the doing of which draft deferment was possible.

In both cases the elements of ultimate compulsion were absent. The compulsory registration for work and job orders, the compulsory acceptance of job offers and of workers, the legally binding use of *only* the Employment Service were measures not taken even in the face of this most severe problem of manpower mobilization the nation had ever faced. If such measures were not resorted to at such a time, it is scarcely conceivable that we would choose to do so in peacetime, however much they might superficially seem to promote a more rational organization of the labor market in the interests of the nation's economic strength and growth.

An unpublicized but definite responsibility of the Employment Service is to assist in the project to plan and be ready for immediate implementation of the manpower allocation problems of production and of civil defense if and when a war emergency arises. This function, of course, would have to be characterized by a degree of compulsion appropriate to the state of war in which the nation would find itself.

In the peacetime operations of the Employment Service as such, there is no hint of curtailment of the absolute freedom of both employers and workers not claiming unemployment insurance to use or not to use the placement service or to accept or reject recommendations of the Service as to jobs or workers. Employers have felt some pressure at times to accept veterans, handicapped workers, older workers, or youth, as legislative or executive action has compelled or encouraged the Service to give emphasis to such placements. Employers' requests for referrals of only white or colored workers are, of course, refused as a matter of national and state nondiscrimination policies. In a number of states requests for workers below a certain age would also have to be honored only if the matter of age could be related specifically to qualifications for a particular job.

But there is nothing in the United States similar to the law in England that a request for an able-bodied worker cannot be honored unless the employer has on his payroll the full quota of handicapped workers assigned to him. Nor are workers compelled to accept ancillary services such as testing, counseling, training, etc.

In its function as an agency for unemployment insurance, however, a real element of compulsion enters the work of the Employment Service with respect to applicants for such benefits. They are compelled to register for work at an employment office and to accept any offer of "suitable" employment as a condition for receiving their benefits. As the length of the unemployment period increases, the compulsion to meet this "work test" by accepting a job of a geographical or occupational character not completely consistent with what the worker would choose (as an alternative to remaining on unemployment insurance) becomes stronger.

The requirement of filing of applications for those claiming unemployment insurance benefits exists even in those cases where no one wants him to be given another job. Neither the employer, who wants the worker to stay in "his" labor reserve, nor the worker himself, who wishes to maintain his seniority, fringe benefits, and callback rights, nor the union, desiring to protect those rights for its members, wants the unemployed worker referred to a job if there are prospects of his returning to the one from which he has been laid off and which he considers to be *his* job. However anomolous it may seem to be that unemployment insurance benefits designed as a tideover compensation for those who are unemployed through no fault of their own, but who are *willing* to work and *available* for work, should be provided to workers whom no one involved wants to have available for work, it is an inevitable consequence of the unemployment insurance system as it has developed.

Basing their contention on this fact of compulsory registration of claimants and the increasing downgrading of what is considered to be "suitable" work as the period of unemployment lengthens, there are those who contend that this fact of compulsion provides an inequality of treatment of workers and of employers with respect to free choice. For employers are neither compelled to register their orders nor to accept workers referred to them. This is discrimination, these people contend, that shows up as false the general assumption that government agencies are concerned to maintain a "free" movement of labor in the labor market.

The logical deduction of the existence of discrimination is clear. Empirically it does exist. But there is also a discrimination between employers and unemployed workers in the rewards that are available to them for sacrificing the degree of freedom involved in compulsory registration with the Employment Service. The worker thereby becomes entitled to unemployment insurance benefits. The employer, by a similar sacrifice of freedom, thereby would become entitled to—what?

Those unemployed who do not desire to receive unemployment insurance benefits are not required to register, and no one is required to limit his job hunting to such registration. This justification for the alleged discrimination would not apply as strongly in cases such as the receipt of government contracts, where the employer might be considered to be receiving a quid pro quo for his agreement to register all job orders related to the contract work at the public employment office.

In all our contacts with federal, state, and local people connected with the Employment Service, we did not find one who urged even this sort of compulsory registration of job vacancies. Their practical argument against it was that in the long run the placement relations with employers would be on a firmer basis if they were geared to voluntary conviction of the values of the placement service to them, and that their relations with employers and other community forces in connection with other manpower functions would be vitiated if they were perceived and experienced as a compulsion-exerting arm of government. It should be said that many of them expressed the same anxieties about the compulsory function carried out by the Employment Service as a "work tester" for unemployment insurance claimants.

On practical grounds, of course, it is doubtful whether public opinion would continue to support an unemployment insurance system at all unless this assumed protection of the system against malingering were provided. The chief popular arguments against unemployment insurance in the beginning was based on this prophecy of malingering. The strongest attack on the system today is that, in spite of the "work test" provided by registration and the willingness to accept an offer of suitable work, malingering still exists.

PROS AND CONS OF FREEDOM OF MOVEMENT

The causes for this dominant adherence to voluntarism and freedom of choice, aside from the situation relative to unemployment insurance claimants, scarcely need elaboration. It is built into the values of individual liberty that by common consensus we believe to be essential to the maintenance of our way of life and work and our institutions. In the exercise of that private freedom, enterprises and trade unions and other organizations and even individuals, of course, face others with choices that are far from free. But the government interferes with this free choice directly at its peril. Indirectly it does so through laws and agencies. But we have found no tendency on the part of any who influence policies of the Employment and Manpower Services even to desire a situation in which they could plan and direct and manage the allocation of labor by any other means than through presentation of the facts about alternatives, genuine persuasion with respect to the most appropriate of those alternatives in the light of the workers' or employers' own circumstances, the improvement of workers' qualifications freely to choose among those alternatives, and then allowing the decision to rest with the parties involved. Nor are they desirous of winning a larger share of the market by any means other than having a better service to offer which encourages voluntary use of that service.

Moreover, there has come to be accepted the reasonableness of one of the chief present-day inhibitions to movement, callback rights and seniority and fringe benefit rights. It is considered unreasonable to ask workers to forego these. To the workers, these vested rights look as important as a security measure as does a new job or a new possibility for jobs, particularly in view of the fact that without these, experience tells them no job is secure.

What is infrequently mentioned, but well understood, as justification for voluntarism is that the maintenance of free choice of jobs and workers is our most important check on the possibility that the best of economic planning may result in decisions which lead to the destruction of other values we prize, social and political as well as economic values. Actually, we do not know what certain values, which can be affected by the movement of labor, are worth in comparison, for example, with economic productivity. What, relative to that, is the value of the maintenance of local culture and institutions, of the maintenance of the critical numbers and diversity necessary to support and develop it, of family solidarity, of invention of local and personal adaptations when customary ways fail, of freedom to choose and face the consequences of choice, of refusal to amplify, by movement to the cities, the maladaptations of concentrated urban and industrial living? Even if we could estimate the relative values and give the prize wholly to economic strength and growth, we have no assurance of the omniscience and unerring wisdom of those who plan to achieve greater economic productivity. Under the circumstances, the rights of the individual to decide for himself at what and where he shall work and of the employer to decide who will work for him are the sort of basic check on such evaluations and plans which we can ill afford to cast aside.

We would be dodging the issue, however, if we did not take account of some of the factors that cause a more compulsive management of the labor market to become attractive.

The temptation to accept a "managed" labor market is obvious and, as we have seen, is effective in times of war because the demands on the economy are so heavy and civilian manpower is in such short supply. But if free choice is inadequate in wartime, some may ask, is war the only crisis which makes perilous the waste of manpower, the failure to employ workers at their highest potential? And in any case is it safe to have no preparatory conditioning of workers and employers for those emergency situations in which it is impossible to allow freedom of choice to govern? If that end could not be achieved through completely voluntary choice when the need for sacrifice of personal preference in the national interest was so obvious and compelling, can it be achieved when such motivation is lacking?

The temptation arises when pockets of large and persistent unemployment develop. If there are shortages of labor elsewhere in the economy for which these unemployed people can be trained, and then moved to areas where their labor can be used, should we honor their desire to stay where they are or not to take the training?

Our traditional trust has been in the offering of wage incentives of sufficient size to attract people to where job openings are increasing and to induce them to overcome their natural resistance to moving. This has a direct bearing on increasing the wage level in the expanding industries needing workers, a level which is probably in line with increasing productivity there. But that impetus has a tendency to spread to areas where productivity increases are not equivalent to the wage increases and hence to produce inflationary "wage-push" pressures there. What degree of "encouragement" of worker movement is required to take the pressure off the normal large wage differential incentive as the chief means of inducing movement? Although this argument related to inflation prevention has been used by certain labor leaders in Sweden in justification of "stimulating" greater movement of labor, it has not been employed to justify openly "managed" movement. We have seen no indication that American labor union leaders are inclined to forego the advantages to their members in the classical economists' solution of the area labor shortage problem by reliance on competitive wage offers to reduce such shortages.

Another reason inclining some to favor more "management" of labor movement is implicit in the question, "How much compulsion with respect to workers' choice of jobs and of employers' choice of workers is required to preserve the consumers' choice of goods?" Is it possible that consumers and workers cannot simultaneously have free choice? If, for example, workers disemployed from industries which consumers have left high and dry choose to remain where they are and live on unemployment insurance benefits or have some kind of relief works or new industry brought to them, the consumers' choice is limited to that extent. They, the consumers, *must* "choose" to have nothing, or to accept the products (say, roads or grade crossings or drainage projects) resulting from relief works, or whatever products are put out by industries encouraged to move in or by firms receiving defense orders.

Another temptation to employ a degree of compulsion in the movement of labor arises from the same circumstance referred to above as an advantage of free choice, namely, a check on the possible negative impact of planned economic operations and growth on other prized values. This check would be no advantage if it were not effective. But it is. All plans for a dynamic economy involve the necessity for the movement of resources. And the success of the best-laid plan can flounder on the rock of the failure of workers to move in support of the labor requirements of the plan. That is the reason it is self-evident that any spokesman for Soviet Russia is talking through his hat if he claims that there is no need for compulsory measures in the allocation of labor if a centralized plan of economic operations and growth is to be realized according to that plan. No private enterprise would claim it can realize a systematic plan for production, profit, and expansion and at the same time allow any employee to choose his own job and every foreman and supervisor to choose his own workers.

So to the extent that centralized planning becomes an approach to economic strength and growth, not only the temptation, but the necessity to exercise control of the movement of labor becomes imperative. Those who urge this approach would be less than honest if they did not admit that the chances of carrying through their plans to their specified goals were inversely proportional to the lack of success in planning for and implementing the movement of labor. Having little confidence in the probability of free enterprise through free choices of enterprisers to reach any specified 'over-all goals, they would be inconsistent (or lacking in knowledge of the interaction of economic factors) to leave the movement of labor to the absolutely free choice of individual workers and employers.

Our own inclination is to rate these considerations increasing the temptation to manage the movement of manpower as of secondary importance to the maintenance of freedom of choice as a principle of operations. This inclination is reinforced if one considers the impact on the Employment and Manpower Services of departure from the voluntary principle.

IMPACT OF MANAGED MOVEMENT ON THE EMPLOYMENT AND MANPOWER SERVICES

The impact of moving toward more compulsory measures in the development, allocation, and utilization of manpower would undoubtedly have, over the long pull, damaging effects on the Employment and Manpower Services. Even if it were possible to obtain from the federal and state legislatures (and both are involved) grants of power making that possible, the resulting public outcry could well become the domestic political issue of the decade. Added to other criticisms of the services, it could well reduce them to what the Employment Service alone was in the 1930's, a handmaiden of relief works and, later, of unemployment insurance.

The only possible (and even so, not very probable) public tolerance for ultimate interference by government in freedom of choice would be in cases where voluntary choices had resulted in such obvious and costly personal failures that direction of movement from some source other than the individual was probably necessary. Yet even then, although the general public was not immediately interested, it soon would be, when the cries of protest arose alike from unemployed workers, unions, and employers. A public employment service could improbably survive such a protest.

Even this threat is not the most important. The administrators of the services would have reduced for them the now dominant condition of their survival and development, that they have to legitimize themselves and their work, obtain the resources for their operations from Congress and the state legislatures, and increase their use among workers and employers, by an excellence of services that encourages these supporting and "consumer" sources freely to choose to give such support to, and make use of, those services. The wartime exhilaration of Employment Service administrators from their sense of making important economic decisions and having the power to insist on their acceptance, and from the privilege of controlling the satisfaction of workers' and employers' desires, is not a motivation possible of maintenance in a peacetime society in which opportunity is considered to be a matter either of chance and choice or of one's own making, rather than the result of the benevolent designs of someone else.

The only possible departure from the free-choice principle of operation is in a situation of national emergency so critical that those involved voluntarily choose to forego their freedom for the time being.

THE CONDITIONS OF "FREE" CHOICE

The continuance of reliance on free choice for an economically efficient movement of manpower resources has, however, a major implication for the mission of the Employment and Manpower Services. Reliance on a principle of operation is reliance on a cliche unless the services are geared to the removal of obstacles to its implementation. "Free choice" is not implemented by its proclamation, but by successful efforts to make realistic the word "free" in that phrase. This leads to the consideration of the next issue related to the concept of the mission of the Employment and Manpower Services to facilitate the rational movement of labor in a free labor market.

We can put this issue positively by saying it is the mission of the Employment and Manpower Services to provide the conditions in the labor market which make possible a truly free choice of jobs and workers. A listing of these conditions indicates the significance of this mission and the consequences of accepting it as a guideline for the kinds of activity the services necessarily would engage in. Following are the conditions:

1. *The availability of free facilities for bringing employers desiring workers and workers desiring jobs together.* The operation of these facilities would seek to establish the further conditions of free-choice movement indicated below.
2. *Reservoirs of workers' applications and of employers' orders adequate in volume and in the geographical, industrial, and occupational scope to provide employers and workers with a range of alternatives among which "free" choices can be made.* Unless the reservoirs of both applications and orders are ample and varied and approximate as closely as possible to representing the full range of types of workers and types of jobs available in the labor market with regard to occupation, industry, and geographical location, there is little reason to speak of choice, to say nothing of "free" choice. The offer of a choice called "free" is an anomalous claim to the degree that alternatives are restricted within the narrow limits now existing.

We (rightly, I think) steer clear of compulsory application and registration of vacancies as a means of amplifying
this coverage and hence the reservoirs of alternatives. But the
abnegation of compulsory techniques in filing applications
and job orders and in urging acceptance of the matching of
the two proposed by the Employment Service does not lessen
the crucial importance of the adequacy of the applicant and
job-opening reservoirs themselves. In this connection the improvement of "clearance" procedures and of the more-than-
local applicant and job-opening data necessary to satisfy the
requirements of balance in a larger-than-local labor market
is an effort toward widening the boundaries of free choice
for both workers and employers. Choice, to be free, should
not be limited to alternatives available locally.

3. *The provision of workers and employers with adequate information about the details of the present and future labor
market and labor force so that their choice can be free with
respect to the relative promise and security of the employment relationships available.* A choice based on ignorance of
the general conditions of demand and supply, their trends,
and their probable future in the labor market is not a "free"
choice. This is particularly important for youth, since, after
a bit of experimentation, the occupant of an occupational or
industrial job gets marked as such and is less free to move.
This information would have to be backed by adequate collection, analysis, and understandable presentation of both
current and predictive labor market and labor force facts.

4. *Precise and thoroughgoing information about, and analysis
of, the employment potential of workers and of job requirements, and any needed guidance as to where that potential
can be used or as to where the qualified workers can be
found, so that any choice made can be realistically free.* An
unrealistic choice may be made "freely," but it is an expression of the kind of freedom that is more likely to lead to
frustration and failure than to satisfaction and success, for
both employer and employee. This information and guidance
must be backed by application and order taking (and tools
for their recording) which are both comprehensive and pene-
trating in their provision of data for the assessment of worker
potential and employers' needs. It also requires the availability of effective testing and job-analysis techniques as aids
to the obtaining of such data.

5. *The opportunity for workers to develop skills and qualifications which make a "free" choice possible when a job opportunity is offered.* This condition emphasizes the need for training, retraining, and vocational education geared to the nature of present and future job opportunities. There is an increasing chance that the occupational structure will change as a consequence of skills required by developing technology. When that happens, people broadly trained vocationally and those narrowly trained for a particular present-day occupation are not equally free to change. This emphasizes the need for close and influential contact of an Employment and Manpower Service, in possession (hopefully) of the facts of technological trends and their impact on occupational developments, with the vocational-education people. It also emphasizes the need for retraining of adults and the same close and influential contact between retraining agencies and the Employment Service. A worker is not free to choose in the face of shifts in demand for qualified workers if he can come to an opportunity only with the skills he has acquired from a working experience before the shift took place.

6. *The reduction of restrictive costs of movement for individuals and their families so that movement otherwise desirable and acceptable to workers or employers is not hampered.* There is no freedom to choose a job to which one cannot afford to move. This is a touchy issue at the moment involving the provision of relocation allowance of various kinds, the provision of housing, and the liquidation of present property holdings. Several kinds of such efforts are to be found in a number of countries. They are most highly developed in Sweden. Among the efforts made to reduce the economic inhibitions to movement to another locality are the following:

Travel allowances for the worker for transportation to the new job and for removal of his family and belongings.

Family allowances granted when accommodation for the family cannot immediately be provided in the new locality. The family staying behind is generally in need of compensation for extra expenditure.

Starting allowance granted to cover the living costs until the first pay day.

Decisions on travel allowances can at present be made in Sweden by the local employment offices, while decisions on the other allowances are left to the county labor board in question. Geographical mobility is in some cases promoted by the board's building *temporary housing* in areas with expanding economic activity. Also the anticyclical allocation of housing subsidies is utilized not merely as a stimulus to production in general, but with reference to particular localities where the need for housing has developed as a result of the privately promoted expansion of employment. To date the proposals for the provision of such removal allowances and subsidies have received a chilly and negative reception in the United States.

On grounds of principle it is objected that there is already tremendous over-all movement of labor in the United States, the costs of which are financed by private individuals and firms. Unless a means test were to be applied, what would prevent this now privately borne cost from being unloaded onto government? To be sure, cost is an inhibition to movement otherwise desirable both from the point of view of individual, firms, and the general productivity of the economy. But is there not a limit to subsidies that governments can or should provide to make possible a free choice or even to gain a productively advantageous allocation of the work force?

The Swedes contend that, quite apart from the principle of making a freer choice of movement possible, it is less costly for government to subsidize movement of an unemployed worker to a job in which he becomes a productive worker, or in order that he may take training for such a job, than to continue to pay him unemployment insurance or to provide relief works. And the regulations for the payment of such allowances, on the whole, support the probability that the issue is considered to be not one of transference from private to public cost bearing, but one of alternative costs to government. The choice is focused on the economic and cost advantage of substituting movement benefits for maintenance-in-idleness type of benefits.

Moreover, there is no more inclination in Sweden (or, for that matter, in any of the other eight European nations which provide movement allowances to unemployed workers) than in the United States to subsidize anyone who wants to or has a chance to move, or to supplant private investment in movement by public subsidies. Regulations to assure this vary, but they nowhere contain a needs test. For example, in order to qualify for traveling and removal allowances in Sweden the following must be ascertained:

a. That the worker is unemployed or certified by the Employment Service as about to be unemployed.

b. That the Employment Service certifies that there is no work likely to be available in the local labor market and that his removal is judged necessary for labor market reasons.

c. That he will work in another place, and that the Employment Service in the place of destination certifies that the job is open and that manpower from outside that locality is necessary to fill it.

d. That the employment cannot be considered as a transition between different working places of the same concern.

e. That the payment has been approved before the journey began.

When family allowances and starting allowances are involved, additional safeguards are provided. This is no loose handout to any and all comers.

Another objection on principle is that the reduction of the costs of movement is in reality a way of avoiding the necessity for firms to offer high enough wages to overcome all personal, social, and economic inhibitions to movement. This, it is rightly contended, is the traditional way in which a free enterprise economy works, and to reduce the necessity for this is to provide cost-saving advantages to employers at the expense of wage disadvantages to workers. The point is well taken. Whether it is a telling objection depends on the premises upon which the judgment is based.

Involved here is the question of whether manpower policy is separate from, or integrated with, general economic policy aimed, for example, at controlling inflationary forces. The higher and more attractive wages offered will come from industries in all probability in a situation of productivity which makes such wages possible and reasonable. But the competition for workers will necessitate an increase in wages in firms not in that favorable situation and, therefore, have a tendency to lead to a chain reaction increasing the wage-push influences on inflation.

Our own feeling is that, in the light of the limited proportion of the work force affected under the regulations, both the objection and the answer to it are sound only if the quantitative impact of the movement encouraged or made likely by movement allowances is perceived in terms far more sizable than it is likely to become.

Another objection on principle is that the economic costs of movement are a very small part of the inhibitions of a personal and social nature which retard mobility or the inclination to move. This is true enough. But is that an objection to dealing with *that* inhibition? Interest rates are only one consideration among many in affecting the decision to build a residence or a plant; the cost of a plane, rail, or steamship ticket is only one consideration affecting the decision to take a vacation in California or France; the tax rate in a community is only one consideration affecting the decision to establish an industry there; the wage offered is only one consideration affecting the desire of a worker, a government official, a trade union officer, or a professor to take a particular job. Yet we feel justified in an effort to encourage these decisions by eliminating whatever inhibiting effect is present in interest rates, transportation costs, taxes, and wages, well knowing that the decisions will be affected by a host of other and varied personal and social preferences of the decision makers.

Most of the difficulties, however, which appear to have influenced legislators on this matter are practical administrative problems to which they have found no satisfactory answers, plus the fact that the volume of movement in the country would seem to negate the assumption that enough more was necessary to make it worth while to develop headaches and stomach ulcers in trying to solve those problems. The administrative difficulties are real enough, although it is difficult to defend the proposition that the capacity to face them and solve them is any less characteristic of American than of foreign legislators and administrators. And the volume of movement in general is no guarantee that movement of particular people to satisfy particular labor needs from places where they are not needed is both socially and economically desirable.

The foregoing discussion is not intended to provide a case for movement allowances as a part of the Employment and Manpower Services. But it does provide an illustration that the openings for thought about developments in those services are influenced by the concept of the mission of those services within which developments are considered.

That the workers' economic costs, which these measures attempt to reduce, severely restrict otherwise desirable movement is clear. It is equally clear that free choice of movement is, in the light of these costs, possible only for either the economically affluent or the footloose (and sometimes restless) individual relatively unburdened with economic responsibilities to anyone save himself. If the mission to establish the conditions of truly free movement of labor is to be taken seriously by the Employment and Manpower Services, such cost-reducing efforts would greatly amplify the type of activity incorporated within the responsibilities of those services.

7. *The availability of Employment Services to workers before they are unemployed so that their choice is, as labor market theory assumes, between jobs, as well as between a job and no job.* The very condition of being unemployed is the most serious handicap to free choice faced by workers, for, unless a worker has ample tide-over resources upon which no other pressing claims are made, he is forced to take the first port in a storm. Every success in carrying out the measures to prevent unemployment discussed in Chap. 3 is, therefore, a contribution to freedom of movement.

8. *The enlargement of job opportunities in areas where they are declining, before they have declined so long that unmovable workers have lost their value as productive workers.* The longer the unemployment continues, the narrower the freedom of choice becomes. Truly heroic efforts are required of the Employment and Manpower Services and of the related redevelopment of depressed area efforts if the long-term unemployed are to "choose" a degree of movement that has the slightest claim to being labeled "free."

The movement of permanent industry (in contrast to temporary public or relief works, or distribution of government orders) to a depressed area, or one likely to become so, is an even more hotly debated issue than that of providing subsidies for moving workers away from those areas, although they are sometimes taken as alternative ways of approaching the labor surplus problem. Since this solution of an imbalance in the labor market is not normally considered within the horizons of labor market policy in this country, its extended discussion here would be premature if not inappropriate.

The issue, however, will inevitably become sharper and more insistent. Projects of this sort are carried on now by Chambers of Commerce, municipal governments, and state planning commissions. Federal grants, loans, and advisory and technical assistance are available under certain circumstances, normally underscoring the fact that a dangerous degree of labor surplus is already in existence. The initiative normally lies with the local community. The response of the state and federal governments is a response to those needs in order to avoid a continuation of a surplus situation which has already become, and not merely threatens to become, deplorable from the point of view of the deterioration of the business and industrial life of the community, of tax revenues therefrom, and of the productive skills and morale of its unemployed workers and their families.

The over-all anticipation of and planning for the rational and balanced growth of the economy by means of any but voluntary location of industry involves the probability of a degree of centralized decision-making we are loath to employ. Moreover, it involves an assumption of wisdom on the part of centralized decision makers that we are disinclined to make.

The experience of regulated decision-making in countries, particularly England, which has had some noticeable success in this matter, does not provide much ground for overcoming such reticence. The size of subsidies, loans, tax rebates, etc. necessary to stimulate "voluntary" acceptance of the centrally determined places where industrial development is desirable is considerable. The requirement of building permits from the Board of Trade, whose decisions to grant or refuse them are based on plans not to expand where the labor force is tight and to encourage expansion where the labor force is redundant or obviously in surplus to local demand, is a kind of regulated allocation of resources which underscores the hesitancies recorded above.

Interestingly enough, however, the administration of such location or relocation of industry schemes has been accompanied by a widening, in the minds of those concerned, of the conception of the forces at work in the operations of the "unseen hand," which presumably takes charge of such matters when decisions are left to private individuals. The full range of alternative and opportunity costs which must necessarily be the concern of private investors has become more clearly understood by government planners, for whom such costs are not only economic but social and political as well. The need for taking into account, as a governing factor, more than the existence of labor shortages and surpluses, indeed, of more than the other economic resource factors, has become more obvious. Sociology and psychology as well as economics have been necessary to explain favorable and unfavorable responses to plans and decisions. The legitimacy of expressions and actions of workers, their families, social and political leaders in communities and regions, employers, trade union officials, and political representatives in Parliament and local councils, expressions and action which are understandable only in such terms, has had to be recognized.

The fact has been brought home to the government regulators that communities and a nation are more than labor, product, and money markets; they are whole organisms affected by and affecting the behavior in those markets. On the basis of this experience they could be of great service to all engaged in the development and operation of Employment and Manpower Services and of other agencies devoted to increasing the economic health and growth of the nation, if they were to set down for wide distribution these lessons which some of them have learned.

A summary statement of this aspect of the conception of the central mission of the Employment and Manpower Services may be suggested. The Employment and Manpower Services are instruments for encouraging and facilitating the adaptation of the labor force to changes in the nature, manpower needs, and location of the nation's productive enterprise. They do that by facilitating the occupational, industrial, and geographical movement and mobility of workers in the labor market. In the performance of this mission, (1) reliance shall be placed on the free choice of jobs and workers by workers and employers, respectively, and (2) positive measures shall be taken to provide those conditions in the labor market which make that choice realistically free.

SUMMARY

The second issue with respect to the central mission of the Employment and Manpower Services focuses on whether their role in relation to the movement of labor and the organization of the labor market shall emphasize freedom of choice or planned management, and, if the first, what efforts are necessary to assure freedom.

Along with the movement and mobility of capital, the movement and mobility of labor is the "expansion joint" in our economic facilities necessary to assure an economy governed ultimately by the consumers' free choice of goods.

On general principles, and in the abstract, there is unanimous acceptance of the idea that it is a central mission of the Employment and Manpower Services to facilitate the movement of labor. The issues arise when an operational definition and clarification of that function is attempted.

The first issue is whether we shall leave workers and employers absolutely free to make use of the Employment and Manpower Services or not, as they wish, and absolutely free to accept or reject any solution to their respective problems proposed by the administrators of the services.

The governing emphasis in the United States has been upon that freedom. It has been severely modified only in time of war, and then the compulsive features have not extended to absolute control. That degree of control used was established in co-operation with representative policy committees. The sanctions were indirectly, rather than directly, geared to specific violations. The regulation was implemented primarily with respect to the employers' hiring practices.

The regulation of workers' choices was, of course, implied in the regulation of employers' choices. Otherwise, "persuasion" only was used with respect to the workers.

In the peacetime operation of the Employment and Manpower Services as such, there is no hint of a desire to curtail freedom of choice for employers and for workers not claiming unemployment insurance. Employers have felt some pressure to accept the services of certain hard-to-place groups and veterans.

In its function as an agency for unemployment insurance this general principle is violated. As a condition of continued receipt of benefits, claimants are compelled to register, and to accept a job which can be interpreted as "suitable" by a tribunal.

The causes of the prevailing predominant adherence to voluntarism are these:

1. Necessity of conforming with values of the general culture.
2. The basic justice of permitting unemployed workers to retain connection with jobs in which they have vested rights and benefits has been increasingly recognized.
3. Individual freedom of choice of movement is regarded as a check on economic planners who may not consider certain values as important to people as those, say, of productivity.

There are those who are inclined to urge a greater degree of compulsion. The temptation arises from the following factors, which are very persuasive to some people:

1. Generalizing from the need demonstrated in time of war, they envisage other crises calling for maximum manpower mobilization and utilization.
2. The reluctance of unemployed workers to move from places where there is no work for them.
3. The desirability of reducing the load on wage differentials large enough to induce voluntary movement, in order to avoid the chain reaction inflationary effects of the use only of that incentive to movement.
4. The possibility that consumers' free choice of goods and the workers' free choice of jobs simultaneously is an impossibility. They place higher value on the first freedom.
5. The realization that central planning for economic stability and growth can flounder on the rock of free and unmanaged movement of labor.

The impact of the organization of manpower allocations along more planned and managed lines would be almost entirely disadvantageous for the Employment and Manpower Services. The political reaction could well reduce them once more to being the handmaidens for relief and unemployment insurance agencies. The stimulus the administrators receive now to improvement in the quality of their services would be removed or greatly weakened.

The disadvantages to the Employment and Manpower Services of adopting a "managed movement of manpower" orientation are considered compelling. But if "free choice" is to be the orientation, the necessity of improving the conditions making for "free" choice become apparent. Operationally the Employment and Manpower Services, guided by a mission to facilitate movement through "free" choice, would be concerned with efforts to establish at least the following conditions of freedom:

1. Provision to workers and employers of free facilities for coordinating their needs by the establishment of an' employment relationship.
2. Enlargement of the volume and the geographical, industrial, and occupational scope of workers' applications and employers' job orders.
3. Provision to workers and employers of adequate information about the present and future labor market and labor force.
4. Provision to employers of adequate analyses (including testing and job analysis) about the employment potential of

workers, and to workers of job requirements and of guidance as to how the two can be effectively brought together.

5. Provision of opportunities for the development of skills and qualifications which makes a "free" choice possible when job opportunities are offered.

6. Provision of various types of removal allowances which reduce the economic costs of otherwise desirable and acceptable movement.

7. Provision of Employment and Manpower Services to workers before they are handicapped by the very fact they are unemployed, laying stress on the preventive aspects of the efforts of the services.

8. The enlargement of job opportunities particularly in areas of declining employment to avoid the condition of the unemployability of the hard-core unemployed.

In summary, the definition of the second major aspect of the central mission of the Employment and Manpower Services is as follows: to facilitate economically desirable free adaptation, movement, and mobility of labor, through reliance on the free choice of jobs and employees by workers and employers respectively, and through positive operations in the labor market to provide those conditions of choice which make it realistically free.

NATIONAL AND LOCAL
LABOR MARKETS

Chapter Five Implicit in many of the issues raised in the foregoing chapters is the question of what the operational field of the Employment and Manpower Services should be,
because decisions and actions with respect to such issues will hinge
on how broad or how narrow the concept of that operational field is.
Is the emphasis to be placed on the national as well as on local and
regional labor markets? Is the emphasis to be placed on developing
manpower and employment facilities for the whole range of occupations, industries, and institutions or only for those areas of the labor
market not served by existing facilities?

It is obvious that these emphases are not mutually exclusive.
Nevertheless, important consequences follow from neglect of either
emphasis and from a commitment to one or the other as the primary
emphasis.

In this chapter we consider the concept of the operational field for
the Employment and Manpower Services by reference to the national
or local labor market issue. In Chap. 6 the concept of operational
field is considered by reference to the issue of comprehensive or only
gap-filling coverage of occupations, industries, and institutions.

INSTITUTIONAL ADAPTATION TO EXTENDED PROBLEMS

Institutions established to meet social and economic problems normally are brought into existence to serve the needs of relatively small groups living within a relatively limited geographical area. As the relationships extend outward and the area of contacts broadens, the problems faced by these institutions change, not only in size, but in nature. Adapted originally to the character of the narrower operational field, the methods employed are not always effective in the larger field. Yet there is a reluctance on the part of the beneficiaries of these institutions to modify their essential character. This tendency is apparent in the case of the services which are the focus of our present interest. And naturally so.

There is a traditional expected American way of developing organized means for dealing with problems facing people as a group as the size of the group increases. The evolution of means is expected to begin with invention by individuals, and move through adoption and modification by voluntary associations and enterprises, through local community elaboration, through state and regional to national amplification and support. At each successive stage, modifications are made in, and additions are made to, the organized facilities to fit the problems faced by the unit of government involved and the needs facing the unit of the population which that government was designed to serve. This process of evolution is apparent to some degree in every institutional field, economic, political, educational, religious, military, recreational—indeed in all except, very understandably, the family.

It has been one of the inevitable accompaniments of this process that, as the horizon of problems has widened, those responsible for the shaping and operating facilities at the next comprehensive level have had to face the resistance to change on the part of those responsible for facilities at the next lower level of comprehensiveness. Consequently, the former have frequently fretted at the opposition to their plans and programs, opposition carried on in the name of the preservation of individual initiative, local autonomy, states' rights, etc. It should be expected that opposition on such grounds will be raised against the concept of national labor-market-oriented Employment and Manpower Services.

But there have been, and are, advantages as well as disadvantages in this situation. Lacking dictatorial powers, those concerned with plans and operations at the more comprehensive level have had successively at each step to persuade individuals, then those whose primary functions and loyalties were geared to voluntary associations and enterprise, local communities, and states, that there were problems faced by all involved at each successively more comprehensive level that were not the mere adding up of the more individualized and localized problems, that the problems were different in nature, not just in number. Moreover, they have had to persuade them that the facilities required to meet these problems were not just a collection or a loosely affiliated set of facilities previously developed to meet the more individualized and localized problems. What was possible, then, became a function of the degree of consensus which could be obtained. The process of achieving that working consensus comes near to being the operational definition of the democratic process, preserving alike the significance and stimulus to individual and local initiative and adaptation on the one hand and the possibility of moving ahead, *by mutual consent,* in an attack upon the solution to problems peculiar to the more comprehensive unit of government and population.

These values are worth preserving. They are stated here to make clear that, in arguing for increased emphasis on the national labor market as an operational field for the Employment and Manpower Services, there is no intention to discount the importance of effective and efficient attention and adaptation to the problems peculiar to local, state, and regional labor markets. Nor is it intended to substitute national initiative, planning, and direction, for that appropriate to the character of problems at the grass roots.

NEED FOR SERVICES GEARED TO LOCAL PROBLEMS

The arguments for strong Employment and Manpower Services geared to local needs are irrefutable. This is where the employment relationship, the facilitation of which is the major practical objective of each and every one of the services, takes place. Placement, counseling, testing, research, employer services, vocational education and training, creation of job opportunities, rehabilitation, maintenance and mobility benefits, all have as their end objective the establishment and maintenance of the most productive employment relationships possible. And the vast majority of those relationships are established between particular actual or potential workers and particular actual or potential employers whose work is carried on in a particular local labor market, and under the peculiar conditions of production and facts of labor supply and demand existing there. Those conditions are different in California, West Virginia, Georgia, Hawaii, Iowa, Arizona, North Carolina, Colorado, Connecticut, and New York. They are different in New York City, Rochester, Elmira, Ithaca, and Port Chester. To the specific work-a-day adaptations required in these relatively localized labor markets, no national labor market manager can bring the required experience, skill, knowledge, wisdom, and capacity to elicit the co-operation and confidence of the flesh and blood people whose behavior is involved.

It was the folks living and wrestling with the problems of these local labor markets who set up and developed the first placement offices, the first efforts at vocational education and training, the first attempts at fact-gathering, and the creation of job opportunities. There is no reason to believe that the present generation of people living in, and acquainted with the needs of, local areas have any less sensitivity to those needs, or less of an urge to meet them, particularly if the sense of responsibility for solving local problems and the pride in doing so is not weakened by blurring the image of the local labor market which people of a somewhat provincially limited experience (that is, most of us) can be expected to have. We could ill afford to lose the initiative and urge to work at local problems which has been stimulated by the concern for and pride in solving local and state labor market problems, particularly since that is where most of labor market events do, and will continue to, take place.

The big volume of business for all the Employment and Manpower Services is going to be focused on the removing of local imbalances between the supply of and demand for labor, and between the number requiring services and the available facilities for providing them locally. In the area of placement, for example, the great bulk of exchange of orders and applications will take place locally. The orders from "outside" labor-shortage offices will, in the great majority of areas, be *supplementary* to the local stock of orders as long as the principle of freedom of choice in the movement of labor is maintained. The number of applicants requesting transfers to other places will always be supplementary to the number wishing employment in the home locality.

What is true of placement is likewise true of the other services. The greatest number of customers for retraining and for workers who have been retrained will be workers and employers who foresee the possibility of establishing an employment relationship with each other locally. Vocational training and counseling will be geared, on the whole, to bringing youth into successful contact with employment opportunities in the local areas where the training is received and the counseling given. (There are growing exceptions to this rule, of course, particularly in rural areas.) It is true of research and information activities. It is the research which portrays the present and prospective local labor market, labor force, and labor development facilities which count in providing a suggested local pattern for actual operations and programs. These local data, of course, can be summarized for something called a national labor market, but, as such, they will not be used to the same extent as their local components for planning actual operating projects in particular localities. One of their chief (and most important) functions on the national level is to create in the minds of those able to initiate and finance general employment facilitating programs at that level, as well as locally, a willingness to act. Particularly when the size of unmet needs over the nation are statistically disclosed, is the reaction, "For crying out loud, ain't it awful," a good stimulator of Congressional and executive determination to respond to the challenge, "Let's do something about it." Nationally summarized local data should, of course, be able to point the way as to what needs to be done.

When something is done about it by administrators appointed to the task, the doing involves the capacity on the part of 1900 local Employment Service managers and their staffs to get the co-operation of literally millions of employers and tens of millions of actual and potential workers, tens of thousands of local trade union leaders, local mayors and aldermen, educators, sponsors of welfare agencies, etc. Those co-operators are primarily concerned with the local market with which they are best acquainted. The national labor market is a hazy oblong blur to them, no matter how adequate its statistical description. If their interest and effort are to be brought forth, it will be because they can visualize the needs that call for the kind of action *they* can take. And that, by and large, is within the local labor market.

There is an even more compelling reason why consideration of local labor market factors must be thoroughly emphasized in any employment and manpower program. A local labor market is only one aspect of a local community, even of that community's complex of interdependent industrial business and other economic institutions. The whole order, structure, and dynamics of economic activity in a community has a very particular character. Those activities related to employment and manpower problems take their place not merely alongside of, but in reciprocal relationship to, that unique complex of resources, transportation, production, communication, marketing facilities, demographic characteristics, economic values, and relations with external economies. All these ways of work and life are subject to control within a particular power structure in the community which has its reciprocal relations with those outside the community. Not only the character and structure but the operations of labor market agencies will of necessity be geared in with this local complex. Otherwise, their chances for effectiveness as public services are nil. No single pattern of Employment and Manpower Services and operations can fit in with, and be effectively and consistently serviceable as one element in, the economic processes of these varied localized systems.

Moreover, communities are not just places where people work, but places where they live. And living involves the integration of relations at work with other relations which in total make up the web of life for the folk of that community. The interaction and interdependence of life in the work place, in the family, in the political arena, in the churches, in neighborhood and interest group associations, in the schools, in the places where seller meets customer, and in all other private and public institutions results in a unique community which is more than the sum of its parts and which is reinforced by a culture and sense of membership which gives stability to that whole.

Communities vary in the degree to which all these aspects are well integrated, but in every community there is a strain toward consistency and toward the adaptation of each aspect to all the others. Modifications in any one will become effective not in isolation and in terms of standards pertinent to that aspect alone, but in terms of the degree to which it fits in with and strengthens the whole.

Modifications in the labor market operations can either strengthen or weaken the community, not only as a place to work, but as a place to live. For example, the movement of labor into or out of a community has an effect upon the critical number needed for participation in other areas of community life, needed for balance, initiative, and effort along the whole front of community social, economic, familial, political, recreational, and religious activities. The condition of that balance, initiative and effort on the whole front will, in turn, affect the productiveness of employment relations and other labor market activities in that community.

There is no lack of recognition of the importance of emphasis on the local labor market on the part of officialdom in Washington. The former Secretary of Labor reinforced the position repeatedly taken by the directors of the Bureau of Employment Security and the United States Employment Service when he said of one of the most important of the Employment and Manpower Services:

> A modernized employment service must assume that the action front will remain as it is now—*within the local office*—operated by the states, but also as an integral part of a national system of employment offices.

For all these reasons the emphasis on the local labor market as the operational field is important and not likely to be neglected.

LOCAL LABOR MARKET INTERESTS

Another reason the local labor market is not likely to be neglected is that there are powerful forces and pressures set up to protect the interests of people in each local market from encroachment of any who might be unaware of those interests or inclined to discount them in an attempt to implement a national labor market policy.

The forces resistant to any concept of a national labor market which would lead to more efficient allocation of manpower resources in the over-all interests of a stronger and growing national economy are deep-seated and real. It is not the concept of a national labor market in the abstract which is the object of resistance. That object is the action-implications disadvantageous to local labor market interests, which it is feared might follow from emphasis upon that nationally oriented concept.

Most of the resistance is related to the movement of labor from one locality to another, from less productive to more productive uses, which it is (rightly) assumed would be an accompaniment to an increased emphasis on the effective operation of a national labor market.

Resistance arises from the disinclination of workers and their families to leave the familiar place of work and life, to face the disassociation from family and friends, to take a probable loss in disposing of the home, to forego seniority and accumulated benefit rights, and to undertake the costs of movement in the face of an unpredictable degree of job security in the new locality. Resistance arises from employers who dislike to see their labor reserves depleted. (An interesting positive interest of employers in the alternative of the movement of jobs to workers is in the bringing into the community of industries which employ women. It is assumed that since these women will be the wives or daughters of male workers, a further factor will be added to inhibitions of the latter toward moving.) Even where labor shortages exist, employers in the shortage area face a gamble in bringing in workers from a distance and investing in training and induction. Resistance arises also from local trade unions who may find their "scarce commodity" advantage reduced by in-movement of skilled labor or its development for "their" jobs through retraining. Resistance arises from politicians to the loss of constituents resulting from out-movement of labor. Those interested in the maintenance of community institutions have been known to oppose such out-movement on the grounds that it can reduce participants and leaders in those institutions below the critical number needed for their dynamic life. Local elected representatives and taxpayers do not look favorably upon the devotion of local facilities, personnel, and funds to the training of youthful or adult workers who then may utilize their newly acquired skills in another locality. Any government effort to encourage movement of labor by helping to bear the cost of that movement, or of any training in preparation for it, is resisted by those conservative successful people who see in such an effort the assumption by government of a cost traditionally borne by individuals.

A national labor market policy and its implementation will have to meet such resistances and take steps to reduce their retarding effect upon the occupational and geographical movement of labor needed for maximizing the most productive utilization of that labor.

NEED FOR SERVICES GEARED TO NATIONAL PROBLEMS

The arguments for conceiving of the operational field of the Employment and Manpower Services as the *national* labor market, however, are equally compelling. One argument stands out from all the rest. The operation of those services must be geared to political and economic events and developments which take place on a national scale and which have, not only manpower and employment effects, but components as well. The elimination of international trade restrictions, the development of other reciprocal economic and political relations of the United States with other nations, the adoption of a national full employment policy and national efforts to implement it, a national defense program with its distribution of orders for products, preparations for manpower mobilization in a national crisis, the federal encouragement and support of education and of scientific and industrial research, a federal antidiscrimination effort, and a national youth program are examples of action taken at the national level which have manpower and employment effects and whose successful outcome depends on manpower and employment factors.

Moreover, private efforts for expansion or movement of industry, for increasing the speed and volume of communication and transportation, for enlarging the units of productive and distributive organization, and for the development and utilization of new techniques and automated tools of production have tremendous manpower and employment effects on the economy as a whole. Agencies of the labor market are poorly equipped to deal with such problems if the operational field to which they are geared is merely a local labor market. The very mobility of families in the country (one in five moves every year) is a fact not only affecting, but affected by, the changing character of the occupational structure of the national labor market. The growth of regional cities, the megalopolis, outmoding many traditional state boundaries, is also a factor emphasizing larger than localized employment needs. Neither the initiation nor the results of these national events and trends are limited to specific localities or states. All of them, of course, have an impact, although differently felt, on the thousands of local labor markets.

An emphasis, moreover, on the adaptation of the Employment and Manpower Services in response to national needs is essential in order that those who plan and operate such services shall gear their programs to amplifying the *benefits* of the nationally significant events and developments just named. Those whose eyes and interests are focused chiefly on the nature and problems of their own local, or even state and regional, labor markets are concerned chiefly with *difficulties* presented by these developments. They do not have the opportunity normally to take into account these national developments in their plans and programs except as a dark threatening cloud before the storm breaks locally and faces local people with the need for remedial measures to reduce the injury to the employers and workers with whom they deal. The result is that administrators in local labor market areas are necessarily concerned with the negative manpower problems created by these over-all national developments. And their representatives in Washington get their chief impression as to the kind of manpower and employment measures required from the transmission to them of these problems which are facing their localized constituencies.

Now there is no denying that these problems exist locally and that remedies have to be found. Nor is it sensible to ignore the fact that these localized headaches add up to a big national headache, both economically and certainly politically.

But the national developments we have spoken of are intended to create primarily opportunities, not problems, opportunities for economic strength and growth of the nation as a whole. And they do just that. Consequently, they present the Employment and Manpower Services with opportunities for a positive nationwide development and maximized utilization of our human resources, as well as with the necessity for protecting them, in particular places, from the ill effects on employment security. But these positive opportunities and advantages, as they affect manpower and employment, will be realized by virtue of adjustments and reallocation of resources, including manpower, within the labor market as a whole. These changes will be accompanied by disturbances of ways of work and life in particular local places, some good and some bad from a human, as well as from a local economic, point of view. The realization of benefits will require adjustments within an area broader than a community. It will require, for example, long-range programs of vocational education and training of young people and occupational retraining of adults, who may never use their preparation in the local areas where it is received. It will require a general training facilitating the possibility of future occupational *change* as well as immediate and specialized occupational *performance*, the type of training local interest groups, including employers, are unlikely to invest in, since it may not pay off immediately in profitable production and local employment. To realize benefits will require the loss of manpower in some communities where it is underemployed in terms of its potential and the removal to communities where it can be more productively employed. Realization may, therefore, require the encouragement and financial support of movement of workers to move away from the community in which the support is given. In other words, the realization of advantages from these national events and developments is geared to interlocal-labor-market affairs, or, in other words, to operations within the national labor market.

The emphasis on the national labor market as an operational field is essential, therefore, in order to provide a leadership for the Employment and Manpower Services which is alert to and concerned with exploiting, for the nation's benefit, the positive opportunities residing in the national events and trends named, as well as remedying the localized damage attending them. That emphasis is essential in order to conceive and plan the services to facilitate the interlocal-labor-market and manpower adaptations and adjustments that will be required. It is essential in order to enable men to see the employment and manpower problems and opportunities of the nation steadily and to see them whole. Only if they do so will their thought and action hold an appropriate and respected place in the thought and action of those whose decisions affect these over-all national policies and activities intended to increase the economic strength and growth of the nation as a whole.

Whether we like it or not, an increasing number of decisions, policies, and programs which affect our lives are being made at the national level, in response to national needs, and are being carried out by a national mobilization and activation of resources. All of these decisions, policies, and programs have manpower and employment components and effects, and the Employment and Manpower Services, if they are to make their maximum contribution to economic health and growth, must operate consistently with them, that is, from a national labor market point of view. The direction and utilization of manpower resources can no more be governed by purely local interests and objectives than can our natural resources, our monetary resources, or our transportation and communication resources.

Moreover, there is a growing need for private decision makers and action takers, employers, trade union leaders, educators, researchers, and for local and sectional political leaders to think broadly in national interest terms. This means that they would not only evaluate the impact of their decisions and actions on the national interest, but consider the contribution to their localized activities of the nation's over-all strength and growth. The concerns and activities of all these private decision makers are affected by the public approach to our employment and manpower problems. If the approach is geared to the national labor market as an operational field, that provides one more influence, one more experience, which stimulates them to lift their sights in their private affairs to the level of the national interest.

The orientation of the services to a nationwide operational field was achieved when the crisis of war was upon us. At such times it is not difficult for men to know that the horizons of community interests are broader than the range of hills at the borders of the town. The question here raised is not whether we face a crisis in national security equal to that faced in 1918 and 1941. It is, rather, the question as to whether the adaptation of the services to nationwide labor market developments ought not to be expected as a normal on-going process, not just a development awaiting a crisis for its forced initiation.

ADAPTATION IN SERVICES IMPLICIT IN
THE NATIONAL APPROACH

We have discussed the operational field issue in general, although not abstract, terms. The issue can be sharpened by focusing now on the implications of taking a national labor market approach for the operations of several of the services which we have included in the roster of Employment and Manpower Services.

The service most obviously affected by the local or national operational field emphasis is the placement service. Accordingly, it will receive the greatest attention in the discussion which follows. But since, to a large extent, all the services are, or should be, designed to lead to the maximum employment of our people at the maximum of their productive capacity, the enlargement of the boundaries of the labor market to be served requires an accompanying amplification of all these services so that they are geared to facilitating employment adjustments made within the framework of the larger national labor market.

Counseling cannot be based on knowledge of the job requirements and opportunities of merely the local and closely contiguous labor markets. The facts and trends in the nationwide opportunities for work and the qualifications for work must be readily available in sufficient detail to enable counselors to bring to bear on every case the full range of possibilities available, and probably to be available, in the national labor market. And their counseling must concern itself with the nation's productive needs as well as the needs of specific clients. Interviewing and testing must be adequate for the discovery of the potential of prospective job holders for occupations existing or likely to exist anywhere in the nation.

Research and the distribution of information concerning labor force and labor market facts and trends will have to be based on patterns of fact-gathering which are uniform and comparable for all local and regional areas and capable of summation in a way to indicate precisely described characteristics of both the demand and supply for labor wherever imbalances are apparent in any area of the country and in the nation as a whole. The subjects for research will have to place increased emphasis on factors encouraging or discouraging labor mobility residing in the attitudes of workers, employers, community leaders, and politicians; increased emphasis on study of economic developments affecting the long-range character of labor supply and demand for the nation as a whole, and the differential impact of these developments on the several geographical, industrial, and occupational areas of the nation's economy; and increased emphasis on reliable prognostic indicators of probable shifts in both the short-range and long-range supply of and demand for labor.

Vocational education and training and *retraining* will need to be guided, not solely by present shortages for labor in particular localities or states, but by those existing and developing anywhere in the national economy, and by the preparation, not just for presently available work, but by that required for adaptation to changes in the occupational structure taking place in the nation as a whole.

The creation of job opportunities will need to be geared not merely to the relief and renewal of particular distressed areas, but to the positive expansion of the nation's productive capacities, wherever that can be accomplished most effectively.

Maintenance benefits like unemployment insurance and aids to movement of labor will have to be considered not merely from the point of view of helping particular people in particular places to meet the costs of unemployment, retraining, and movement, or from the point of view of keeping as intact as possible the local or state funds available for such assistance. The essential concern, where public agencies are involved, is the most economical and efficient allocation of public funds enabling those receiving benefits to make a freer choice among alternative ways of finding more productive outlets for the utilization of their labor power, outlets more satisfying to themselves and more beneficial to the nation's economic strength and growth.

All of these services contribute to the establishment of the most productive employment relationships, which is the precise objective and function of the placement service. Hence, when the implications are considered, for that latter service, of the national labor market concept of the operational field, the other services will feel the force of those implications also.

IMPLICATIONS FOR THE PUBLIC PLACEMENT AND TRAINING SERVICES

A wholehearted emphasis on the national labor market might conceivably have as its objective, so far as placement and training efforts are concerned, the making available to every employer in need of permanent workers, the total national supply of workers, or at least of unemployed workers, whose qualifications fit his requirements.

Likewise, every person desiring a job would have available to him for his consideration all unfilled job openings in the nation suited to his qualifications. If selection for and engagement in a training or retraining program were to be considered as similar to selection for and engagement in gainful work, the same universality of possibilities for training might be considered the appropriate concomitant of a national labor market emphasis. It is unlikely, however, that even the most enthusiastic supporters of the national labor market concept have in mind anything as utopian as this, but only a development of the placement and training services which moves in that direction, and a reduction of barriers to such a development.

Their interest in the direction of development, rather than in some absolute perfection of achievement, is mirrored in the questions they pose: "Is the rational national movement and training of labor less important in peacetime than in times of war, when the whole nation was looked upon as a source of supply for workers required in particular places for production essential to the nation's needs?" "Should the Employment Service be concerned primarily with temporary joblessness to which adaptations usually can be made locally, or also concerned with that resulting from those large economic changes whose impact on employment is more continuous and lasting, changes which burst the boundaries of local, state, and regional labor markets, changes the adaptation to which can seldom be accomplished by attempts to balance the local supply of and demand for labor?" "The expansion in production that we count on to promote economic growth involves both increasing need and decreasing need for labor in particular labor markets. Can the waste of manpower and its irrational utilization involved in this unevenness be avoided unless the operational field for the placement and training of labor is the nation itself?" "A frequent catchword for the national emphasis is, 'the proper coordination of local-labor-market-oriented placement and training services to meet the nation's needs.' What is meant operationally by the phrase 'proper coordination,' and who shall determine the nation's over-all needs when it comes to the movement and training of labor?"

Even if we seek the answer to these questions in a development of placement and training services which only moves in the direction of serving the national labor market, it is desirable to be clear about the factors which have to be dealt with if and whenever that emphasis is made.

The first of these factors is that the demand for labor is of importance equal to or greater than the supply of labor in determining the scope of possible employment adjustments, and that the demand existing or possible of creation in any particular labor market is frequently insufficient for the establishment of an equilibrium, and certainly the most productive equilibrium. The national labor market problems, whether they be surpluses of labor, reflected in the unemployment, underemployment, and waste of manpower, or a shortage of certain kinds of manpower which places brakes on economic development, are produced and solved, as far as employment is concerned, primarily by the private decisions of millions of employers. The supply of labor, the capacity for and the desire for work, do not initiate, except indirectly, the fact of employment. Employment is initiated by job orders from employers. Employers' decisions—to increase or decrease production, to expand or reduce or move their productive facilities, to change from labor to capital intensive modes of production—create the fact of shortages or surpluses of labor. Demand rather than supply is the direct initiating factor in the creation of an employment relationship.

Now our present conception of the scope of Employment and Manpower Services does not include any systematic widespread attempt to influence the demand for labor. The administrators of those services, on the whole, must wait until those private decisions creating or reducing demand are made, and then adapt their activities as best they can to facilitating the operation of, first the local, and then the national labor market, with respect to supply of labor. Unless the Employment and Manpower Services incorporate tasks relevant to the creation of job opportunities, they are handicapped in bringing the supply of and demand for labor into balance even in a local, to say nothing of a national, labor market. In view of the essential contribution of the volume of demand to the possibility of finding the most useful employment for the available supply, it is not probable that comprehensive services designed to bring productive order and balance into a national labor market can exclude from their functions a share in the promotion of job opportunities on a national scale.

Moreover, in view of the reciprocal impact on each other of the decisions and actions affecting the demand for labor and those affecting the supply of labor, the operational field for the Employment and Manpower Services must be large enough to make use of the adjustment possibilities offered by private decisions establishing a demand for labor in many areas, not merely a limited local one.

The second factor affecting the movement toward a national labor market concept of the operational field for the placement and training aspects of the Employment and Manpower Services is that there is an unsatisfied demand for certain kinds of skilled labor, in widely scattered areas, from employers who, if that supply were available, are in a position and willing to increase production and employment. When workers are in short supply, decisions on allocation must be made, and those decisions, particularly if made for a national labor market, would necessitate some just and workable system for establishing priorities.

Even in a nation with three million unemployed, there are shortages of labor in critical, and chiefly skilled, occupations. Not only are there jobs which are not being done because qualified workers are not available in the immediate locality, but many of these are bottleneck operations which, if performed, would have a multiplier effect on the opening of less skilled jobs ancillary to the skilled jobs. But the distribution of scarce manpower resources among employers making competing manpower bids beyond the available local supply requires a principle for priorities.

Even in wartime, when an overriding interest in satisfying military needs encouraged employers to put up with the sacrifice of their personal and local interest, the establishment of priorities was a ticklish business and gave rise to allegations of favoritism and blind bureaucratic decision-making. The removal of *whose* shortages, either by transfer of workers or by training, is in the national interest? Should expanding and dynamic-growth-potential industries get first call rather than industries which are static or declining? Should expansion be encouraged in the South or decline prevented in New England? Should expanding export industries or domestic producers have first call on the available short-supply manpower? What about the encouragement of growth in densely populated urban areas as opposed to semirural areas? Should recruiting of workers by employers from outside the local labor market be permitted or even encouraged by the local employment offices?

It is political dynamite for government officials to give answers to such questions in peacetime. That *allocation* will not be made overtly by a public agency in any period save wartime. The allocation will be a result of comparative persuasiveness on the part of employers competing for that scarce supply. We count on the private resolution of pluralistic private claims to resources, rather than on a scheme for directing those resources to those industrial and geographical areas in which a central decision-making body determines that growth in the national interest is desirable. In such a nation it would be political suicide for a government to assume it could establish planned priorities for the allocation of those resources that would simultaneously meet the tests of mutual consent and the national intent.

Yet answers will inevitably be given to such questions, in deed if not in word, if officials become concerned with the most rational movement of labor in a national labor market to accomplish over-all national economic goals. And the problem is that the results of those deeds will be taken as the intent of policy. The wider the boundaries of the labor market in which employment adjustments are made, the more and larger will be the potential conflicts among claimants for manpower which is in short supply, and the more government agencies will lay themselves open to the charge of "managing" manpower allocation.

We may not be convinced that an "unseen hand" guides the resolution of private decisions as to production and employment in local labor markets toward the achievement of balance and adaptability in the national labor market serving the national interest in over-all economic strength and growth. But we are committed to counting on that resolution, nevertheless. That commitment restricts the possibility that managers of public placement and training facilities will be able to make judgments and decisions as to the most desirable encouragement of labor movement in the interests of achieving the most productive utilization of labor in a national labor market.

There are, however, things we can do to shore up the unsteadiness of that "unseen hand" so strangely moved by private decisions. For example, we can make private decision makers more aware of and concerned for the facts affecting the maximum utilization of the nation's manpower, more conscious of the implications of their decisions for, and their impact on, that objective. And we can make available to them the kinds of labor-market and labor-force information which can encourage their action in the direction of that objective. And services whose operations are consciously oriented to the requirements of a national labor market have a greater possibility of utilizing manpower productively.

In the third place, there is no single type of national labor market, operationally defined. This is true even of local labor markets. Members of different occupations and those occupying different status positions in an organization have different horizons bounding the labor markets to which they relate themselves and to which they feel themselves attached. The great majority of workers and employers seek jobs and workers, respectively, that are to be found within an easy commuting area. This is the popular conception of a labor market. Within those boundaries there are differences also, but these do not concern us at the moment, although they affect the operations of local employment offices.

At the other end of the spectrum is the national, or even international, conception of a labor market considered appropriate by the occupants of certain occupations or positions. Employment is sought wherever in that extensive market the most satisfactory terms can be found, and employers seek employees wherever they can be found. Business and industrial executives, highly qualified technicians and staff people, professors, and research workers are typical examples of those for whom the labor market is perceived in national, and even international, terms.

The occupational trends in the United States, responding to managerial and technological innovations, seem to be supporting the probability of an enlargement of the numbers who will in the future seek jobs and workers in this wider national labor market. This is an important factor with which those who plan, support, and operate the Employment and Manpower Services need to be concerned if they would implement a positive and active labor market policy and program.

The implications of this trend for the placement, placement-related, and training services is that, although the bulk of their operations will seek to provide a balance between supply and demand in the immediate labor market, there will be increasing opportunity and need for gearing their placement, counseling, training, information efforts, and testing to the facilitating of labor movement and adjustments within a more extensive national labor market created, not by definition, but by actual free choices of job seekers and the providers of jobs. This requires both a continuous study of occupational trends and their mobility characteristics and the development of interlocal and interarea facilities for movement of people, facilities which can be adequate only within the framework of a national-labor-market-oriented service.

A fourth factor with which national-labor-market-oriented Employment and Manpower Services, especially those related to placement and training, must deal is the lack of standardization of job requirements and worker qualifications, a lack increasingly evident as the boundaries of the labor market are extended. This problem has a significant bearing on the practicability of a placement "clearance" device being proposed by some enthusiastic supporters of a national labor market concept. They are urging the automation of the record-keeping and exchange of job order and training opportunities information on the one hand and job applications on the other. They envision, for example, a punch-button operation in which the receipt of a particular job order would be followed by an automatic search and retrieval process among the cards of a total number of job applicants, much like the process which takes place in some airlines when a prospective traveler, say in New York, seeks a reservation on Flight 51 from St. Paul to Mexico City on March 15. This speeding up of the search process is highly desirable, particularly when the concept of the job to be done is the balancing of supply and demand in the national labor market.

The analogy, however, with the airplane trip market is interesting but not too convincing, for the difference in the standardization of the data in the airline and Employment Service is marked. In the first, the categories used by the airline service are specifically and simply labeled, and both parties mean the same thing by "Flight 51," "tourist class," "March 15," "St. Paul," and "Mexico City." Labor market data is not so clear-cut. Not only are the worker qualifications which the employer seeks and the job specifications which the worker believes he can meet more numerous than the variables in the airline service, but they lack the preciseness and clarity and even a meaning consensus characteristic of the airline data. With some exceptions such as, for example, height, years of schooling, eyesight, an operation requiring the use of two hands, etc., it is not infrequent that words defining job specifications and personal qualifications mean different things even to different employers and certainly to a prospective employer and prospective employee.

This does not mean that a more rapid and comprehensive screening cannot be done with respect to the location of workers and jobs that have certain clearly, consistently accepted, and quantitatively measurable dimensions. But it does indicate the chance for errors in the matching of the two. And the wider the boundaries of the labor market in which the search is made, the greater the chance for errors, the greater their cost, and the greater the need that they be avoided.

The lack of standardization of data relevant to establishing an employment relationship is one handicap to conducting national labor market operations whether or not, of course, the process is automated. The variations among order and application takers employed by the Employment Service in the intensity and accuracy of their record-keeping is another. Possibly the obvious observation that rapid and comprehensive search can be only as effective as the adequacy of the original data exchanged permits would be a stimulus both to standardization and adequacy of recording. But a continuing stumbling block would still be the undeclared conditions held by workers and employers as essential to their mutual agreement on an employment relation, conditions determining their decisions, but not sufficiently expressible and quantifiable to record on a card.

These comments on automated placement of workers and selection of trainees are made only to indicate that, as the labor market area is extended, the problems of adequate information recording, standardization, and exchange are multiplied. The standardization and nonquantitative-terms problems are not ones to retard the efforts underway to experiment with more expeditious exchange of job and applicant information now being carried on by the Employment Service. Nor do they supply an excuse for a failure to face the challenge of a type of employment adjustment which utilizes the potentialities of a national rather than merely local labor market. They are simply problems to be solved.

Closely related to the data adequacy and exchange problems just named are two others that can be mentioned briefly. Operations in a national labor market bring into sharp focus conditions of employment other than job requirements and worker qualifications which vary greatly from one part of the country to another and which bear on the appropriateness of the referral of a worker from one locality to another, however perfect the fit of his apparent qualifications with the job. These factors include working conditions, salary, fringe benefits, housing, and transportation provision, standards which are important factors in a worker's choice of a job. Employers are also interested in a number of personal factors not normally recorded on an applicant's card. For any long-distance clearance, it is highly desirable, if not absolutely necessary, that specific and detailed information about such factors be available, first to provide the worker and employer a basis for judgment as to the desirability of an employment relationship, and second to provide the Employment Service administrators with a basis for judgment as to the appropriateness of assisting to establish that relationship in the light of public policy. In a local labor market the ease of arranging for face-to-face exploration of these factors between the parties makes their detailed recording less necessary. Moreover, the manager of a local employment office and the placement staff are familiar with the going local conditions. In addition, a reduction or simplification and systematization of the burden of an overwhelming number of orders and applications which must be handled, if the volume of opportunities for applicants and employers is expanded, is an obvious administrative problem.

Finally, the larger the operational field, the more vital becomes the element of speed in processing. The lengthening lines of communication and the increase in the number of reservoirs of orders and applications which can be tapped are, however, in themselves handicaps to speed. Attention will have to be paid to elements in the process which affect the rapidity of appropriate services. These include, of course, the techniques of data processing and retrieval. They include lead-time gains which could be made by a system of warnings from employers of major employment changes. Our services do not even have the advantage of the forewarning voluntarily agreed to by employers in Sweden of the employment changes they contemplate in the immediate future. If that warning could be given, particularly in the case of large-scale curtailment or expansion of operations, the removal of the enterprise to another location, or the extensive introduction of labor-saving devices, there would be some possibility for the Employment Service and the Office of Manpower, Automation, and Training to place that problem in its national setting and to lay the groundwork for adaptation through movement, retraining, or both, in a way which would strengthen the productive forces in both the local and in the national labor market. Another informational element affecting the rapidity of interlocal labor market adjustments is the foreknowledge of which workers are most likely to respond to the opportunity to move when it arises. Finally, the attention to matters affecting rapidity of such movement may well include a possible reconsideration of the necessity for certain devices to protect the local interests before moving beyond the local labor market for jobs or men. These matters will come to the fore when we consider the present arrangements for expanding the operational field, particularly those related to the so-called "clearance" procedures.

THE PRESENT SITUATION IN
THE UNITED STATES

To what degree are the existing Employment and Manpower Services adapted to the needs and requirements in the national labor market? The answer is that with the exception of the direct placement services, research, preparation for war mobilization of manpower, and numerous and important services to other national agencies, there is very little evidence that the services have moved very far in that direction. Brief statements can be made, therefore, about most of them on this score before we consider in more detail the placement clearance system.

Employer services, of course, include aid in recruiting beyond the local labor market and the furnishing of labor-market and labor-force information available concerning conditions beyond the local market. Otherwise, as is to be expected, they are operated to meet not simply local needs, but even more specifically, individual employer needs.

The creation of job opportunities, as far as the Employment and Manpower Services are concerned, are almost wholly limited to participation in local area development projects which are stimulated by and geared to the relief of the local rather than the national unemployment problems.

Vocational education and training is, as we have seen, subject to only indirect influence from the Employment and Manpower Services, whether at the federal or state levels. In view of the fact that direct control of curriculum, facilities, teaching, and administration are by local and state governmental agencies, it would not be surprising to find objectives and programs and operations geared to whatever analysis of problems in their local jurisdictions were available, and to local and state political pressures. The Employment Service, through the distribution of its labor market and labor force trends information, attempts to broaden the horizons of local authorities as to prospective educational and training needs for young people in the light of their search for work in a field which comprehends the nation. In some states their efforts have led to notable results in lifting these horizons at least from local area to state and regional levels. But if the more effective balancing of supply of and demand for labor in the national labor market is to become a major objective of vocational education and training, the need would seem apparent for a far more energetic and comprehensive program of "stimulation" directed toward local and state authorities, and toward federal educational agencies which, in turn, have "stimulating" functions.

Programs for retraining the unemployed have been planned and carried out almost entirely by reference to needs related to the kinds of unemployed and the needed occupational qualifications discovered within local labor markets. Given the understandable, and basically sound, legislative admonition to retrain the unemployed only for jobs that promised to be available (and this taken normally to mean available locally), this concentration on concern with the local labor market is all but inevitable. And as long as retraining programs are sponsored and carried through ultimately only by local and state authorities, it is unlikely that the needs of any but local and state areas will be served. As a matter of fact, the concept of the need for retraining to make more effective the balancing of supply of and demand for labor *nationally* is virtually nonexistent in operational terms. It is difficult to find even any statement of the need presented by a national labor market for retraining which is not merely an adding together, a summation of, demonstrated or claimed needs of particular local labor markets.

Unemployment insurance benefits were originally conceived solely in terms of a more respectable form of relief for workers laid off for short spells with prospects of returning to work in the same local labor market. If any concept at all was present of the utility of such benefits in the organization of the labor market, it was related to their help in the maintenance of a local "labor reserve," ready again to become active when a cyclical upturn in demand for labor became a fact in that locality. It was a labor reserve, however, for, at most, a local labor market. In reality, unemployment insurance is conceived by local individual employers to be a device for maintaining *their* labor reserve. This concept is emphasized by experience rating and by bargained-for supplementary unemployment benefits. To some extent they consider that *they* have a fund, available for the maintenance of *their* labor reserve. Very naturally they want those funds administered by people with whom they and their fellow employers have some direct influence. That desire will continue to be one of the restraints on a conception of unemployment insurance as a tool of *national* labor market policy.

Federally financed extended unemployment insurance benefits have actually been used in the same way and to shore up state funds weakened by unexpectedly large claims. They have been conceived as performing the same relief to individuals as the state-financed benefits. Some reciprocity in the payment of benefits in one state (particularly an adjoining one), the right to which had accrued to individuals because of a work record in another state, has developed. But the same minimal relevance to labor market adjustments characterize these arrangements.

Only recently have we begun to consider the payment of unemployment insurance benefits and federally supplied maintenance allowances to assist training and/or relocation, as devices facilitating adjustment of supply and demand in the labor market. Since this approach to benefits as useful to assist needed occupational and geographical movement in order that men and jobs may be brought into better balance is so new, little comment as to its status is possible.

Moreover, since training, as we have seen, is itself oriented to service
to local labor markets, it could scarcely be expected that we have
thought very deeply about the relation of benefits paid in connection
with it to the facilitating of adjustments within the framework of a
national labor market.

That analysis and appraisal of the place of benefits not solely
as a relief-to-individuals device but as a positive instrument in the
facilitating of an efficiently operating national labor market needs to
be undertaken.

Services to other agencies, particularly national agencies, have
many national labor market aspects; we name only one of the most
important. The Bureau of Employment Security (employment service
and unemployment insurance) supplies to other national agencies
charged with providing a picture of conditions in the national labor
market those statistical evidences gathered in the course of operations or by special research projects. These statistics are the basic
stuff of many of their reports on the state of the nation economically.
These agencies include Office of Manpower, Automation, and Training, Bureau of Labor Statistics, Council of Economic Advisors, Joint
Economic Committee, Senate Labor and Public Welfare Committee,
House Education and Labor Committee, and others. These agencies,
particularly the first three, have, of course, additional national information providing functions for which they are solely responsible.

NATIONAL ORIENTATION OF
EMPLOYMENT SERVICE

This brings us to the *placement and placement-related* procedures
of the Employment Service in connection with which positive steps
have been taken to meet the needs of the labor market which certainly move beyond the borders of local communities and states and
in some cases approximate those of a national labor market.

At least five developments of procedures within the Employment
Service move in this direction.

THE COUNSELING, TESTING, AND PLACEMENT
OF STUDENTS

The conception of labor market opportunities made available by
the Employment Service to prospective first-job holders in many high
schools in nearly every state of the union is normally that of the
nation, particularly with respect to counseling. The same orientation

applies to services to students in co-operation with college counseling and placement agencies. One of the real contributions of the Employment Service to such high school and college centered efforts is the view of the national occupational outlook and labor market developments that they bring to the field of opportunity which the student can contemplate. The occupational outlook presented to both high school and college students, of course, makes reference to that in their own communities and states, but it does not stop there. Particularly will the increasing efforts being made with rural youth, for whom there exists little alternative to disappearing rural jobs, inevitably involve an emphasis on interregional placement and training for more than locally needed work qualifications.

THE PLACEMENT SERVICE PROVIDED IN CONNECTION WITH THE NATIONAL MEETINGS AND CONVENTIONS OF SCIENTIFIC AND OTHER PROFESSIONAL SOCIETIES

The range of applications and job openings cleared in this convention service is as national as the range of locations in which the members of these societies live and are employed, i.e., countrywide. In 1962, nine societies were provided these national convention services. The record of the first six is as follows: Employers listed 6455 openings for professionals, and 3416 referrals were made. Salaries offered ranged from $4500 to $18,000. The record of placements and acceptances are not available on a national basis but are included in reported state totals.

THE ANNUAL WORKER PLAN FOR AGRICULTURAL AND FOOD-PROCESSING MIGRANTS

This plan for organizing, in a tandem series, a number of jobs to which migrants, with certainty, may move after each employment contract is finished, is in my judgment one of the most inventive and soundly conceived plans for interstate employment that could possibly be devised. It has been particularly effective on the South and Middle Atlantic Coast and in the Far West and Southwest. In carrying out the 1961 program, contact was made with 9200 migrant worker *groups* consisting of 204,000 individuals from 34 states.

THE PROFESSIONAL OFFICE NETWORK

This plan for making potential jobs available to professional people, and potential workers available for consideration to those desiring professional services, on a nationwide basis, was instituted in March 1956 after pilot projects and experimentation in eight northeastern states, the District of Columbia, and Puerto Rico. Initially the plan was to provide for a flow of unfilled orders and unmatched applications for the local office to a central "key city" office in each state charged with responsibility for attempting a statewide effort to find openings or recruit applicants. Beyond that there was an exchange of still unmatched orders and applications among the "key cities." The next year this was expanded into a nationwide operation, and by 1963 there were 121 professional network offices strategically located in cities in all sections of the United States.

In these cities are located lists of professional and managerial applications and jobs which originated in one of the 1900 local employment offices but could not be matched there. The requesting employer had in each case approved out-of-the-area recruitment, and the applicant, of course, had indicated his willingness to move.

Professional or managerial applicants can be listed immediately in the network city by registering at the nearest Employment Service office if no suitable and satisfactory job opening is on file at their local office.

Here, then, is a model for a truly national labor market Employment Service devoted initially, very naturally, to facilitating professional and managerial employment in connection with which both employers and employees consider the national labor market to be their appropriate field of search and opportunity.

It is available for expansion as new occupations come into the classification of those whose participants consider their employment relationship opportunities to be national in scope.

INTERAREA RECRUITMENT (CLEARANCE)

The Professional Office Network is actually a specialized occupational aspect of the Interarea Recruitment System. The original Wagner-Peyser Act authorized the establishment of a system of "clearance" between the states. During World War II, this activity became of greatly enlarged importance. It developed rapidly into an effective process for facilitating the unusual degree of labor movement required for wartime production. It has continued to be a significant part of the operations of the Employment Service, and its administration has been continuously improved. Together with the Professional Office Network, the Interarea Recruitment System aims to make available to all workers the job opportunities for which they are qualified available anywhere in the United States, and to make available to all employers the qualified workers to fill their jobs to be found in any part of the country. The system operates through a series of steps, searching for jobs and workers in the next most comprehensive labor market when supply and demand cannot be matched in the more immediate labor market. In spite of certain limitations on this ambitious objective, to be named presently, this clearance, or Interarea Recruitment System represents a closer approximation to a systematic attempt to gear placement services for all workers to a national free labor market than that existing in any country with whose Employment Service we are familiar. Its elements can be briefly described:

Step 1. Offices of direct clearance. In certain areas there are a number of local employment offices in near enough proximity (even though they are on opposite sides of a state line) so that they have been authorized to deal directly with each other when their employer orders are insufficient to provide employment for their applicants or vice versa. Orders and applications are "cleared" directly with those other local offices which in the judgment of the initiating manager have greatest probability of supplying unfilled openings or unemployed qualified workers, as the case may be. If no results are obtained, the order may be extended by the next step.

Step 2. Clearance within the state. The state administrator, upon request from a local office indicating that they have been unable to match an order with a worker, either from their own resources or those available in offices of direct clearance, may put the order in intrastate clearance. The state administrator, on the basis of available information, exercising his best judgment as to where among the local offices the workers will most probably be found, transmits the order to these offices. If a favorable response is received from any of them, further negotiations are carried on between the two local offices concerned.

Step 3. Clearance between the states. If the state labor market has not been able to supply the worker or workers needed, the state administrator then initiates clearance between the states. He selects those states most likely, on the evidence of current information, to have available qualified workers. He may obtain from regional and national offices required information about the current state of labor demand and supply, by occupation in specific areas, to help him in making this selection. He then transmits the order to the administrators in those states, who in turn submit it to local offices within their states. Upon receipt of a promising reply from one or more of these local offices, direct negotiations between the two involved local offices are initiated.

Inter-labor-market clearance is also facilitated by a state inventory of job openings. When an attempt to fill an order is unsuccessful locally or through the resources of those offices in direct clearance contact, the order is sent to the state administrator for inclusion in this inventory. The inventory is issued every two weeks. Copies are sent to all local offices within the state and to their offices of direct clearance in adjoining states, as well as to all state administrators, the U. S. Regional Offices, and the United States Employment Service National Office.

A local office, upon receipt of the inventory, can check its files and negotiate directly if it has qualified applicants ready to move. The local office having applicants desiring to move may also request its state office to search the inventories from other states.

Here, then, is at least a theoretical provision for every participant desiring to consummate an employment relationship to have at his disposal the job openings and the manpower available in not only local, but in increasingly wider labor markets, and ultimately in the national labor market. That this is not merely a theoretical provision is indicated by the fact that during the six years from 1957 through 1962, close to 850,000 placements were made through the utilization of this interarea recruitment service.

DEPARTURES FROM NATIONAL LABOR MARKET CONCEPT

Some of the departures from a national labor market concept of this procedure can almost be inferred from contemplating the above description. Following are a few which have been reinforced by comments of administrators and users of the Employment Service.

The system is first of all a service primarily for employers, although of course it eventually seeks out a worker to whom the finding of a job is a welcome service. Unlike the Professional Office Network, which lists both applications and orders, in the case of the interarea recruitment service, the name of the applicant remains in the local office until he is found by the search process. It is not accurate to say, therefore, that all unfilled jobs in the national labor market are available to him, for his knowledge of them depends on the accident of the search process coming upon his card in the files.

A moment's thought will reveal the problem here of keeping manageable the size of the files for the millions of registrants in the several offices at successive levels of comprehensiveness under the present hand sorting and search methods, and of keeping the lists corrected for placements made. The system does, however, make ultimately available to employers qualified applicants from all parts of the national labor market. We have already suggested, moreover, that the Professional Office Network system is available for expansion if it develops that the performers and the employers of labor in other occupations demonstrate a tendency to consider the national labor market their field of operation.

In the second place, *at every stage* (save in the case of the distribution of the state inventory of job openings) *there is a judgment exercised by the manager or administrator as to which local or state offices shall receive the order for consideration.* The result could then very well be as follows:

> *Step 1.* Order sent by local office managers to one out of three offices of direct clearance.
>
> *Step 2.* Order sent from state administrator to six out of 36 offices in the state.
>
> *Step 3.* Order sent to four out of 50 other state offices, and then by the four state administrators to ten out of the 100 local offices in those states.

It is accurate to say, therefore, that the employer is offered access to that labor force in those local and state segments of the national labor market where, in the judgment of local and state Employment Service administrators, the desired workers are likely to be found.

Here again we see what is probably an administrative necessity at work. Back of it is undoubtedly the common-sense judgment that there is no point in flooding the desks of local and state administrators with job orders for, say skilled lumberjacks, if that community or state has no forestry industry. Moreover, the judgment is unlikely to be of the "snap" variety or merely an expression of the administrator's or manager's intuition. There are rules about this exercise of judgment. It is supposed to be made after examination of labor market reports, recent clearance activities and results, occupational and industrial data, and other current data on the condition of labor supply and demand. The purpose is to have the order considered by only those local offices which have what appears to be a potential supply of the kind of labor desired. Furthermore, no one in his right mind would suggest the multiplication of paper work in offices where the

chances are one to 1000 or one to 100 that the process would lead
to any results. The necessity for selective judgment in order to avoid
this does, however, highlight the importance of making certain that
the judgment is based on accurate and quickly available data about
labor supply and demand, and that it is insulated from the necessity
for weighing political pressures in the determination of what states
or localities will be "selected" for submission of the order.

A third observation that can be made is that a primary intention
appears to be the consideration of local interests. These local interests
are frequently both that the unemployed in the local area shall have
first crack at jobs in that local area, and that local reserves of labor
shall not be tapped from the outside until the would-be tapper has
exhausted all possibilities closer to home. There are, of course, considerations, other than the protection of such local interests, in the
requirement that an order shall not be put into clearance before it
is evident that it cannot be filled from the unemployed in the local
or immediate area labor market. But this is the consideration which,
if not honored, is most likely to produce employer and political pressures critical of this aspect of the work of the Employment Service.

Nevertheless, the rules mentioned above for the operation of the
clearance procedure make it a slow and cumbersome process. Economists who look upon the Employment Service as a necessary facility
to bring the labor market closer to the economists assumed ideal of
a "perfect" labor market (as it unquestionably does) can note these
added prospects of imperfections residing in the Employment Service
process itself.

It is unlikely that the speed and smoothness of movement in the
labor market will be increased by the complete removal of these
"imperfections" which appear to make administrative sense and to
be based on administrative necessity.

There are possibilities for increasing that speed and smoothness,
and they are being, and have been, developed and applied as experience grows. The clarification and standardization of both order and
application data and forms; the more careful exploration and recording of an applicant's willingness or even desire to move; the
improvement of the labor supply and demand data, its accuracy and
up-to-dateness in a form making quick and accurate judgments as
to where the greatest possibility of successful submission lies: these
are all practicable steps to be continued. Automation by use of tele-
type and ultimately electronic recording, sorting, and retrieval of
application and order data has been suggested. At the present time
an experimental development is taking place in the Pacific Coast and
adjoining states region in the step-by-step introduction of such auto-

mated methods. The problems involved will be revealed for attention, the improvements required be made, and the results in more rapid and efficient services considered. If successful, the developments can be extended to other regions.*

Here, then, in the Employment Service are developments that have gone far to realize in practice the concept of an operational field encompassing the national labor market. They include: (1) vocational counseling and placement for youth, (2) the national convention placement services to the professions, (3) the annual worker plan for migrant agricultural and food processing workers, (4) the professional and managerial office network, and (5) the interarea recruitment or clearance process. It remains to bring the other services, such as vocational education and training, retraining of the unemployed, employer services, the creation of job opportunities, the administration of unemployment insurance and other benefits, into a program and operational phase which is geared to the same concept of a national labor market. It remains to provide the integration and co-ordination of all Employment and Manpower Services at the federal level so that they reinforce each other. It remains to focus all services on a united effort to develop the required manpower to maximize productiveness in the economy and to facilitate the genuinely free movement of labor to that employment so that it is not wasted but put to work at its highest potential, within the framework of a national labor market.

NEED FOR A NATIONAL LABOR MARKET EMPHASIS

The need for positive emphasis on the national labor market is reinforced by three facts:

1. There are other economic policies and programs which are nationally conceived and directed to the problems of the

---

* An interesting sidelight on this experiment recently came to our attention. A weekly magazine, very widely distributed among employers, recently ran a feature article on the experiment with automatic data processing in the California area of operations. The article had a critical tone geared to the "bureaucratic tendency to waste the taxpayers' money on impractical schemes" theme. Apparently California employers drew a different conclusion to the effect that the Employment Service was on the ball in updating its methods and hence likely to be of real service to them, for the Employment Service, after the article was published, experienced an upsurge in orders for technical and professional people, with salaries in many cases in five figures.

total nation rather than of its sectional and local areas. They affect and are affected by the policies and programs in the employment and manpower field. The integration of all of these at the national level is difficult, if not impossible, if policies and programs of the Employment and Manpower Services are not oriented to the same national operational field as the others.

2. There are national employment and manpower problems, factors, and facility needs which are not mere summations of these matters as they are found in local communities, but which are unique to employment relations for the nation as a whole.

3. The conditions in and operations of the national labor market set limits or provide opportunities for what can be achieved in local labor markets.

It perhaps should be restated that the emphasis in this chapter has not been a plea for supplanting a local labor market concept of the operational field with that of national labor market. A marriage of the two emphases would be the appropriate metaphor. People live and work in local communities, and the employment details of their daily lives are affected by the conditions and processes of their local labor markets and the decisions and actions of the participants therein. There can be no such thing as an effectively operating national labor market while local labor markets are operating in an ineffective way.

Nor do we intend to suggest an inflexible set of national plans, programs, and procedures to which the offices in all local labor markets shall conform. The objective of a national labor market policy and program in relation to local labor markets is not a precise specification of every last detail of operations, or even of emphasis, among various services in those local markets. The objective is to provide flexibility to meet realistically local labor market problems in response to local awareness of and analysis of what those are. The objective is to undergird local efforts and strengthen them by the results of an adequate and realistic handling of the problems characteristic of a national labor market. But it is also an objective that labor market problems which are brought to the fore by national events and conditions, and those whose solution is improbable or impossible by adaptations confined to local areas, shall be tackled by Employment and Manpower Services whose operational field is legitimately considered to be the national labor market.

SUMMARY

In the United States, the traditional evolution of the means for dealing with problems experienced by increasingly enlarging groups begins with the invention of the individual, and moves through the elaboration of that invention by voluntary association and enterprise, through successive levels of local and state government, to the amplification of those means by the national government. Resistance is offered as each more comprehensive unit of government seeks to adapt measures to the group problems faced at that level. This resistance has certain advantages as well as disadvantages, however. It makes it necessary for the determination of ends and means to be a matter of consensus formation and mutual consent, with the consequent possibility that localized needs will be well considered and better met, and that simultaneously progress in ends and means at the more comprehensive level will be based on the consent of those who must ultimately participate in their realization and implementation. There is no intention here, therefore, of suggesting a substitution of a concept of an operational field defined as a national labor market for one defined as a local labor market.

The arguments for strong Employment and Manpower Services geared to local needs are irrefutable. The vast majority of employment relations are established within the conditions characteristic of local labor market operations and the facts of labor supply and demand existing there. The initiative and effort of local people created these services in the first place, and their continued initiative and effort are required for the continuous development of those services. The big volume of business for all the services is going to continue to involve circumstances and transactions at the grass roots. The administrators who eventually bring policy and plans out into life are the local managers, and their success in each case requires cooperation with thousands of people whose horizon is the local labor market. Labor market operations are only one of the processes of community life affecting, but also affected by, the totality of those processes. The specific requirements for their integration to provide an effective working whole community in thousands of different unique local situations can never be understood and acted wisely upon solely by central directors of services removed from daily and intimate contact with those situations.

There is no lack of recognition of these arguments for the strengthening of local services by those in Washington, and, if there were, there are plenty of pressures arising from local sources which can effectively impress them with the "error of their ways." These pressures are mostly related to the geographical and occupational movement of labor which might appear desirable in the national economic interest. They include the plain disinclination of workers to move. They include the fear of employers that they may lose their labor reserves, of local trade unions that they may lose their "scarce commodity" advantage, of politicians that they may lose votes and have their constituency reduced, of community leaders that the life of community institutions will suffer, of local representatives and taxpayers that they will pay for training and other services from which their community gets no return, of conservatives who are loath to see central government assume responsibilities traditionally carried by individuals and local communities.

But the arguments for conceiving of the operational field of the Employment Services as the national labor market are equally compelling. There are political and economic events and trends which take place on a national scale involving national policy and programs which affect and are affected by policy and programs in the employment and manpower field. There are private decisions of free enterprisers (including the automation of their technical processes and the movement from one locality to another) which have manpower and employment implications and effects which cannot be dealt with solely on a local or state basis. The mobility of families and the development of megalopolis are matters, neither the initiation or effects of which nor their implications for employment are local in scope. Those whose vision of the Employment Services they operate is purely locally oriented see these developments as threats and are inclined to local protective action. The positive exploitation of the opportunities for economic strength and growth which the national events and developments offer requires initiative and effort within the framework of a national labor market concept. The same conclusion pertains to other participants in the labor market. The increase in their tendency to gear their activities to the national interest will scarcely be promoted by a governmental program of Employment and Manpower Services which is not conceived and operated toward facilitating the effective operation of the national labor market.

Each of the Employment and Manpower Services faces the need for adaptation when its operational field is considered to be the national labor market. Counseling, interviewing and testing, research and the distribution of labor market and labor force information, vocational education and training, retraining for the unemployed, the creation of job opportunities, maintenance benefits like unemployment insurance, training allowances, and subsidies for movement to other localities share with the placement services themselves the need to gear their services to the most effective development and allocation of the labor force in the interests of national, and not merely local or statewide, economic strength and growth. A number of the requirements for adaptation were named.

It is the Employment Service, however, which feels the strongest impact of the necessity to operate with an eye to the effective functioning of the national labor market. Most advocates of the national labor market emphasis do not envisage a situation in which every worker would have available to him every unfilled job in the country, and every employer would have available every worker qualified to perform in the job or jobs he has to offer. But they do urge movement in the direction of that situation. It is well, therefore, to consider the kinds of factors which are likely to affect movement in that direction.

The first of these factors is that the demand for labor, that is, private decisions to offer jobs, rather than the supply of labor is what normally initiates an employment relationship. If balance of supply and demand is to be achieved in the national labor market, the area in which adjustments are to be made and the area in which orders and work applications can be sought must broaden beyond the local and state areas, and it is probable that more employment-creation functions will have to be allocated to the Employment and Manpower Services.

The second factor is that the larger the area of adjustment, the more necessary becomes a just and acceptable principle for priorities for allocation, among employers, of labor in scarce supply. In a free-enterprise economy no centralized government dares to announce that it has a policy with respect to such priorities, but its deeds create what the word does not proclaim. Deed will be interpreted as intent.

In the third place, workers, and the employers of workers, in different occupations and organizational positions have varying perceptions of the size and extent of a labor market within which they should seek their opportunities and resources for an employment relationship. Only a small proportion conceives of a national (or international) labor market as that field. The number who do so, however, is increasing and will continue to increase, and the placement services will, more and more, have to facilitate their search for jobs and workers in the national labor market. Those aspects of the service geared to this nationwide clearance of orders and applications will necessarily come in for heavy duty.

A fourth factor is the difficulty of standardizing the data on job requirements and worker qualifications and of recording, storing, and retrieving that data speedily and accurately, a difficulty that becomes increasingly apparent as the field of operations moves outward from the local to the national labor market. These difficulties were illustrated by indicating the difference in the possibilities of automating the making of airline reservations, and the closing of an employment contract transaction.

Closely related to the data recording and processing problems are those related to the amplified kinds of data which are required when employment transactions are carried on over the longer distances characteristic of a national labor market. Conditions of employment and personal characteristics of the applicant which can be left to face-to-face confrontation of the prospective applicant and employer must now be recorded and available for accurate transmission.

In addition, the facilitating of interlocal labor market movement in the face of the enlarged opportunities and jobs available in a national labor market requires attention to the technical simplification and systemization of the burden of handling what well might be an overwhelming number of orders and applications arising in the enlarged market.

Finally, the larger the operational field, the more vital becomes the matter of speed in processing. Elements in the process of interlocal labor market movement which were related to that speed were briefly named. They included automation of the clearance process, warnings from employers of prospective major employment changes, ascertainment of likelihood of an applicant's willingness to move, and a policy with respect to the protection of local interests opposed to the inter-labor market movement of workers.

The present situation concerning the degree of adaptation of the Employment and Manpower Services in the United States to the needs of a national labor market operation was described as relatively weak in most of the services with the exception of the Employment Service. The predominant orientation of employer services, creation of job opportunities, vocational education and training, programs for retraining the unemployed, unemployment insurance, and training and mobility allowances is toward operations for the benefit of local labor markets.

Chiefly with respect to research and statistical reporting and with respect to the placement and placement-related services have serious steps been taken to implement a national labor market approach to employment and manpower problems. The five major going programs of the Employment Service that give evidence of that approach are as follows:

1. The counseling, testing and placement of high school and college students.
2. The placement services provided the professions in connection with the annual national meetings of the professional societies.
3. The annual worker plan for agricultural and food-processing migrants.
4. The national professional and managerial office network.
5. The interarea recruitment, or the clearance procedure.

A number of characteristics of the clearance procedure resulting from administrative necessity and the need to avoid antagonizing local interests were named. These limit the accuracy of the statement that the clearance procedure provides a completely adequate national-labor-market-oriented placement service. Nevertheless, the three-step procedure, in which an employer's order, impossible to fill locally, is brought into contact with progressively more comprehensive labor markets, until well-nigh the national labor market has been explored for qualified workers, plus the distribution to every state administrator of the bi-weekly unfilled openings inventory was characterized as the nearest approximation to a truly national labor market placement service found in any country with which we are familiar.

The steps which have been and are being taken by the Employment Service to make these national-labor-market-oriented services more adequate and speedy are notable. They include, for example, a large-scale experiment in the automation of the clearance process.

There remains a large task, however, in making the operations of the other services more consistent with those required by the nature of a national labor market operational field. There also remains the necessity of integration and co-ordination of all the services at the federal level. There remains the need to focus all of them on a united effort to develop the required manpower to maximize productivity in the economy and to facilitate the genuinely free movement of labor within the framework of a national labor market to that employment in which labor can be used at its maximum potential.

There can be no compromise with the policy of accepting the national labor market as the operational field for the Employment and Manpower Services. There are other economic policies and programs which are nationally conceived and directed to the problems of the total nation, with which the Employment and Manpower Services need to be integrated. There are national employment and manpower problems, factors, and facility needs which are unique to employment relations for the nation as a whole. The conditions in and operations of the national labor market set limits or provide opportunities for what can be achieved in local labor markets.

At the same time, there can be no success in cultivating the total field in a nation of this size and with its traditions of federal-state relations unless local labor markets are operating effectively, and there is flexibility within very general national policy for the exercise of local initiative and action in response to local awareness and analysis of local manpower and labor market conditions. From the point of view of local administrators, the purpose of emphasis on the national labor market in concept and action is not to supplant but to undergird their efforts and to expand the amount of elbow room they have for solving their local problems of labor surplus or shortage.

COMPREHENSIVE AND
GAP-FILLING SERVICES

Chapter Six We have defined the operational field for the Employment and Manpower Services in geographical terms. It can also be defined in occupational and industrial terms, and by reference to the agencies providing services to particular groups. The question is this: to what occupational and industrial groups shall the efforts of the Employment and Manpower Services be directed? Shall it be to each and every one of them? Or shall it be only to those which are not served by other labor market facilities? Both questions are answered in the affirmative, but, of course, by different people. This situation grows partly out of the fact that a difference of opinion and even conviction exists on the basic issues with respect to the mission and operational field of the services. It is difficult even to suggest a sound policy with respect to the extension, maintenance, or limitation of the occupational operational field of the services until there is some basis for that policy which flows from the choice made about putting primary emphasis on the nation's economic or individual's social welfare, on managed or free labor market facilities, and on national or local labor market coverage. Another reason is that there are already, in the field, placement and counseling services, at least for some of the occupations, and those managing them raise objections to the intrusion of what they call a competitor. Their vested interests are at stake. These objections are on occasion voiced through political representatives.

In a study of the documents and widespread discussions with the creators, administrators, and potential "customers" of the services, we have come across strongly held but multiple points of view on the principles which should govern this occupational coverage of the services. Consider some of the consequences of policy following from each of these principles.

113

SERVICE UNEMPLOYMENT INSURANCE CLAIMANTS

The first and narrowest principle is to limit the occupations served to those represented by unemployment insurance claimants, and then only when those claimants are involved. This principle is the least likely to meet any opposition from any popular source, since the placement services of the Employment Service have been related to unemployment insurance since its inception. Moreover, the principle, superficially at least, meets the interests of employer taxpayers in getting as many unemployed as possible out of the group that are depleting what they consider to be *their* funds by drawing benefits. The principle appears consistent with a social service mission that provides attention for those who need it most and trusts that others will take care of themselves.

We have already discussed the chief objection to this principle in considering whether the placement efforts should concentrate on the hard-to-place, or on the normal run of workers and on those for whom the demand is greater than the supply. Adherence to the "claimants principle" involves a reduction of the range of occupational skills and volume of workers available to employers and of occupational openings available to workers. We also noted the impact of any such policy on the image of the Employment Service, reducing the probability that the voluntary submission of applications and orders would supply the most desirable range of choices to employers and workers, respectively.

There is no question raised here about the propriety of and necessity for attention to placing those claiming unemployment insurance. The principle under discussion is *limitation* to this group. That group in a country which has an unemployment insurance coverage as broad as in the United States will always provide the largest number of customers for the public placement services. Indeed, one way to expand the natural operational field for those services is to extend the coverage of unemployment insurance.

SERVICE THOSE OCCUPATIONS MOST IN NEED

Another principle which would probably meet popular acceptance is to concentrate on those occupational and industrial groups of claimants or others unemployed who need the services most. From the points of view both of income and of the availability of alternative placement facilities, for example, it would be assumed that domestic, casual, and unskilled industrial labor need a public placement service more than the occupants of professional, highly technical, or management occupations.

That perceived degree of relative need is an understandable, but nevertheless unproved, assumption even when need is defined as personal need of the individuals involved. If account is taken of the need of the economy, either locally or nationally, for effective movement of the workers in every productive occupation, this principle is wholly inadequate. Its acceptance is likely chiefly among those who identify the public Employment Service as a social welfare or relief agency.

SERVICE ANYONE WHO WANTS IT

Very little popular opposition would be raised presumably to the third principle that anyone who walks through the door and asks for it has a right to placement service. This point of view, which implies a status for the Employment Service as a "responder," if sincerely held, appears to relieve those who plan and operate the Service from responsibility to think further about the matter. The decision is made by the initiative of the customer.

But can the managers of the Employment Service pass the buck in that fashion? If the people who "come through the door" represent a range of occupations inadequate to enable the Employment Service to encourage employers to extend the range of occupations for which they seek to obtain workers through the Service, what then? If those who come through the door do not constitute a supply of labor actually or potentially possessing capacities needed to bring productive balance into the local and national labor market, what then? Moreover, the very tendency to "come through the door" will be determined by the prior decision of the Employment Service as to the range of occupational and industrial groups it will seek to serve. The tendency of employers to want or to use the Service will be determined by the prior decision of the Employment Service as to the range of occupational jobs it will seek to fill. That decision cannot be passed off on the customer, although the response in applications or orders, to which they are stimulated by it, determines whether the decision can be translated into results.

STAY OUT OF OCCUPIED TERRITORY

The hottest issues related to the policy with respect to the occupational and industrial operational field center around the principle that the Employment Service should cultivate only those areas of the labor market in which no other placement and vocational counseling service is available. If some other agency has taken on the responsibility, or is exploiting the opportunity for profit or service, the Employment Service should stay out of such occupied territory.

Objections on these grounds arose, at the very beginnings of a public employment office effort, from those making a living out of the employment problems of workers and employers in the casual or day work and in the migrant labor markets. The Employment Service today has established a sufficient scope of service in those areas so that we need not concern ourselves with it at this time, other than to note that the protest against infringement on private enterprise is not new.

Likewise, in the area of factory production workers there is some continued activity among both fee and non-fee-charging agencies. It is all but universally accepted, however, particularly because of the relation of the unemployment of these workers to unemployment insurance, that their placement is a legitimate and desirable operational field for a public employment service. In earlier times, and in some areas of the country today, certain trade associations performed, and do perform, a service, welcomed by some employers, of screening out "undesirable" applicants.

There are, however, six other occupational groups, the service to whom by a public agency is still challenged with some heat. These are the following:

1. Service occupations, both domestic and institutional.
2. Clerical, retail, and similar occupations.
3. First jobbers, high school and college.
4. Professional and highly skilled technical occupations.
5. Management occupations.
6. Crafts (including maritime).

The first five of these occupations are an operational field for fee-charging agencies, and the natural objection of the managers of those agencies is that government is competing unfairly with private enterprise, since no fee is charged by a public Employment Service. We find little merit in this argument for three reasons. The first is that to abdicate the area, on the grounds that the occupants of these occupations can get service for a price from a private employment office, is to discriminate against them. The only basis on which public provision of free Employment and Manpower Services can be provided some, and denied to other, citizens is on the ground that the latter don't need it and can afford to pay for it. This would be consistent with a social welfare and relief service, and those holding to this concept of the mission of the Employment and Manpower Services could square such discrimination with their concept. We do not hold to that concept.

The second reason is that there is no compulsion on anyone not to use a fee-charging agency if he finds that it provides a better or more effective service than the free public one, or even if it does not and he just believes in supporting private enterprise at a personal cost to himself.

The third and most important reason is that manpower allocation and development is related to other economic health and growth problems of the nation. No private fee-charging agency can be expected to have a major concern for those problems. The greater the emphasis given to this economic role of the Employment and Manpower Services in defining their mission, the more reasonable becomes the justification for the maintenance of public free Employment Services to all occupational and industrial groups, in spite of the fact that fee-charging agencies are available to supply individuals with those services at a price. Lacking that emphasis, however, the decision on this particular policy issue is a matter of who can marshall the most votes—from the legislators and from the customers.

Some are inclined to debate the issue on the basis of relative quality of service offered by the fee-charging and public free agencies. This is a debate that will always end in partisan claims rather than in decisions, persuasive to the managers of one or the other type of agency, to go out of business. In any case, there is no arbitrator with power to make the decision, save the applicant or the employer who does or does not make use of the agencies on the basis of his perception of their relative merits for his purpose. We are ready to let the decision as to relative quality of service rest with the potential users.

The public Employment Service has a labor market function to perform for the community and national economy, as well as for individuals. The first function involves the necessity of cultivating an operational field in which all occupations and industries are represented. The a priori decision of the Employment Service, if it is to perform that function, must be to cultivate that comprehensive field. Whether or not it can successfully do so in the face of a similar cultivation of certain occupational and industrial fields by fee-charging agencies may appropriately be decided by the decisions of customers in those occupations, on the basis of whether it does or does not provide a service which meets their requirements.

STAY OUT OF TERRITORY
OCCUPIED BY FREE SERVICES

The challenge of encroachment on private territory arises not only from fee-charging agencies but from placement and counseling agencies run for the benefit of their membership or beneficiaries without charge. First jobbers leaving high school and college, professional and highly technical people, management, and crafts served in employment matters by unions are among those for whom employment and counseling services are available (although unevenly throughout the country) on a no-charge basis. The most vocal of these challengers are those serving the high school and college students, the associations of high school and of college vocational counselors and placement officers. Indeed, the recent outcry of the college association that the Employment Service is "trying to put them out of business" has introduced an emotional and potentially political tone to the debate which threatens to becloud the basic issues. Placement services of professional associations and trade unions, trusting in the relative prestige with their own members of their services, are not so vocal in their opposition to the public Employment Services as "competitors." Indeed, in some cases they have requested that the Employment Service provide special facilities for the occupations whose occupants they represent.

In this case the challenge cannot be met on the grounds of an equal right to publicly provide free Employment Services, for normally no fee is charged by such private agencies. But the third point related to the fee-charging agencies, stated above, i.e. that point relative to the broader function of the public service, does hold, and to an even greater extent here. For these occupational groups served by such associations are frequently those whose performance, and hence whose placement and movement, are key elements in the operation of a labor market in a way that contributes to economic health and growth, a result which, in turn, improves the job openings and job security for all occupations. That broader function of the Employment and Manpower Services is reduced far out of proportion to the numbers involved if the proper operational field is limited to casuals, migrants, production workers, domestics and other service workers, and clerical and retail workers, who have no fraternal associations interested in assisting them in their employment problems.

UNLIMITED AND CO-OPERATIVE SERVICE

One suggested solution to this problem is that there be no universally applicable policy to undertake services to these groups. If Harvard or the high schools in Waterbury have effectively functioning vocational counseling and placement services for their graduates, let the Cambridge and Waterbury offices of the Employment Service concern themselves with groups not so well served. If Jackson College and the high schools in Lincoln Center have no such services, let the Jackson and Lincoln Center offices of the Employment Service supply them.

This seems reasonable if the mission of the Employment and Manpower Services is limited to vocational counseling and placement and is focused on meeting the needs of individual employers and potential workers. But we have not been satisfied so to limit the horizons of that mission. Those horizons encompass the needs of the community and the national economy for strength, stability, and growth. While implying no compulsion on individual choices, those latter needs point to the desirability of those choices being made in the full light of the present and future occupational outlook and in the light of the full range of present and developing work opportunities and need for particular skills in the total economy.

Now it is possible and probable that in some instances those who administer the counseling and placement services in, for example, educational institutions provide students with such a comprehensive range of choice. But it is also possible that their efforts do not provide the students with a presentation of the realities of the general occupational outlook and with the opportunity to come in contact with the job offers other than those made by the limited number of recruiters from large companies who are permitted to interview students and for whom appointments have been made by the college or high school placement officers. Is it not possible that the Employment Service can increase the effectiveness and scope of the services of those officers by supplying them, and even coaching them with respect to, the labor market and labor force information in its possession; by placing at their disposal, in the case of college students, the Professional Office Network system; by amplifying the openings available to include those offered by the smaller employers not in a position to send recruiters; etc? Far from "putting such officers out of business," such assistance would amplify their field of business to the benefit not only of the individual students involved but of the productive enterprises in the country.

What is indicated here is co-operative relations with the educational placement and counseling officers through reciprocally beneficial supplementation of each other's effort. Far from eliminating their valuable services from the field, such supplementation would amplify those services in a way improving chances of accomplishment of the economic mission that must always weigh heavily with the public Employment and Manpower Services. There is no reason to suppose that the value of the work of the educational offices will suffer by the stimulus this co-operation would provide for their administrators to include the public interest in economic strength and growth among the objectives guiding *their* efforts also.

The same co-operative offer of supplementary service might well apply to those professional and trade union agencies which are providing placement and/or counseling services for their members.

PRACTICE PRAGMATIC ENTREPRENEURSHIP

A principle suggested by the foregoing discussion is that of filling a gap in Employment and Manpower Services whenever and wherever it appears in a community or the nation. In addition to continuously improving services for those groups about whose servicing by a public Employment Service no question is raised, let the managers and administrators keep on their toes in surveying the field and keep on the lookout for such gaps.

This pragmatic approach is actually that taken by the most dynamic and initiative-filled managers and administrators of the services on all levels, federal, state, and local. If we survey the occupational and industrial field served by the Employment Service, for example, in the 1930's and compare the fields in which beginnings at least have been made today, we cannot but be impressed with the entrepreneurship displayed. The record, of course, is uneven, as is the record of any enterprise which relies on entrepreneurship and private initiative as a driving force in its development. Entrepreneural skill and energy is unevenly distributed among Employment Service personnel as it is among industrial, business, and educational personnel. At the root of the unevenness is not only the fact that the degree of initiative varies among administrators, but that the services that initiative develops in some places are already in existence in others, and that the degree of co-operation in, or opposition to, their development varies from one community and state to another.

We can list only a few of the expansions in services resulting from that find-the-gaps-and-fill-them approach. In 16 states centralized placement services are available for teachers, primarily in primary and secondary schools, but in some places in colleges also. The initiation of clearing-house services for hopeful instructors and researchers at the scientific association meetings is in the same occupational area. Registries for nurses and social workers are not uncommon. Recently in Los Angeles, 46 professional associations joined in requesting placement service from the Employment Service. The development of the Professional Office Network dealing with professional and managerial occupations, resulting last year in around 200,000 placements, is evidence of entrepreneurship of a high order.

The special importance of the hotel, restaurant, and garment industries in New York City stimulated special emphasis on meeting that need.

We have already spoken in another connection of the annual worker plan for migrant agricultural and food-processing workers in states and between states where these occupations furnish a major labor market problem.

Efforts to meet a growing unserviced need for counseling, placement, and vocational training of young persons for whom there is, and will continue to be, a decreasing need on the farms are being made in an area where the public services will meet few "competitors." In my visits to the states, the evidence was clearly apparent that these services to youth rate high in the entrepreneural activities of state and local administrators.

While not attempting to do more than establish co-operative relations with unions where they have well-established hiring-hall facilities for their craft members (primarily in the building, maritime, and entertainment occupations), exchange managers have found opportunity for amplified service in communities where such union facilities were inoperative.

There is much to be said for this entrepreneural initiative-in-filling-gaps approach to the expanding of the occupational territories considered to be the appropriate operational field of the Employment Service. Initially, since it leads to the exploitation of virgin territory and to the performance of services not existing or insufficiently supplied, it arouses less opposition than initiative making an impact on territory already occupied with varying degrees of effectiveness by other agencies.

It goes without saying that such entrepreneurship is equally applicable to the maintenance and improvement of services to groups already among the "customers" and to the seeking out of new groups to serve. And it needs to be exercised in the light of the requirement for performing the central mission assigned to a public Employment Service.

If to the guideline, "Expand Employment and Manpower Services for those occupational areas where services are weak or nonexistent," there are added a couple of qualifying phrases, the principle would provide a stimulus to initiative more likely to implement the central economic strength and growth mission of the services. Those qualifying phrases could be: "Wherever those services contribute to the more economically effective operation of the labor market, and to a greater degree than the same amount of effort and resources devoted to strengthening the services already being provided under existing programs." The mere development of new or increased services to particular occupational groups is no guarantee of progress toward more effective performance of the mission of the Employment and Manpower Services to promote the economic strength and growth of the communities and the nation. Resources for publicly supplied services are not unlimited. The most effective use of those resources of money and staff is most likely if decisions as to their distribution, and indeed as to their expansion, are made and justified by reference to the essential mission they are expected to perform. Otherwise, the expanders of the services into new or enlarged fields of operation may come to be characterized by a phrase which Santayana used to describe another group of people. "Fanatics," said Santayana, "are those who redouble their efforts when they have forgotten their aim."

Another qualifying phrase might be "When in the light of the tradition and quality of existing free services it would not appear to be a better use of available resources to establish co-operative relations with and strengthen those facilities now in operation." If the medical or hospital association provides an effectively operating service for nurses or medical technicians, if the state board of education does that job for teachers, if trade unions are doing adequate placement work for their members, public funds may well be devoted to .co-operation with them and to the provision of better placement facilities for others not so well served. There is no reason, however, why the named facilities and the Employment Service both could not benefit from providing orders and applications to each other when either is in short supply or these cannot be matched from those registered with the agency having the problem.

THE CASE OF CIVIL SERVICE

A special problem concerns the present near monopoly of the federal and state civil service commissions with respect to government employment. On the surface the interest of government officials in promoting as wide as possible use of the Employment Service by private enterprises would seem to be inconsistent with maintaining its own Employment Service, i.e., a civil service commission, for its own employment process. But this is deeply embedded both in tradition and in current practice. There are special requirements for screening and selection for employees who are going to be related to politically important occupations. The coverage is well-nigh universal (although quality varies). Nevertheless, it is questionable whether the issue as to the present relationship of the two services is moot, or will remain unchanged with time. Even now the Employment Service is called on for aid in emergencies. And as the stature of the Employment Service in the professional field increases, there will develop mutual relationships for providing information on civil service openings, registration of applications, and preliminary screening of applicants.

In the light of the very great needs for development in the other occupational areas, however, and in the light of the workable quality and extent of the placement procedures in the civil service commissions, government service jobs filled through them would scarcely appear at the moment to be the most appropriate field for entrepreneural activities of the administrators of the Employment Service.

We would make no judgment about the desirability or appropriateness of entrepreneurally stimulated efforts to expand or strengthen the Employment and Manpower Services in any particular occupational area. But it does seem reasonable to suggest that both the makers of the proposal to do so and the opponents of that proposal should base their arguments on a major premise defining the central mission of the services as one of advancing the health, the strength, and the growth of the economy, and on a minor premise defending the proposition that the proposal did or did not perform that mission better than any alternative.

OTHER MANPOWER AND
EMPLOYMENT SERVICES

The operational field questions relating to occupational and industrial coverage are raised chiefly with respect to the placement services. A briefer notice may, therefore, be taken of the questions as they relate to other services.

On the whole, it can be said that the same principle of unlimited and comprehensive occupational coverage applies to these other services with equal justification. Once it is accepted that the mission of the Employment and Manpower Services is oriented to the development and utilization of the nation's labor force in the most productive manner and to facilitating the national as well as local labor market processes so that the free movement of labor contributes to the same end, nothing less than such comprehensive coverage can be defended.

Those services such as *counseling* and *testing*, which are really a part of the placement process, must obviously be oriented to the same occupational and industrial range.

Research and *information* services cannot even be limited, either locally or nationally, by the considerations applying to placement and counseling services, namely, that other nonprofit efforts are being made. For even the value of the co-operative relation suggested for the placement and counseling services assumes the availability of information about labor market and labor force facts and trends that, to be serviceable, must present a whole, and not a partial, picture. There are no private research agencies, academic or otherwise, which can organize and support the continuous, comprehensive, and uniform data collection required for meeting the problems of a national labor market.

The efforts to *stimulate labor demand* will focus in different communities on different occupational groups, but a national effort will be concerned with all of them.

Industrial services to the employer must take account of whatever occupations are utilized in his operations.

The need for *rehabilitation* can have its incidence in the occupants of any occupational group.

If *benefits* of either unemployment insurance or those related to the encouragement of economically desirable mobility are to be serviceable to the effort to place men in the jobs and occupations most fully utilizing their actual or potential skills, there can be no occupational limitation on their applicability. In this connection it should be noted that unemployment insurance coverage, while not directly occupationally discriminatory, is so industrially, and indirectly occupationally, in its exclusion of agriculture and domestic service, and an only partial coverage of nonprofit institutions. There are other issues, of course, involved in this case, but if the functions of the various Employment and Manpower Services are to be mutually contributory to one another, there is not only logic but necessity in raising the question of the desirability of identity of occupational coverage.

The case of *vocational education and training*, including apprenticeship training and on-the-job training, is more difficult to assess. Taken together, they provide a large share of the facilities for whatever development of manpower resources we have. As such, the education and training given in hundreds of thousands of schools, institutions, unions, and places of work must, therefore, be directed toward all occupations needed by the productive processes of the economy. The question here is not solely a matter of comprehensiveness, but also of emphasis, whether the emphasis being given to preparation for certain occupations and the quality of such preparation is consistent not only with the relative present demand for workers in the several occupations but the probable future demand. Since all these facilities are not at present integrated into an over-all employment and manpower program and agency, the best that can be done at the moment is for the managers of the Employment and Manpower Services to stimulate those who operate such facilities to supply the kinds of education and training most likely to fit young people for work in the light of that present and future demand situation.

One development deserving of serious consideration is the pre-apprenticeship course, preliminary to apprenticeship training proper in any craft, which in a number of places in England has reduced over-all apprenticeship period from four to six years to two to four years. The experiment is in its infancy, but the addition of this number of productive years to a worker's life is not to be ignored as a factor contributing to the nation's economic strength and growth.

Another development, to the promoting of which those managing vocational, educational, and training facilities could well be stimulated, is the revamping of the curriculum to supply students or trainees with that basic general knowledge and skill that could form the most promising capacity to move from occupations that are likely to become outdated by the advancing developments in international and domestic marketing and in automation. These developments result today in manpower waste, because vocational education and training acquired in the past have been directed to providing workers with the skill to carry on through life in a single type of job. The future will increasingly require this basic general knowledge and skill, not only as a basis for a present livelihood, but as a foundation for flexibility in adapting to changes in the occupational structure to be met in the future.

Retraining for the unemployed, for upgrading the potential skills of the employed, and for shortage occupations is a relatively new venture for the federal, state, local public Employment and Manpower Services. On the whole, the occupational and industrial coverage has been determined by an assessment of the probable availability of local job openings when the training is finished, and of the skill potentials of recruits for training. These are sound principles, the observance of which keeps the retraining efforts grounded in reality. It is to be hoped, not that these principles will be abrogated, but that they will be amplified by reference to a conception of the more nearly unlimited occupational and industrial character of a labor market larger than the local area.

Moreover, the effort made by any conceivable use of existing facilities, equipment, and teaching staff, or any likely to be set up and acquired with public funds, is a drop in the bucket relative to the need of the whole economy and the potential of the nation's unused or underused manpower for satisfying it. *The great reservoir of facilities, equipment, and teaching resources for this purpose is in the plants, offices, fields, and forests where the great volume of retraining is presently done and always will be done.* We would predict that any major breakthrough in the solution to our manpower retraining problems, systematically geared to increasing the nation's economic health and growth, will be accomplished not by government agencies alone, but by a partnership of these with the facilities and staffs available in the productive enterprises of the country.

Subject to the particular circumstances indicated in this section, it may be suggested that the policy premise with respect to the occupational operational field set forth below applies to all the Employment and Manpower Services.

CONCLUSION RELATIVE TO ALL SERVICES

The conclusion which seems reasonable in the light of the considerations discussed above is this. The operational field for the Employment and Manpower Services with respect to occupational coverage should be, in general, unlimited. The services should concern themselves with every gainful employment occupation in every industry contributing to the productive strength and growth of the economy, whether or not the occupation and industry are served in some places and to some degree by other facilities, fee-charging or free. It is necessary to do so in order to fulfill their mission as defined, to make the field of job oportunities as wide as possible and the volume of available employees as large as possible. It is necessary in order to develop the supply of manpower potential of an economy which needs all occupations, although not to the same degree, in every labor market area. It is necessary in order to adapt the supply of and demand for labor to each other in such a way as to maximize the application to work in gainful employment of the highest productive potential of the nation's manpower.

Where existing free Employment and Manpower Services are available in particular areas (none save those for government occupations are available in all areas) entrepreneural consideration can well be given to the establishment of co-operative relations of the Employment Service with the agencies concerned so as to amplify the opportunities for jobs and workers available to both, and to make it possible for the private agencies to improve their services in the light of the opportunities offered by and the needs of the national labor market.

The touchstone for decision in all cases is what allocation of existing or potential resources is most likely to advance the performance, through public *and* private facilities, of the mission of the Employment and Manpower Services to promote economic health, strength, and growth of the communities and the nation.

SUMMARY

The issues raised with respect to whether the operational field of the Employment and Manpower Services shall involve comprehensive coverage of all occupations and industries or only those not served by existing private facilities primarily, but not exclusively, affect the placement services. Approximation to consensus is made difficult because policies on the central mission and geographical operational field of the services are not clear. A further difficulty arises from the opposition of other agencies in the field to encroachment upon "their" territory, an opposition sometimes backed by political pressure.

A number of principles as to occupational scope are proposed in certain quarters. These are as follows:

1. Service only to unemployment insurance claimants.
2. Service to unemployment insurance claimants and other unemployed who most need the service, from the point of view

of lack of personal resources and the nonavailability of alternative facilities.

3. Service to anyone who wants the service.
4. Stay out of territory occupied by fee-charging or free private services.
5. Stay out of territory served by non-fee-charging private agencies.
6. Unlimited service in general to all occupations, but cooperation with non-fee-charging agencies where they are functioning effectively.
7. Unlimited and pragmatic entrepreneurship as a supplement to effective operation of services within existing occupational coverage.

The first three principles are not acceptable, because, as a basis for operations, (a) they do not provide for a reservoir of orders and applications sufficient to give adequate service to clients and to the nation, and (b) they reinforce an image of the services as relief agencies, an image unlikely to stimulate any increase in the range of orders and applications needed either adequately to service clients or to fulfill the central mission of the services to contribute to the health of the economy and the free movement of labor within the national labor market.

The fourth principle of no competition with existing private agencies was rejected, so far as fee-charging agencies are concerned, on three grounds: (a) There is no basis for discrimination, in provision of a free public service, against workers in some occupations, merely because those occupations are normally better paid, other than that the free public service is a relief service. (b) There is no compulsion on anyone not to use the fee-charging facility if he finds it more advantageous to do so. (c) Restriction of coverage to occupations not served by fee-charging agencies would eliminate a group of applicants and jobs needed to fulfill the central mission of the Employment and Manpower Services.

The fifth principle, staying away from occupational territory served by free agencies, was rejected as a general principle, for these occupations are essential and key elements necessary to the organization and operation of productive enterprise in the economy, and, therefore, essential foci for Employment and Manpower Services. Moreover, the provision of such free private services (for example, to high school and college students and members of professional societies and craft unions) is uneven both in amount and quality over the country.

The sixth principle was accepted with certain reservations. It suggested that, while occupational coverage should in general be unlimited, co-operative and reciprocally supplementary working relations might well be established between free private and public placement and counseling agencies to their mutual advantage. In particular it is likely that the labor market, labor force, and occupational outlook information as well as coaching in their significance and use, which the Employment Service can supply, would be advantageous to the free private agencies both in increasing the value of their services to their clients and in amplifying their contribution to the national interests in economic health and growth. Similar values would be involved in the broadening of the job opportunity alternatives which the Employment Service would be able to provide.

The seventh principle, that of pragmatic entrepreneurship, as a supplement to effective maintenance of services to occupations now served, is that actually practiced by the most dynamic and initiative-filled administrators of the services on all levels, federal, State, and local. In applying this principle, the managers of the services keep their eyes focused on developing needs for their services and move in on areas where either there are gaps in the services or those available are ineffective. A number of examples of such entrepreneural action were cited as evidence of the value of this principle as an operational guide.

It seemed desirable, however, to warn that, in spite of the value of the dynamic initiative such an operating principle was capable of stimulating, there is need for qualification of its application in order to assure a furthering of the central mission of the Employment and Manpower Services and the most efficient allocation of not unlimited governmental resources of money, facilities, and staff. The suggested statement of this entrepreneural principle was, therefore: "Supply employment and manpower services for those occupation areas where services are weak or nonexistent (a) wherever those services contribute to the more economically effective operation of the labor market, and to a greater degree, than the same amount of effort and resources devoted to strengthening the services already being provided under existing programs, and (b) when in the light of the tradition and quality of existing free services it would not appear to be a better use of available resources to establish co-operative relations with, and to strengthen, those private facilities now in operation.

It appears most practical and desirable to deal with the special case of civil service occupations by reference to the second of these qualifications.

The conclusion was expressed that on the whole the same policy of an unlimited and comprehensive occupational and industrial operational field was relevant to all the Employment and Manpower Services: counseling, testing, research and information, stimulation of demand for labor, industrial services, benefits, vocational education and training (including apprenticeship and on-the-job training), and retraining for the unemployed.

Some modifications or elaborations would need to be applied to the present character of certain services in order to follow this guideline: unemployment insurance benefits are indirectly discriminatory against certain occupations in those industries excluded from coverage. Apprenticeship training and vocational education are in many cases oriented toward a single-track preparation for immediate use in a particular occupation rather than for the almost certain shifts in the skill content (or indeed the elimination of some) of those occupations in the future.

Occupational coverage of federally supported retraining courses for the unemployed and for upgrading the skills of the employed have, understandably enough, been geared to immediate and localized needs, as it is probable such institutional retraining must be. The opinion was expressed that the major breakthrough in retraining will be likely to come, not through government agencies alone, but by a partnership of these with the facilities and staffs available in the productive enterprises of the country.

The policy which appears essential with respect to the definition of the operational field of the Employment and Manpower Services relative to occupational coverage and "competition" with other agencies in the field is, accordingly, as follows:

> The operational field for the Employment and Manpower Services with respect to occupational coverage should be, in general, unlimited. The services should concern themselves with workers and employers in every occupation and industry contributing to the economic strength and growth of the economy, whether or not the occupation and industry is served in some places and to some degree by other fee-charging or free facilities. Where existing free private employment and manpower services are available in particular areas, the most efficient allocation of resources, as well as the most progress in fulfilling the central mission of the services, makes desirable the establishing of mutually beneficial relations between these and the public services. In every case the touchstone of decision is what allocation of existing or potential resources is most likely to advance the performance, through public and private facilities, of the central mission of the Employment and manpower services to promote the economic health, strength, and growth of the nation.

INITIATIVE AND
RESPONSE

Chapter Seven
In recent years a phrase has been introduced into the discussion about the numerous Employment and Manpower Services, a phrase which suggests a dynamic leadership role for them in the area of labor market activities. That phrase is "an active and positive labor market policy and program." It suggests a concept of the role of these services in which their administrators take the initiative in analyzing the need for their activities and promoting adaptations to that need rather than merely responding to the pressures and demands made on their energy, time, and activity by public executives, legislatures, and other government and private agencies. It suggests an awareness and recognition not only on the part of these administrators, but on the part of government officials responsible for bringing order, strength, and growth into the nation's economy, that the labor market is an area of economic activity as essential to the achievement of that result as are the money market, the product and commercial markets, and the area of fiscal and trade policy and practice. It suggests that the Employment and Manpower Services are positive instruments for initiating measures to promote the health and growth of the nation and not just the repairers of damage to the labor market participants caused by the developments initiated by the decision makers and actors in these other markets.

131

The question, then, is raised as to whether the Employment and Manpower Services shall be initiators or mere responders, whether their administrators shall themselves be the architects and leaders of the programs and operation that implement the mission we have discussed, or whether they shall be the hewers of wood and drawers of water for other architects and initiators of miscellaneous economic and social welfare policies and programs.

It should be said at once that in using the word "responders" we are thinking of response to demands, pressures, and requests which come from *other* individuals and agencies who have programs of their own to promote. Initiative is, in one sense, of course, a response, a response to need or to a problem or a challenge. The contrast drawn here is between a function to analyze, appraise the nature of, and *initiate* action to meet, those needs and problems, and a function merely to provide assistance to others in *response* to the pressures and demands brought by those others who have initiated their own programs.

Moreover, in raising this question, we are not inferring a negative evaluation of the administrators of the services from the point of view of their lack of initiative in carrying on their work. It is to be expected, in a system of agencies at the federal, state, and local levels which ultimately functions through 1900 local offices, that there would be wide variations among those in charge in the degrees of initiative they display. Our concern here, however, is not only with what these people do, but also with what is expected of them, what status they occupy in the minds of leaders in the legislative and executive branches of government, in the minds of employers and trade union officers, in the minds of educational, political, and social leaders concerned with employment and manpower problems. Are those who operate the services expected to initiate action for themselves and for these leaders, or are they looked upon as merely responders to assignments and pressures initiated for them by these leaders? It should be obvious, of course, that the nature of this expectancy as to what the administrators of the services *should* do is not unrelated to the observation of what they have done and are doing.

THE SITUATION IN THE UNITED STATES

Historically and at the present time, the status of the Employment and Manpower Services is best described in terms of the second of these functions. The accomplishment of the central mission of the services as described in the previous chapters is important to the

nation and to every one of its citizens. More specifically, it is import
to the executive branch of the government charged by both C
gressional and popular mandates to provide full employment, econoi
stability, and growth. It is important to Congressmen who feel a responsibility for meeting the employment and unemployment problems of their constituencies and the nation. It is important to the
several Cabinet members whose departments have been charged
with various economic, social, and political responsibilities, and who
are reaching out for more worlds to conquer. It is important to the
managers of enterprises on whom we count principally to keep the
wheels of production turning, without which production those mandates are impossible of fulfillment. It is important to the workers
whose human energy is still a major factor in that production and
whose compensation provides the means for completing the pro-
duction-consumption-production cycle. It is important to that five
to six per cent of the workers in our labor force who, on any day, have
no work to do. It is important to the trade unions who have a mandate from their members to protect and improve the security of their
job opportunities and income. It is important to the families of both
the employed and the unemployed and the communities in which they
live. It is important to the many relief and welfare agencies in those
communities. It is important to the citizens of every nation whose
economic welfare and growth are tied to our own.

Every one of these groups, save the last, has ideas about the way
in which the Employment and Manpower Services in the United
States can help them. They make their demands for such service. The
demands and pressures are not always consistent, and are frequently
in conflict, with each other.

The issue here raised is whether the direction and kinds of action
taken by the Employment and Manpower Services shall be merely
a response to whatever demands or pressures are brought on them
by all of these people who have an interest in what they do and
how well they do it; or whether the responsible managers and administrators of those services, from their intimate experience with
the facts of life in the area of their operations, shall be charged with
the responsibility to provide dynamic initiative and leadership, not
only in setting their own course and pursuing it, but in influencing
the actions of other groups and institutions in the community and
nation, which actions have a critical bearing on the possibility of
achieving full employment and economic strength and growth.

In putting the issue in this way we are not intending to suggest
that response to demands and pressures is never an appropriate guide

to what shall be done, but that such responses can be made in a way consistent with the kinds of programs and operations and emphases necessary to discharge a responsibility for initiative and leadership of an integrated attack upon the nation's employment and manpower problems.

THE ALTERNATIVES ILLUSTRATED

The issue can be focused more sharply by setting out alternative kinds of action which could conceivably be taken by managers and administrators of the services in the face of several situations. The first of each pair of alternatives named below would be action characteristic of a status as responder, the second, of a status as initiator and leader. As in our discussion of the central mission and the operational field of the Employment and Manpower Services, the alternatives are not mutually exclusive. The issue is not really one of either-or, but of both-and. Yet it is also a matter of where the emphasis shall lie when policy decisions must be made which involve conflicts between alternative possibilities.

DISTRIBUTION OF SUPPLY OF LABOR— CREATION OF DEMAND FOR LABOR

There is always present in a community and in the nation as a whole a supply of workers who are out of work and needing jobs or wanting to change jobs. The Employment and Manpower Services could consider it their task to analyze the qualifications of the people making up that portion of the supply who seek the help of the Employment Service and placing them as rationally as possible to the extent that the job openings listed with them make it possible. Or they could, in addition, take the initiative in the effort not only to increase the volume of job openings on their list, but to maintain the present demand for workers in their area and in the nation and to stimulate and participate in efforts to maintain and increase the size of that demand. Several efforts of the latter sort can be named: participation in and active support of efforts to bring new industry to the community if such efforts are underway; if not, then to initiate them; assistance to managements facing problems in utilization of manpower, problems making continued operations unprofitable; stimulus to vocational training which provides the kind of manpower resources which attracts industry to the community, and which gives confidence to future initiators of productive enterprise that the qualifications and skills essential to their manpower requirements will be available; attention to helping employers figure out how they can use particular hard-to-place groups.

This is, of course, at the local level. At the state and federal level the administrators of the Employment and Manpower Services, especially those concerned with training and with the Employment Service, can, if given the job, contribute much in the way of initiative in the development of employment-producing programs, indicating where they can be set in motion best to further the national economic health, and when they ought to be initiated in order to anticipate and prevent unemployment rather than to allow the situation to become so desperate that local political representatives demand attention to the problem.

Initiators will be concerned with efforts to maintain and create a demand for labor as well as to distribute an existing supply to the extent possible given the existing demand, that is, presently available registered job openings. The Employment and Manpower Services make their contribution to the nation's economic health and growth by facilitating the most productive possible employment engagements in the labor market. An employment engagement is a bringing together of a unit of labor supply and a unit of labor demand. The initiator in an active labor market program will be concerned with amplifying and improving the quality of both kinds of units.

Referrals—Recruitment

A closely related possibility is (a) to respond to existing employers' demands for workers by referring the best available applicant candidates they have in their files, or (b) actively to recruit the kind of workers needed through advertising and personal search, including extending their search beyond their immediate labor market. This choice to go beyond referring people in their files and to recruit people raises a lot of opposition from fee-charging agencies, especially when the Employment Service uses newspaper ads in the process. Also there is opposition from employers at times, because it is entirely possible that the advertised job might be attractive to one of their good workers. But it is difficult to conceive of an initiative-taking Employment Service operating effectively unless it does more than refer people in its files in response to local job orders.

OPERATIONS, GIVEN EXISTING DESIRE FOR SERVICES AND
THE AVAILABLE SUPPLY OF SERVICES—RESEARCH AND
STIMULATION AND INITIATION OF BETTER-ADAPTED SERVICES

Every day when local Employment Offices open for business, there
is a certain volume of applications and usually a somewhat more
limited number of job orders. But this is not the only imbalance
they face. There are a certain number of people desiring testing and
counseling, and a certain number of available staff to perform those
services; a certain number of people who could do work if they
could be trained for it, and an existing number of facilities and institutions equipped to provide that training; a certain number of young
people getting, or wanting to get, vocational education, and an existing volume of institutions to provide it, approximating in varying
degrees to the quality of education required by productive enterprise; a certain number of people who have expressed their willingness to move to places where there is a shortage of workers, and an
existing number of places outside the locality which are seeking
workers and of resources available for movement of people to those
places.

It is conceivable that the managers of the Employment and Manpower Services could take a look at these immediate imbalances, and
work out the best balance they could before they close up shop, in
other words, respond to whatever operating conditions they were
immediately faced with. That is a minimum effort which they will
have to make in any case. But they could also be engaged in the
kind of current and prognostic study of the facts and causes of those
conditions of imbalance that would enable them to take the initiative,
or to stimulate others to take the initiative, on long-range efforts to
correct that imbalance, to prevent it before it happens, or to deal with
it more effectively when it does. Such effort to improve, for example,
institutions for vocational education, for training, for inter-labor-
market movement of workers, is not one limited to individual localities and states. It requires action at the interstate or federal level also.

PROVIDER OF CALL-IN HELP—CENTER OF ORGANIZED
EMPLOYMENT AND MANPOWER EFFORTS

There are, as we have indicated, a number of groups and agencies,
local, state, and national, to whom the activities of the Employment
and Manpower Services are relevant and useful. Particularly useful

are the activities related to placement, counseling, testing, research, and training. Societies established for increasing the opportunities of and for mitigating the problems of youth need those services. Agencies for relieving and rehabilitating veterans, the aged, the handicapped, the minority groups, and new immigrants need the placement, counseling, and testing efforts of the Employment Service. Community industrial development agencies need not only the foregoing efforts, but the kinds of labor market and labor force data essential to those efforts, which are supplied by the daily operations of the Employment Service and unemployment insurance or by prognostic surveys made better to plan their activities. Retraining organizations and agencies, both public and private, also need that information in order to determine what it is sensible to train for. Moreover, they need the skill and knowledge of the placement interviewers, counselors, and testers to select the most likely candidates for training. They need someone on the spot whose full-time occupation is concerned with the employment prospects and requirements locally and beyond the community to keep the training process realistic in terms of those prospects and requirements, and to follow through and co-ordinate the many details of the training process. They need the follow-up placement activities to assure that the trained person has the chance to put his newly acquired skills to work. Vocational education and apprenticeship programs need, in order to keep their curricula and processes up to date, the counsel of the experience of Employment and Manpower Services operators, local, state, and national, who are in close touch with current and future trends in technological, and hence occupational, structure developments. Schools and colleges can improve the quality of their counseling and placement activities by making use of the knowledge, skill, and facilities of the Employment Service. Employers, agricultural, industrial, and professional, unless they want to fly blind or undertake expensive surveys of their own, must depend for their forward planning of operations and investments on the labor market and labor force data available in no other place as adequately, comprehensively, and continuously as in the files and reports of the Employment Service. Government statistical and planning agencies also would find it wasteful and costly to duplicate the fact-finding efforts of the services. Politicians, from mayors and aldermen and governors and legislators to the President of the United States and Congressmen, know that, without the effective co-operation from the Employment and Manpower Services, their desire to whip the problem of unemployment and to gain the political advantage following a successful attack on that problem is wishful thinking. Experience

has taught the heads of government that the mobilization of productive strength in times of national emergency and war is dependent
on the effective knowledge, experience, and efforts of the Employment Service to marshal and allocate the manpower resources for that
effort. Such needs result not only in demands upon, but opportunities
for, the expansion and increasing usefulness of the Employment and
Manpower Services.

The managers of those services can wait until they are called on
for information, advice, and service, wait for requests arising from
these unco-ordinated needs and demands; or they can, from their
vantage point at the very heart of the manpower and employment
problem, locally and nationally, take the initiative and seek to become the central stimulating and organizing instrument for the employment and manpower efforts of the community, state, and nation.
Each local employment office and its staff can conceivably be the
employment and manpower development and allocation center and
the labor market operations and research center for that local area
and the co-ordinator of its relations with other labor markets. And
there should be in the Department of Labor in Washington a focusing, integrating, and co-ordinating Employment and Manpower Administration to perform that function nationally.

The Employment and Manpower Services in the United States
have received such requests for help and have responded to them. It
is appropriate and necessary that they do respond. The administrators
have not had to wait long. But because not all of these demands are
consistent with the maintenance of effective effort, particularly in
connection with placement activities, this is one of the critical problems facing the Employment Service. It is desirable to reduce this
conflict among demands. It is one of the reasons it is so important to
get more clearly established in the minds of the public and the leaders
of the institutions concerned with the development of manpower
resources, in the minds of worker and employer users of the services,
in the minds of economic planners and developers, and in the minds
of politicians the central appropriate mission operational field, and
the status of the Employment and Manpower Services. The programs
and activities of the services as they exist today have "just growed"
like Topsy in response to every demand from these sources which
could be made effective. Especially effective have been those that
came from legislative mandate and executive order and political and
interest group pressure. Such demands have come, at different times,
for "co-operation" from the Employment and Manpower Services to

implement programs for veterans, depressed areas, hard-core unemployed, youth, older workers, handicapped, migrant workers, immigrants, minority groups, workers threatened with automation-generated
unemployment or that resulting from results of tariff reductions, to
carry out community development efforts, to provide statistical studies
and reports, to mobilize and allocate civilian manpower in time of
war, to provide Selective Service with a table of priorities, virtually
to manage retraining, and to make unemployment insurance malin-
gerer-proof, etc.

THE PARTICULAR CASE OF UNEMPLOYMENT INSURANCE AND EMPLOYMENT SERVICE

Particularly troublesome to the development of an effective and
efficient Employment Service, in the minds of many, has been the
allocation to that service of the responsibility for using its placement
procedures for providing a work test for the unemployed receiving
unemployment insurance, and for making effective the campaigns for
finding jobs for the hard-to-place, particularly those receiving unemployment insurance. The image thus created of an "unemployment"
office, they claim, has retarded the use of the service by workers and
employers, limiting the Employment Service reservoirs of applications
and job orders so that the development of an Employment Service
paralleling the needs of the total labor market was difficult if not
impossible.

Not all agree with this appraisal, and it is currently a hot issue
in the relations between state and federal officials, and between the
Bureau of Employment Security and certain outside pressure groups.
There are some who contend that being a "work tester" for unemployment insurance places a heavy tail on the kite of an effective Employment Service. Debates on appropriation bills in Congress indicate that
some Congressmen think the Employment Service is justified chiefly
as a work test agency. Some service relationship of Employment Service
to unemployment insurance in this respect is probably going to remain. And in our judgment it should remain. Unemployment insurance is only one of the types of financial benefits which will ultimately
be recognized as essential to a full manpower and employment program, particularly when it comes to the establishment of types of
allowances which create the conditions of free choice and ability to
take training or move to places where jobs are available. These

financial benefits, as well as unemployment insurance, are essential aids to the development and operation of other Employment and Manpower Services. Any move to separate unemployment insurance from the other services would move away from the integration we are seeking. In addition, it would make necessary the establishment of another benefit-dispensing and -controlling administration for administering, for example, training and movement allowances, a job perfectly possible of performance through the present unemployment insurance machinery. But one of the big problems of making the Employment Service a spearhead of a dynamic employment and manpower policy and program is how to keep this service function in response to the need to eliminate malingerers as benefit receivers from getting in the way of the accomplishment of its mission as a manpower developing and placement agency.

POSITIVE RESULTS OF DEMANDS FOR SERVICE

The initiators of these many and varied economic, social, and political efforts had no over-all focus of motivation and purpose except, "Here's a big problem, let's do something about it." In every case, of course, there was the implicit assumption that there was not only a political responsibility for, but a political advantage in, doing something about it. Since employment was a central factor in all of these programs, the expectancy very appropriately arose that the Employment and Manpower Services should do something about that aspect of the problem.

The Employment and Manpower Services, however, have responded and grown in the face of those calls for servicing these unco-ordinated projects and programs, although at times their administrators must have felt punch drunk from the impact of the multipurpose demands and the shifting organizational arrangements and lines of accountability which, on several occasions, have accompanied the allocation or reallocation of functions.

In making that response, a great amount of experience has been accumulated by the administrators of those services about the nature of the labor market and the requirements for organizing and facilitating its processes. Perhaps the time has come for those who man the employment and manpower agencies, local, state, and national, to be charged with responsibility for bringing that experience to a focus as to what those requirements are, and for taking the initiative and leadership in stimulating and setting in motion the kinds of community, state, and national activities designed, not merely to find jobs for people, but to find those which use their greatest potential, to develop that potential when present skills do not fit present and future job requirements, and to make jobs and stabilize those now available.

Make no mistake about it, there are places where the state and local managers and other officials of the Employment Service have gone beyond the adaptation-to-others'-request process to seize the leadership in making their offices the center of initiative for employment and manpower operations in their regions. Many insist that they would like to do much more, and would, if staff resources were adequate. The same thing is true of the leadership of the Employment Service at the national level. In the face of the lack of any integrated and co-ordinated over-all national employment and manpower policy and program, the Employment Service national leadership, supported by many forward-looking state and local administrators, has labored since World War II to amplify and develop that program so that there was not a complete vacuum in this matter in the United States. The amplification was on the whole justified as an extension of and necessary support for the basic job of the Employment Service to bring men and jobs together, but to do so in a way which would result in the maximum utilization of manpower resources at their highest skill potential. The development of the rationale and philosophy for that amplification and the attempt to gain acceptance for it in the states has been a stimulating contribution to the concept of an integrated set of Employment and Manpower Services.. It has had its effect at the operational level although, as is to be expected, to varying degrees in the several states and local areas.

That leadership, however, has had to be assumed. It has never been clearly and specifically allocated to the managers and administrators of the services. It has had to be exercised against a concept in the minds of public officials and legislators that the Service is simply a helper agency, a servant available to shoulder any task in the employment and manpower area they felt it desirable to have set in motion. It has had to make progress within the habit patterns of traditional federal-state relations, a budgeting formula which took inadequate account of nonroutine and not easily measurable expenditure of staff time, a lack, on the whole, of recognition by legislators and federal and state officials of the significance of the new approach, and a persistence of the image of the Employment Service in the mind of potential users as an adjunct of unemployment insurance.

We waste a rich resource of experience and know-how for improving the effective operation of the labor market as a key factor in promoting full employment and economic growth if those who man the Employment and Manpower Services are assigned the status merely of responders to the demands for services coming from those who, in order to carry out the programs they have initiated, need their help.

INITIATIVE IN THE EMPLOYMENT AND MANPOWER FIELD

There is nothing wrong about the Employment and Manpower Services' occupying the status of responders to the needs of other groups and agencies and trying to make that response as helpful as possible; nothing wrong, *except* that it does not exhaust their potential as contributors to the development and most effective use of our manpower and hence to full employment and economic growth and to the genuinely free choice of workers and employers with respect to the movement of labor.

Educators do not exhaust their potential for doing the job they are capable of by merely responding to requests for the kind of teaching and research their students, the public, or its political representatives demand. Religious leaders do not exhaust their potential for doing the job they are capable of merely by providing the kinds of sermons and spiritual service their congregations want. Managers of industry and business do not exhaust their potential for doing the job they are capable of merely by devoting themselves to what the consumer wants, or thinks he wants, and doing their best to furnish that. Fiscal and monetary officials do not exhaust their potential for doing the job they are capable of merely by responding to the demands of citizens as payers of taxes or users of money. Nor do even political "representatives" exhaust their potential for doing the job they are capable of merely by responding to the pressures brought on them by their constituents.

Response to the demands of the market place is an example of smart, accommodating, and often reward- or profit-promising operations, but scarcely a sufficient characteristic of responsible fulfillment of mission in that market place, whatever its nature. There is an opportunity and a responsibility that goes with experience and knowledge in a particular area of activity, a responsibility for initiative and leadership, if for no other reason than that the demands of the consumer normally come from experience to date, while their long-range interest is tied up with anticipation of an adaptation to the future. And there is a duty and opportunity resting with legislators and executives, who delegate responsibility for effectuating public policy and performance in these areas, to allocate initiative, and the authority to take it, where experience and knowledge are to be found.

Those who operate and direct the Employment and Manpower Services have more unbiased experience with and objective knowledge of the nature, trends, and future of the local, regional, and national labor markets and labor force than any group of people in the country. Where that experience and knowledge is inadequate and incomplete, they are in a better position than anyone else, from the very nature of and contacts in their full-time jobs, to obtain what is needed. There is not only an opportunity, but a responsibility, to focus that experience and knowledge on the stimulating of, and leadership in, local and national efforts to make the conditions and operations of that labor market contribute to the economic health and growth of the community and nation.

There are several considerations which support this conclusion as to the responsibility for and allocation of leadership in labor market affairs, in addition to those already named. Leadership requires necessarily an anticipation of needs; and anticipation, if beneficial, must be based on adequate knowledge of probabilities. Moreover, that knowledge can not be based on information which is spotty and discontinuous. No individual or private enterprise is able to survey these probabilities with sufficient detail, coverage, and continuity to indicate the probable future developments in the labor force, the labor market, and the changes in technology, occupational structure, etc. affecting the general problems of employment and the adequacy of our human resources. Incidentally, the present skill surveys and other prognostic studies of the Employment Service and the series published by governmental statistical agencies are not completely adequate in these respects, either. But they can be made so. One reason they are not more adequate is that this type of activity has been considered a supplementary, rather than an absolutely essential, performance of the Employment and Manpower Services in the role of initiator and leadership we are here discussing.

Second, public leadership action in any but a totalitarian society is necessarily marginal to the sum of private decisions and actions which will determine the extent of our economic health and growth.

The decisions and actions by hundreds of thousands of managers of industrial and business enterprises, by millions of investors and their counselors, by tens of thousands of vocational educators, trainers, and counselors, and by millions of individual workers and their unions will be the determiners of that result. But if public leadership is to be effectively given at the margins, it is most effectively given before, rather than solely after, the fact. It is most effectively expressed as initiative rather than as response.

Third, all of these millions of decisions and actions are taken for a great variety of purposes, in many of which the interests of developing and maintaining an effective labor force and a genuinely free labor market have very little, if any, influence. There is need to focus the attention of private and public decision makers and the general public on the consequences of their decisions and actions for the quality of the labor force and the effectiveness of the free labor market, and to suggest the kinds of private and public action which will make those consequences economically advantageous. That function can be only incidentally performed by Employment and Manpower Services regarded as operating primarily as responders to calls for service from other public and private agencies, associations, and individuals.

REQUIREMENTS FOR INITIATIVE AND LEADERSHIP OF THE EMPLOYMENT AND MANPOWER SERVICES

If the Employment and Manpower Services are to take the kind of initiative and leadership suggested here, there are a number of requirements for supporting such a role and assigning to them the status appropriate to it. Those requirements come to a focus first of all in the decisions and actions of the President, of Congress, of the Secretary of Labor and his Assistant Secretaries in the employment and manpower areas, and of the corresponding state legislative and administrative officials. Their concept of the appropriate mission, operational field, and status of these services, their expectancies, their standards of evaluation, their allocations of resources, and their decisions on programs will define the possibilities within which the services may or may not exert initiative and leadership.

Another requirement for effective initiative and leadership is a focusing of the efforts at the national level (as well as in states and individual localities) of the numerous bureaus, departments, and agencies concerned with manpower and employment problems. It is useless to expect initiative for an integrated national effort without a focusing of administration for developing objectives, policy, plans, and evaluation of performance with respect to that effort. It should be clear that such initiative at the local and the state levels will result only by accident, or by virtue of the foresight and energy of a dynamic individual there, if the organizational guidance and direction or influence from the center comes from a diffuse and multiple set of agencies. We shall further consider this problem in the next chapter.

In discussing this leadership role we have laid particular stress on the key contribution of research, analysis, and forecasting activities, on stimulus of and participation in shaping the course of community development, of encouraging and contributing to the better organization of the employment process in the communities, and of stimulating the adaptation to current and future employment needs by the vocational educational institutions. These activities are, of course, carried on at the present time by the Employment and Manpower Services as time, money, and staff permit. The traditional concept of the services as mere responders to currently expressed needs and demands, however, inhibits the giving of the emphasis and providing of the support to them needed to make the local offices and the several state and federal agencies the initiative-taking manpower and employment centers in the communities, state, and nation.

Moreover, the criteria for evaluation of performance of the activities now carried on within the Employment Service is not geared to the total job and the taking of initiative with respect to it. The most frequently used basis for evaluation is the "penetration rate," a very imperfect measuring rod for appraising even the placement aspects of the services and one with even less relevance to the appraisal of the kinds of activities we have just been discussing. The formula for allocation of funds also stems from this standard of evaluation and, whatever its value as a rule-of-thumb builder of a budget for *next* year's operations geared to the amount of staff time actually used in particular aspects of *last* year's operations, it gives only incidental recognition to anything but routine tasks.

The kind of administrative personnel required for the performance of leadership tasks is difficult and frequently impossible to obtain in the salary ranges provided. Nor are such people always challenged by a service whose main objective appears to many of them to be one of social service and relief. The type of person who needs to be attracted by the services as local manager is one who compares in prestige and influence in the community with, say, the superintendent of schools. Where the employment office manager has succeeded in making his office the community employment and manpower center, he is normally found to be a person of such a stature.

The identification with work testing for unemployment insurance does not encourage confidence in or reliance on employment office managers by workers, employers, trade unions, or public officials for leadership in these employment-oriented services.

Moreover, there is no point in charging the administrators of the services with a leadership and an initiator role if, in practice, they have little participation in shaping the nature of their own jobs. The allocation of new functions or modification of the old would have to be done in full recognition of the status appropriate to initiators and leaders of the kinds of service essential to achieving the mission and role with which they are charged. There is no challenge to exercise leadership on the part of those whose less than infinite energies must be continuously expended in adjusting themselves and their operations to plans and programs introduced by others, and in the introduction of which they have had little if any voice.

SUMMARY

The issue we raise in this chapter is whether the Employment and Manpower Services will be the architects, the initiators, and leaders of the program to carry out their mission, or will be merely the responders to and the hewers of wood and drawers of water for other architects and initiators.

There are so many people, groups, and agencies to which the activities of the services are potentially useful that the demands have been continuous and insistent. Yet the services have constantly been faced with the challenge to go beyond the status of responders. Shall they place applicants as rationally as possible in the light of orders filed, or shall they work to increase those orders and the volume of employment from which more will come? Shall they try merely to face and do what they can about immediately apparent imbalances between the supply and demand for workers, imbalances between the need and the scope and type of manpower agencies to meet that need; or shall they gather, analyze, and put to promotional use the information about the present and future labor market and labor force which points the way to the correction and prevention of those imbalances? Shall they wait to set up the services and operations until they are demanded by a whole set of associations, agencies, and groups interested in some particular segment of the labor force, or until community development agencies, school boards, governors' commissions, or other government agencies come to them for help, or until political decisions tell them what ought to be done by the services to aid a particular program; or shall they be the central stimulating and organizing instrument for such efforts?

The general situation today in the United States is that the Employment and Manpower Services have "just growed" like Topsy in response to every demand from these sources which could be made effective. And administrators have sometimes felt punch drunk from the impact of these demands, some of which were in conflict. Yet, in spite of everything, they have gained an experience and a knowledge of the labor market and labor force superior to that which exists in any other place. The question is whether this experience and knowledge should not now be focused on initiative and leadership in perfecting the resources in, and the operations of, the national and local labor markets. That role is, of course, being carried on by particular managers and administrators, at the local, state, and federal levels, but they have had to seize the initiative. It was not clearly assigned to them by the legislative bodies and executive offices who created tasks for them to perform, nor by the "customers" for whose benefit the tasks were undertaken.

The potential of the operators of the Employment and Manpower Services for maximum contribution to the nation's economic health and growth is not exhausted by their ability to meet demands from other programs to which their services can be specifically and individually helpful. Demands from people in the market grow normally out of past experience, but initiative in satisfying their long-range interests comes from adequate anticipatory knowledge (and its promotional use) of a probable future, a knowledge of which the administrators of the Employment and Manpower Services have the best supply. Public services operate at the margin of the totality of millions of private decisions and actions which determine the health and growth of the economy, and marginal contributions have a greater impact if they are initiatory rather than merely responsive. Merely responsive action is bound to be lacking in focus and direction, because the purposes and motivations stimulating the demands to which the response is made have no uniform nature.

If the Employment and Manpower Services are to perform the initiator and leader role here suggested, there are a number of requirements that have to be met; the most important of these is the recognition by Congress and the Secretary of Labor, and by their state and local counterparts, that there is a status for the services involving the participation of their administrators in decisions as to what they shall be expected to do and how. There is need for an integrated administration rather than a multiplicity of administrations. The standards for evaluation of their services and the formula for the allocation of funds must be consistent with the distribution of time and effort by staff to performing the tasks of initiative and leadership, as well as to performing tasks of a routine operational nature. And the concept of mission and the salary scale must be such as to challenge acceptance of staff jobs in the Employment and Manpower Services by those who are competent to perform as initiators and leaders.

INTEGRATION AND FOCUS

Chapter Eight We turn now to the question of whether the role of initiative and leadership can be operationally effective unless the services are authoritatively integrated, and unless the authority for the direction and co-ordination of all of them is lodged in one of them or in some organ superordinate to all of them.

Our answer is that such allocation of status and authority is essential. When, however, we survey the vast dispersion· in the United States of these tasks that fall logically and necessarily under the employment and manpower umbrella, the first inclination is to throw up our hands in despair at ever achieving any integrated direction and co-ordination. And the allocations of authority are so numerous that the obstacles to their integration organizationally may be well-nigh insuperable. The establishment and implementation of an active, positive, and integrated labor market and manpower policy face many obstacles, particularly when the question is raised as to the organizational assignment of responsibility for achieving integration.

Nevertheless, an issue of such critical importance cannot be ignored. Tables 8-1 and 8-2 represent the present situation of dispersed responsibility and authority for employment and manpower tasks in the United States. These tables disclose 31 distinguishable employment and manpower tasks in which, in the United States and Sweden and in most other European nations, federal agencies have some degree of participation.

149

Table 8-1

ALLOCATION OF EMPLOYMENT AND MANPOWER FUNCTIONS
in the UNITED STATES*

Section I. PLACEMENT AND PLACEMENT-RELATED FUNCTIONS

1. *Local placement: Application and order-taking, analysis, matching, referral*

Group 1: a. B.E.S. (Lab.)

Group 2: b. Civil Service Commission (federal)

Group 3: c. State Employment Service systems

             d. State Civil Service Commissions

Group 4: e. Labor unions and trade associations

             f. Schools and colleges

             g. Professional societies

             h. Relief societies and agencies

             i. Private

2. *Vocational and Employment Counseling*

Group 1: a. B.E.S. (Lab.)

Group 3: b. State Employment Service systems

             c. Government relief agencies

---

* In reading Table 8-1, note the following features:

1. Underlining indicates type of authority possessed by the agency.
   Straight underlining = directive authority and accountability for planning and doing the job.
   Broken underlining = indirect authority by control of funds, provision of tools, assistance, evaluation, etc.
   Not underlined = advisory and stimulating influence, service on request, etc.
   More than one type of underlining = different kinds of authority characterize different aspects of the task.

2. Abbreviations:
   Lab. = Dept. of Labor.
   B.E.S. = Bureau of Employment Security.
   O.M.A.T. = Office of Manpower, Automation, and Training.
   B.A.T. = Bureau of Apprenticeship and Training.
   B.L.S. = Bureau of Labor Statistics.
   H.E.W. = Dept. of Health, Education, and Welfare.
   O.A.S.D.I. = Bureau of Old Age, Survivor's, Disability, Insurance.
   Comm. = Dept. of Commerce.
   A.R.A. = Area Redevelopment Administration.
   Int. = Dept. of Interior.
   Agri. = Dept. of Agriculture.
   O.R.A.D. = Office of Rural Areas Development.
   V.A. = Veterans Administration.
   H.H.F.A. = Housing and Home Finance Agency.
   E.O.P. = Executive Office of the President.

3. Grouping from top to bottom:
   Group 1: B.E.S. Bureau of Employment Security, including Employment Service and unemployment insurance.
   Group 2: Other federal agencies. Those in the Department of Labor listed first.
   Group 3: State and local governmental agencies.
   Group 4: Nongovernmental organizations and groups.

Group 4: d. Professional associations

e. Schools and colleges

f. Private relief and welfare societies

g. Private

3. *Occupational Testing*

Group 1: a. B.E.S. (Lab.)

Group 3: b. State Employment Service systems

Group 4: c. Schools and colleges

d. Private

4. *Development of Placement and Placement-Related Tools* (Dictionary of Occupational Titles, *tests, counseling manuals, procedural instructions and standards, forms, research and survey guides, etc.*)

Group 1: a. B.E.S. and B.E.S. (Lab.)

Group 3: b. State Employment Service systems

Group 4: c. Private

5. *Interarea Placement and Recruitment (Clearance)*

Group 1: a. B.E.S. (Lab.)

Group 3: b. State Employment Service systems

Group 4: c. Professional associations

d. Private

6. *Placement and Hiring of Foreign Labor*

Group 1: a. B.E.S. and B.E.S.

Group 3: b. State Employment Service systems

Group 4: c. Private

7. *Placement and Counseling for Disadvantaged (handicapped, racial groups, aged, youth, etc.)*

Group 1: a. B.E.S. and B.E.S. (Lab.)

Group 2: b. Bureau of Indian Affairs (Int.)

c. Special Asst. on Aging (H.E.W.)

d. Presidential Committee on Employment of Handicapped

e. Presidential Committee on Juvenile Delinquency and Youth Crime

f. President's Council on Aging

g. Presidential Committee on Youth Employment

Group 3: h. State Employment Service systems

i. State and local governmental agencies

Group 4: j. Relief and special group associations

8. *Placement and Other Special Services to Veterans*

Group 1: a. B.E.S. (Lab.)

Group 2:   b. Department of Veterans Benefits (V.A.)

Group 3:   c. State Employment Service systems

Group 4:   d. Veterans associations

9. *Placement for Agricultural Workers, Especially Migrants*

Group 1:   a. B.E.S. and B.E.S. (Lab.)

Group 2:   b. Presidential Committee on Migratory Labor

Group 3:   c. State Employment Service systems

Group 4:   d. Private

Section II.   RESEARCH, FORECASTING, AND INFORMATION ACTIVITIES

10. *Preparation, Analysis, and Distribution of Labor Market and Labor Force Statistics, Current and Predictive*

Group 1:   a. B.E.S. and B.E.S. and B.E.S. (Lab.)

Group 2:   b. O.M.A.T. (Lab.)

           c. B.L.S. (Lab.)

           d. Women's Bureau (Lab.)

           e. Presidential Committee on Status of Women

           f. Census Bureau (Comm.)

Group 3:   g. State Employment Service systems

Group 4:   h. Private

11. *Preparation, Analysis, and Distribution of Information and Forecasts re Short- and Long-Run Quantitative and Qualitative Demand for Labor and Supply of Labor*

Group 1:   a. B.E.S. and B.E.S. (Lab.)

Group 2:   b. B.L.S. (Lab.)

           c. O.M.A.T. and O.M.A.T. (Lab.)

Group 3:   d. State Employment Service systems

Group 4:   e. Private

12. *Preparation, Analysis, and Distribution of Studies of Economic Problems and Trends (including, e.g., impact of automation) Influencing Supply of and Demand for Labor*

Group 1:   a. B.E.S. (Lab.)

Group 2:   b. B.L.S. (Lab.)

           c. O.M.A.T. and O.M.A.T. (Lab.)

           d. Council of Economic Advisors (E.O.P.)

Group 3:   e. State Employment Service systems

Group 4:   f. Academic institutions

           g. Private

13. *Education of Public on Labor Market Matters*

Group 1:   a. B.E.S. and B.E.S. and B.E.S. (Lab.)

Group 2: b. O.M.A.T. (Lab.)

c. B.L.S. (Lab.)

Group 3: d. State Employment Service systems

Group 4: e. Academic institutions

f. Private

Section III. EMPLOYER SERVICES

14. *Industrial Services (other than order filling) to Employers*

Group 1: a. B.E.S. (Lab.)

Group 2: b. B.A.T. (Lab.)

Group 3: c. State Employment Service systems

Group 4: d. Trade associations

e. Private

f. Trade unions

Section IV. CREATION OF DEMAND FOR LABOR

15. *Industrial Development of Communities*

Group 1: a. B.E.S. (Lab.)

Group 2: b. A.R.A. (Comm.)

c. Bureau of Public Roads (Comm.)

d. Defense Engineering and Construction

e. Urban Renewal Administration (H.H.F.A.)

f. Public Housing Administration (H.H.F.A.)

g. O.R.A.D. (Agri.)

Group 3: h. State Employment Service systems

i. State and local commissions

Group 4: j. Private

16. *Location of Investment in Productive Enterprise*

Group 1: a. B.E.S. (Lab.)

Group 2: b. A.R.A. (Comm.)

c. O.R.A.D. (Agri.)

Group 3: d. State Employment Service systems

e. Regional, state, and community associations

Group 4: f. Private

17. *Direction of Government Purchasing and Building*

Group 1: a. B.E.S. (Lab.)

Group 2: b. Various federal departments

c. Particularly Department of Defense and armed forces branches

d. General Services Administration

e. T.V.A. and other such authorities

Group 3: f. Various state and local departments and agencies

Section V. VOCATIONAL EDUCATION, TRAINING, AND RETRAINING

  18. *Vocational Education*

  Group 1:   a. B.E.S. (Lab.)

  Group 2:   b. B.A.T. (Lab.)

              c. Office of Education (H.E.W.)

  Group 3:   d. State Employment Service systems

              e. State vocational education authorities

              f. Local school boards and special authorities

  Group 4:   g. Private

  19. *Retraining for the Unemployed*

  Group 1:   a. B.E.S. (Lab.)

  Group 2:   b. O.M.A.T. and O.M.A.T. (Lab.)

              c. Office of Education (H.E.W.)

  Group 3:   d. State Employment Service systems

              e. State and local agencies

  20. *Training and Retraining for the Employed*

  Group 1:   a. B.E.S. (Lab.)

  Group 2:   b. O.M.A.T. and O.M.A.T. (Lab.)

              c. B.A.T. (Lab.)

              d. Office of Education (H.E.W.)

  Group 3:   e. State Employment Service systems

              f. State agencies

              g. Local school boards

  Group 4:   h. Other educational institutions

              i. Private

Section VI. REHABILITATION

  21. *Rehabilitation for the Handicapped (including operation of "sheltered" enter-*
  prise and archive work for professionals)

  Group 1:   a. B.E.S. (Lab.)

  Group 2:   b. Veterans Administration

              c. Bureau of O.A.S.D.I. (H.E.W.)

              d. Office of Vocational Rehabilitation (H.E.W.)

  Group 3:   e. State Employment Service systems

              f. Municipal and state health and welfare agencies

  Group 4:   g. Other health and welfare societies

              h. Private

Section VII. BENEFITS

  22. *Unemployment Insurance*

  Group 1:   a. B.E.S. (Lab.)

  Group 3:   b. State Employment Service systems

Group 4:   c. Trade unions
           d. Private companies

23. *Financial Aid to Movement (travel, family allowance, temporary starting allowance, etc.)*
Group 1:   a. B.E.S. (Lab.)
Group 2:   b. O.M.A.T. (Lab.)
Group 3:   c. State Employment Service systems

24. *Financial Assistance to Industrial Trainees, Scholarships, etc.*
Group 1:   a. B.E.S. (Lab.)
Group 2:   b. O.M.A.T. (Lab.)
           c. Office of Education (H.E.W.)
Group 3:   d. State Employment Service systems

25. *Financial Assistance to Professional and Other Students*
Group 1:   a. None
Group 2:   b. Office of Education (H.E.W.)
Group 4:   c. Schools and colleges
           d. Private

26. *Housing Related to Movement*
Group 1:   a. None
Group 4:   b. Private

Section VIII. PREVENTIVE MEASURES

27. *Public and Private Works Planning and Setting in Motion before Occurrence of Severe Unemployment*
           a. None

28. *Release and Timing of Private Investment Reserves*
           a. None

Section IX. CONTRIBUTIONS TO OTHER AGENCIES

29. *Advice to and Co-operation with Other Economic Agencies of Government*
Group 1:   a. B.E.S. (Lab.)
Group 2:   b. B.L.S. (Lab.)
           c. O.M.A.T. (Lab.)
           d. Women's Bureau (Lab.)
           e. Office of Education (H.E.W.)
           f. Office of Vocational Rehabilitation (H.E.W.)
           g. A.R.A. (Comm.)
           h. O.R.A.D. (Agri.)
Group 3:   i. State Employment Service systems

Section X. WAR MOBILIZATION OF CIVILIANS

30. *Preparation of Plans for Manpower Allocation and Responsibilities for Implementation in Time of Military Crisis*

Group 1: a. B.E.S. and B.E.S. (Lab.)

Group 2: b. Office of Emergency Planning (E.O.P.)

Group 3: c. State Employment Service systems

d. State and local agencies

Section XI. ORGANIZATIONAL FOCUS

31. *Central Direction, Co-ordination, and Control of All Services*

a. None

(Responsibilities spread among large number of government departments and agencies. Department of Labor has several, but they are not well co-ordinated.)

The Employment and Manpower Services, then, are concerned with:

1. Placement and placement-related functions.
2. Research, forecasting, and information functions.
3. Employer services.
4. Creation of demand for labor.
5. Vocational education and training.
6. Rehabilitation.
7. Financial benefits.
8. Preventive measures versus unemployment.
9. Contributions to other agencies.
10. War mobilization of civilians.
11. Central co-ordinative functions for all tasks.

In the United States, so far as the employment and manpower agencies are concerned, activity is carried on in only nine of these areas, the exceptions being areas 8 and 11.

The federal agencies have three kinds of mandate and authority to carry out these tasks:

1. Directive authority and accountability for determining policy and doing the job.
2. Indirect authority through such devices as control of funds, provision of tools, technical assistance, evaluation, etc.
3. Stimulating and advisory responsibilities only.

Directive authority is lodged in four departments, in three independent agencies, in the Executive Office of the President, and in 13 bureaus and offices within these departments and agencies. *Indirect authority* is lodged in five departments, one independent agency, and

Table 8-2

ALLOCATION OF FEDERAL EMPLOYMENT AND MANPOWER FUNCTIONS*
BY BUREAU AND DEPARTMENT

Bureau or Office	Directive Authority	Indirect Authority	Advisory and Stimulating
B.E.S.	8	19	9
B.L.S.	4	0	2
O.M.A.T.	5	3	5
B.A.T.	0	0	3
Wom. Bur.	0	0	2
Off. Ed.	1	3	2
Voc. Reh.	0	1	1
O.A.S.D.I.	0	1	0
A.R.A.	0	1	2
Bur. Pub. Rds.	0	1	0
Census Bur.	1	0	0
O.R.A.D.	0	1	2
Bur. Indian Affairs	0	1	0
Vet. Bur.	2	0	0
Urb. Renewal	0	1	0
Pub. Hsing. Adm.	0	1	0
Several Defense	2	0	0
Council of Ec. Adv.	1	0	0
Office Emergency Plan.	1	0	0
Civil Serv. Comm.	1	0	0
Gen. Serv. Adm.	1	0	0
Presidential Comm.	0	0	7

Department	Directive Authority	Indirect Authority	Advisory and Stimulating
Labor	8	19	14
H.E.W.	1	4	3
Commerce	1	1	2
Agriculture	0	1	2
Interior	0	1	0
Vet. Adm.	2	0	0
H.H.F.A.	0	1	0
Defense	2	0	0
E.O.P.	2	0	0
Civil Serv. Comm.	1	0	0
Gen. Serv. Adm.	1	0	0
Presidential Comm.	0	0	7

* Functions are defined by reference to the 31 tasks listed in Table 8-1. Where two or more bureaus or offices in the same department have assignments which are related to a particular task, only one assignment is indicated for the department.

in 11 bureaus and offices within them. Responsibility for carrying through action under this indirect authority is lodged in 50 state employment security systems, and in multiple and varying agencies and commissions in the 50 states and thousands of local communities. *Stimulating* and *advisory responsibilities* are lodged within four departments, in nine bureaus and offices within these departments, and in seven Presidential committees or commissions. The objects of stimulation and advice are not only federal, state, and local governmental departments, commissions and other agencies, but various labor organizations, trade associations, private enterprises, voluntary societies and associations, etc.

The Department of Labor has by far the greatest load of responsibility and authority. Indeed, the degree of concentration of tasks in this department considerably modifies the first impression of unsystematic dispersion. The situation is certainly not chaotic, and conceivably may suggest the path to the achievement of a greater integration of the labor market and manpower activities of the federal government. Bureaus or offices within the Department of Labor have either direct or indirect authority in carrying out 20 of the 29 employment and manpower functions in which federal authorities participate in this country. To be sure, this authority is shared with other federal departments in eight of the 20 cases, although the major part of the function is carried out by agencies within the Department of Labor. It has *directive* authority in aspects of eight tasks (B.E.S., eight [seven in Employment Service]; B.L.S., four; O.M.A.T., five, with some dual allocations). The Department has *indirect authority* with respect to aspects of 19 tasks (B.E.S., 19 [15 in Employment Service]; O.M.A.T., three, with some dual allocations). The Department has advisory and stimulating responsibilities with respect to aspects of 14 of the tasks (B.E.S., nine; Women's Bureau, two; B.A.T., three; O.M.A.T., five; B.L.S., two, with some dual allocations).

The Bureau of Employment Security, which accounts for the largest number of task assignments, finds its direct-line authority shared (and sometimes confused) with that of other Labor Department bureaus or offices in the following cases:

1. Preparation, analysis and distribution of labor market and labor force statistics (with B.L.S.).
2. Preparation, analysis, distribution of information and forecasts regarding short- and long-range demand for and supply of labor (with B.L.S. and O.M.A.T.).

3. Preparation, analysis, and distribution of studies of economic trends (with B.L.S. and O.M.A.T.).
4. Education of public on labor market matters (with B.L.S. and O.M.A.T.).

There is also lack of clarity in the degree and extent of jurisdictional authority among B.E.S. and other subdivisions of the department with respect to:

1. Retraining for the unemployed.
2. Training and retraining for the employed.
3. Advice to and co-operation with other economic agencies of government.

Whether or not this wide distribution of employment and manpower tasks at the federal level is to be judged desirable depends to some degree on the desired result which provides the premise for the judgment. At least three results are important: (a) initiation in, and progressive development of, the services, (b) efficiency of operation, and (c) integration and co-ordination of the services. With respect to the objective of integration of the services, the disadvantages of dispersion of responsibility are self-evident. Integration and dispersion provide almost a contradiction in terms. With respect to the efficiency of operations, dispersion is also questionable. Co-ordination of operations must be sought by means of specific, elaborate, and sometimes restrictive agreements between the bureaus and departments involved. It is not an infrequent experience of those charged with formulating and administering these agreements to find that, at times, jurisdictional jealousies and empire-building tendencies provide stronger motivations than efficiency and even effectiveness of ultimate performance. Some wasteful duplication of effort and manpower is an almost inevitable result. From the point of view of obtaining initiative and new, progressive developments in the services, there may be some advantages in a dispersion of tasks, and a placement of responsibility for them in the hands of administrators who approach them from the point of view of the work of several departments, or even several bureaus within the same department. What gets started in a political system, particularly in one which attempts to achieve consensus among pluralistic interests within and outside the government, and which depends more on private initiative than central planning for "figuring out what to do next" and "how to do a better job" is, in part at least, a function of the extent of the horizons which bound the vision of those involved. Any bureaucratic organization, be it geared to governmental, business, religious, educational, or artistic objectives, has a tendency to operate today as it operated yesterday. It is not difficult to find instances in which the invention of new and more effective approaches to a problem, long the task of a particular bureaucratic group, has been obtained by allocation of responsibility for parts of that problem to another, and even to a newly created, group. There is, of course, danger of creating jealousies and in-fighting in this process, danger of overlapping authorities and wasteful duplication of effort; eventually, "things have to be straightened out" and be brought into some semblance of systematic institutional and organizational order.

It is apparent that this desire for initiation and progress lies at the root of some of the dispersion which can be observed, not simply in the employment and manpower functions, which are our immediate concern, but in many other fields of public and private operations. Frequently, however, this is done without awareness on the part of legislators or executives that the tasks they desire to have "initiated" are already being performed with a high degree of foresight, awareness of the ramifications of the problem, and initiative on the part of on-the-job administrators, and that the effective translation of these administrative qualities into broader programs is inhibited by a failure of the legislators and executives to provide adequate resources to accomplish that result.

We do not live in a planned economy whose direction is placed in the hands of an all-wise philosopher king. We may expect, therefore, the process of invention of ways of expansion, improvement, and development of government services to display this unsystematic assignment of functions and a consequent duplication of assignments.

Eventually, someone will sense the need for greater unity of direction and co-ordination of operations, if for no other reason than to avoid the unnecessary costs of duplication. It is not, however, a popular role for a legislator or an executive to play, that is, to suggest ways of rationalizing the operation of functions, the assignment of which has its roots in history, and, in the carrying out of which, vested personal and political interests have developed. Stepping on toes is not a popular political pastime and process. It is much more prestigeful and indicative of foresight and initiative to be the creator of a "new" activity or a "new" agency, than to be the systematizer of already existing activities and agencies. Besides, giving attention to this latter task appears to imply an assumption of omniscience, on the part of the one proposing suggestions, which can very easily be interpreted by his colleagues and the public as the politically undesirable quality of arrogance.

Nevertheless, the long-run advantages following the initiation of new developments are geared to their eventual integration into an institutional organization which makes sense in terms of the effective continuity of productive operations and of their direction toward major long-range public goals.

The above picture of dispersed responsibilities for the Employment and Manpower Services is presented not as a criticism of the way the situation has evolved or of those responsible, but to raise the question as to whether the time has not arrived for serious attention to the advantages of the greater integration of the services as to policy and administration.

PROBLEM OF INDIRECT AUTHORITY

One generalization, other than that with respect to the dispersed allocation of functions, stands out from Table 8-1. An examination of the type of authority possessed by federal agencies discloses a peculiarity of the U. S. system which is crucial for the problem of central direction and co-ordination of these employment and manpower tasks, even if we limit ourselves for the moment to those tasks for whose performance the bureaus and offices within the Department of Labor are responsible. *In the great majority of cases that authority is indirect.* The federal agency in most cases is not a line boss in any normal meaning of that term. At the operational (and to some degree at the policy) level the tasks are carried on by state and local government agencies, and the role of the federal agency is to guide and control indirectly through the persuasiveness of the rewards and penalties it can administer, i.e., allocation of funds, evaluations, technical and advisory help, provision of tools, etc.

For example, all the nine placement and placement-related functions are operationally performed and carried through by state systems of Employment Security, by local offices responsible directly to them, and by staff employed by them. With the exception of the operation of the District of Columbia Employment Offices, the development of placement tools, the administration of extended unemployment and other training and mobility benefits, and certain procedures with respect to the employment of foreign labor, the Bureau of Employment Security has no complete directive authority and must depend on state systems for "co-operation." These state systems consider themselves semiautonomous operationally and policywise. If the state and local agencies acknowledge the necessity for following suggestions from the Bureau of Employment Security, it is because the suggestions seem to them to have merit, are advantageous from their point of view, or because they fear loss of money, whose allocation is made by the federal agency, if they do not.

The same thing is true in the field of vocational education and training, and retraining for the unemployed. Here the Bureau of Employment Security and the Bureau of Apprenticeship and Training have chiefly advisory, stimulative, and supportive responsibilities. The Office of Manpower, Automation, and Training also has that kind of responsibility, as well as indirect authority (shared with others) to "persuade." Only if "adequate facilities are not available" has this office, in collaboration with the Office of Education in the Department of Health, Education, and Welfare, presumably directive authority to operate retraining facilities on its own.

Only with respect to research, information, and education of the public in labor market matters do agencies of the Department of Labor (Bureau of Employment Security, Bureau of Labor Statistics, Office of Manpower, Automation, and Training) appear to have a free hand to plan and carry through on their own what they consider to be good policy and good practice. And this is not the case in all the aspects of this area.

A second characteristic of the total program of operations is that the only existing local offices in which the operations are carried out and can be effectively integrated and co-ordinated at that level are the 1900 employment offices. It is on the manager and staffs of these offices that the ultimate performance of every activity rests, with the exception of the actual conduct of training classes and a few, but by no means all, of data-gathering tasks carried on by the Bureau of Labor Statistics. The managers and staffs of these offices are directly accountable to the Bureaus of Employment Security in the several states and indirectly to the U. S. Bureau of Employment Security.

IMPLICATIONS OF INDIRECT AUTHORITY

This situation raises several questions of an organizational character when we are considering the problem of where the directive and co-ordinative function for the Employment and Manpower Services might most appropriately and effectively focus, always assuming that we are solely interested in the best possible end results.

Where end results must be achieved through semiautonomous and indirectly stimulated and controlled agencies rather than through genuinely subordinate agencies, policy, planning, and operations are well-nigh inseparable. Comprehensive policies are not made by a central authority and implemented by subordinates. Not only will the operating "implementing" agencies insist, except under duress, in making their own policy on certain matters, they must, as the subordinate agents of their own state or local governments, follow policy and plans adopted by the latter.

There is, however, another fact about policy and planning which is coming to be recognized by organizers generally, whether or not the operating agency is wholly or partially autonomous, that is, whether or not it occupies a subordinate status. That fact is that policy is made during operation as well as before operation; plans are remade during operation. Operational units are close to the hard cold facts to which their operations have to be adjusted. In the interest of doing the best possible job in the face of those facts, they make the necessary adjustments. In doing so, they determine what, operationally, the organization's policy and plan will actually be as much as do the specifically designated "policy makers and planners." There is a real sense in which policy and plans are not fully formulated until they are implemented. Specifically designated policy and plan *makers* are realistically only policy and plan *proposers*. The organization's actual policy and plan is what it becomes in operation.

In the face of this reality there is an increasing tendency to provide for participation of those responsible for operations in the determination of objectives, policy, and plans. This is not frequently an authoritative "codetermination" type of participation, but rather a consultative participation. Its objective is (a) to bring policies and plans into the realm of feasibility, given actual operating conditions and other factors influencing ultimate performance, and (b) to assure operators of the representation of their interests and needs in the goals and standards set for them, and hence to increase their motivation to performance consistent with original policy.

If this is true in the relation of policy, plans, and operations in *any* type of organizational hierarchy, it is even more true in the situation we are dealing with, where the power to direct resides in persuasion and in indirect kinds of authority. When we seek a solution to the need for focus in the general direction and co-ordination of the Employment and Manpower Services in the United States, the problem we are dealing with is how to harness the people who are responsible for the administration of the Employment and Manpower

Services, from the President clear down the line, into a team, an integrated team, for the performance of the central mission of those services. That mission is to develop the manpower resources of the nation, to facilitate their employment so that their potential is not wasted, but utilized at its maximum, and to provide the facilities that make choice of movement in the labor market genuinely free; to do this guided by the requirements for increasing the nation's economic health, strength, and growth.

That operation requires, of course, integration and co-ordination at the top and the allocation of responsibilities and authority to achieve that at the federal level. But the tasks that produce the end results are not performed at the federal level. They are performed ultimately where man meets job, and with the men who do the jobs and the employers who offer them. The integration and co-ordination sought is not for the purpose of making the allocation of policy and administrative functions more logical, but for the purpose of getting those functions integrated and performed at the ultimate level where workers are developed, trained for, brought into contact with, and put to work at the jobs which are the dynamic stuff of economic health, strength, and growth. The logic we seek is ultimately not simply the logic of the distribution of policy-making, planning, and administrative positions, but the logic of effective performance of the end tasks which is the only excuse for the existence of those positions. The first logic is the servant of the second.

INSEPARABILITY OF POLICY AND OPERATION

The issues are three, the first of which we have suggested. Can policy as to direction and co-ordination of activities be formulated by any person or group other than one composed of those intimately acquainted through experience with the realistic problems of operation, or at least without the latter's authoritative or consultative participation in the determination of that policy?

FOCUS OF INTEGRATION AND DIRECTION

The second issue is closely related. If we assume that an integrated policy-operational organization of direction and co-ordination of the Employment and Manpower Services is required for effective end results, where shall that directive and co-ordinative function be placed?

We can let our minds range over a number of possibilities, the first two of which will be challenged as impracticable in the United States at the present time. Yet there is value in naming them.

A FEDERAL INDEPENDENT AGENCY

There might be established a Labor Market Board, an independent agency, on the model of that agency in Sweden. The Board would have line responsibility for policy and operation and co-ordination of all the tasks listed in Table 8-1. The evaluation of this type of solution would go far beyond the evidence referred to in this book. Such an organizational arrangement has great advantages operationally, however, not the least of which is the clear-cut recognition of its equality with those agencies dealing with the money market, the product market, the investment market, etc. in the effort to promote the nation's economic health, strength, and growth.

The establishing of an over-all central agency of this sort, to be sure, would be difficult politically in the United States at the present time. The picture of the existing dispersion of responsibility for the various employment and manpower tasks in the United States presented in Table 8-2 suggests this. Those tasks are distributed (disregarding for the moment the degree and type of authority involved) among over 20 federal offices and bureaus, and eight Presidential committees and commissions. These are grouped under six different federal departments and four independent agencies and the Executive Office of the President, each of which has a vested interest (backed by varying degrees of political power) in maintaining the status quo.

Moreover, as we have seen, the normal existing pattern of operation does not involve an allocation of directive authority to the federal agencies, but only indirect authority to influence the action of and gain the co-operation of the several state and local agencies and private associations. In addition, the established pattern and dynamics of that federal-state-local relationship are not the same for the different departments (e.g., the Departments of Labor and Health, Education, and Welfare), or even for bureaus within the same department (e.g., Bureau of Employment Security, Bureau of Labor Statistics, Bureau of Apprenticeship and Training, and Office of Manpower, Automation, and Training within the Department of Labor). It cannot be overemphasized that the realities of this federal-state-local relationship are compelling and constraining in assessing the possibilities of central focus for direction and co-ordination of all activities.

For any over-all co-ordination of the Employment and Manpower Services through the establishment of a Labor Market Board type of operation would immediately raise the question of the federalization of these services, an issue to which we shall return later.

The immediate identification, in the public mind, of the establishment of a new federal agency, in a particular area of economic or social activity, with a trend toward monolithic state socialism is an obstacle in the way of this approach to organizational integration of the Employment and Manpower Services. The establishment of the Federal Reserve Board, The National Labor Relations Board, the original Social Security Board, to name only a few, had to face this obstacle. Yet the increasing obviousness of the impact on the nation's interests in the problems dealt with has, to varying degrees, reduced the potency of the original objection.

A review of the arguments for attention to national as well as to local labor market needs and problems in Chap. 5 will indicate the existence of a similar situation when consideration is given to the question of the type of organizational agency responsible for the effective functioning of the national market. These arguments lend strength to the case for the eventual establishment of an independent federal agency to deal with those aspects of labor market problems which are of truly national significance, to strengthen, co-ordinate, and integrate the agencies dealing with these problems in their more localized aspects, and to bring to bear actively and forcefully the labor market and manpower interests, needs, and contributions, in the councils of those who are shaping over-all national economic policy and practice.

What can be at the moment, however, grows from what is. The several Employment and Manpower Services in the United States are not in their infancy or early childhood. What they shall become, and particularly what organizational integration they, in the future, come to have, will evolve from what they are, and their evolution will be stimulated and constrained by many of the same factors and conditions which have produced what we do have now.

These facts have a constraining effect on present tactics, but they also leave the way open for the expectancy that the growing awareness of developing needs will eventually support a strategy approximating ever more closely to the meeting of those needs. The time is not far distant when it will be recognized that national economic policy cannot be effectively formulated and implemented unless all employment, manpower, and labor market factors are taken into account, not as separate pieces of economic resources and processes, but as integral and interacting parts of the whole. When that time arrives, the need for focusing of responsibility in a single agency for the study and presentation, and prescription with respect to, all such factors, both of supply and demand, will be clear. In no other way can the significance of the impact of economic policy on these factors and the reciprocal impact of these factors on the implementation of economic policy be adequately and usefully represented.

On the basis of the probability, however, that the time is not ripe to initiate the independent-agency type of solution to the need for an active and positive labor market policy and program, what other alternatives are present?

LABOR DEPARTMENT AS THE INTEGRATING AUTHORITY

As indicated in Table 8-2, the present federal public efforts affecting the operations of the labor market and the development and movement of manpower are heavily concentrated in the Department of Labor. An approximation to the establishing of a federal integrating agency might be suggested by this fact. One way of doing this would be to bring into the Department of Labor from other departments a number of activities closely related to the large number of employment and manpower tasks already assigned to the Department.

It will be recalled that bureaus or offices within the Department of Labor at the present time have a primary responsibility for at least 20 of the 29 tasks which are normally considered, in this country, and indeed in most industrial countries, to have a logical and practical claim to incorporation into the employment and manpower complex of public activities. The chief functional areas over which the Department of Labor exercises no, or only incidental, control are (1) creation of the demand for labor (industrial development of communities, investment in productive enterprise, direction of government purchases), (2) planning, direction, and support of public works as a preventive measure against unemployment, (3) housing related to the facilitating of the movement of labor, (4) the actual conducting of vocational education, training, and retraining courses, and (5) rehabilitation.

These functions are all closely related to an active and positive labor market policy and practice implementing the central mission proposed in this book as appropriate and necessary. Would it be desirable and possible to concentrate them all in the Department of Labor?

There are many obstacles to such a concentration of these activities, many of them of the same sort as were noted in the case of the establishment of an independent labor market and manpower agency. In addition, there are problems of political acceptance of the Labor Department as an appropriate "home" for particular activities, and personal and bureaucratic vested interests to consider. Moreover, if the present authoritative relation between federal, state, and local governments and their respective agencies is to be maintained, the different degrees of maturity of these relations, and the different patterns of relationship which have been evolved by, for example, Area Redevelopment Administration in the Department of Commerce, Office of Rural Areas Development in the Department of Agriculture, the Urban Renewal Administration in the Housing and Home Finance Agency, Office of Education and Office of Vocational Rehabilitation in the Department of Health, Education, and Welfare, and by the Bureau of Employment Security and the Office of Manpower, Automation, and Training in the Department of Labor, would present severe problems of rearrangement. Many of these differences are rooted in the varied organizational assignments for getting these tasks performed in the states and localities.

These are not, of course, insuperable problems, but they do suggest that the approach to the integration of the several services, from policy through performance, is not merely one of a reallocation of responsibilities at the federal level either to an independent agency or to the Department of Labor.

Even if there were no political or bureaucratic-vested-interest or practical problems in transferring the expedition of these services to the Department of Labor, the case for their inclusion in that Department's responsibilities is not an unchallenged one.

Transfer of Demand-Creating Functions

Consider, for example, the case of those functions related to creating a demand for labor.

To be sure, Employment and Manpower Services, seeking to maintain an active and positive labor market policy, find themselves operating with one hand tied if their concern is limited to the provision of a supply of labor with no opportunity to promote in particular localities and at particular times the demand for labor.

No employment and manpower agency can be held accountable for the success of an active labor market policy and program unless it has within its control, or has authoritative powers to influence, job-creating as well as job-filling functions, labor-demand as well as labor-supply functions. It cannot be held accountable for the reduction of seasonal, structural, and cyclical employment through that labor market policy and program if its only function is the development, counseling, and placement of a supply of labor. Their participation in that demand process, especially in an advisory and stimulating capacity, can be considerably amplified, and we have suggested it should be so amplified. The desirability of administrative amplification of responsibility for job-creating functions involves more than the desirability of having an integrated labor market agency. But the possibility of such amplification also depends on more than a demonstration of the fact that it is logical. The present situation with respect to the assignment of responsibility in the areas noted above grows out of considerations, some of which are peculiar to the demand functions involved, and to the ways of decision-making and action initiation we have come to believe appropriate in our culture for carrying out such functions.

We depend, for example, upon initiative and energy from a wide range of private as well as government and public interests to promote such labor-demand-creating activities as the industrial development of communities and the encouragement of the most desirable location of investments in productive enterprise. The variety of combinations of those interests, and of the economic, social, political, and demographic factors which shape their expression, raises a question as to whether the officials of any one existing government department, especially at the federal level, can be charged with more than an advisory, stimulating, and supporting role in planning and in implementing plans in these areas. (This is quite aside from the specific question of whether the Department of Labor is the appropriate and acceptable instrumentality.) The basic policy involved is one which is necessarily affirmed prior to the policy with respect to the concentration of all employment and manpower functions and especially demand functions in one department. That basic policy concerns to what degree we shall continue to depend on a consensus among pluralistic interests and on acts of private initiative, both locally and nationally, when public attention is given to increasing or decreasing job openings in particular localities.

Moreover, the variables are many, and their relationships in any particular community and in the nation as a whole are extremely complex, a fact which suggests that centralized decision-making may very easily go astray. We have not developed our models for the multiple variables involved and the programing of these variables to the point where we can assign their analysis to mechanical or human computers. Decisions about community job-producing development and permission or encouragement to private enterprisers to invest are too complex for centralized solution. In particular times and particular localities (and we are not speaking now of *general* demand-producing measures, such as those related to fiscal and monetary policy), that decision is going to result, in the foreseeable future, from a horseback judgment, even if the judgment is encouraged and supported by such quantifiable data as can be fed to a mechanical or human-brain computer. In the area of labor-demand-creating activities which we are discussing, the man on horseback will find it desirable, in the light of the peculiarity and complexity of community interests and forces with which he is dealing, to have his horse in at least the approximate neighborhood affected by his judgment.

Nevertheless, a number of countries (particularly England and France) have experimented with centrally guided industrial development, and investment in enterprise, and hence with job-opportunity-creating efforts, by reference to the need to supplement and reinforce their labor supply efforts with efforts related to labor demand.

Structural unemployment, involving particularly that in mining, fishing, and agriculture, which is normally regionally concentrated, is tackled in part through encouragement or control of the investment in new plants and their movement to particular areas. Seasonal unemployment, particularly in building, agriculture, and forestry, is tackled in part through direction of government orders, the timing of public works and through the release of private "investment reserves." Cyclical unemployment is tackled in the same way. And, in many countries, these are considered appropriate activities related to the function of a labor market agency or agencies, along with, of course, their efforts in the field of labor supply.

In the United States we have the beginnings of such efforts in our area redevelopment, urban redevelopment, and our rural area redevelopment, and in the direction of public works and government purchases. In a country which suffers the persistent level of unemployment and the uneven geographical incidence of unemployment experienced in the U.S., it is very unlikely that the book is closed with respect to the enlargement of this area of labor-market-balancing activities or to the possibility of their direction and organization under the auspices of a central labor market agency.

Even though, because of these many practical difficulties, it appears unwise or impossible to transfer these labor-demand-creating functions to the Department of Labor in the interests of lodging direction of both supply and demand elements of an active labor market policy in the same organizational unit, the need for such integration does not disappear. At a very minimum, some mutual liaison representation in the deliberations over policy and practice relative to both supply and demand functions, liaison relations between the involved departments and independent agencies, can be established. Such a move is desirable and necessary in order that the reciprocal impact of supply and demand on each other shall be taken fully into account and the national interest in a balanced labor market be effectively served.

The direction of government orders not only by reference to areas of persistent unemployment, but in a manner to prevent threatened unemployment is another possibility in this effort to enlarge, in particular situations, the demand for labor. Government procurement policies, of course, must satisfy a number of criteria, interests, and standards governing departmental accountability for economic expenditures, not specifically related to the maximum development and utilization of the nation's manpower. With respect to the control over and direction of such procurement policies, therefore, it is unlikely that we could expect, or reasonably urge, more than an increased effectiveness of the Employment and Manpower Services' voice in a joint determination of procurement policy and practice, so that the achievement of a balance of supply and demand in the labor market be approximated as closely as possible. The ultimate procurement decision itself is not likely to be transferred to an Employment and Manpower agency, whether within or outside of the organizational framework of the Department of Labor.

Closely related to the above areas of employment and manpower activities are the planning, having ready "on the shelf," and the initiation of public works, as at present for the relief of unemployment in those areas certified by the Bureau of Employment Security as in need of that relief, or, hopefully, in the future, as a preventive of seasonal unemployment. It is probable that the contribution of the federal government to this labor-demand-creating effort is more appropriately and effectively made through the agencies charged with this type of work on federal projects, which agencies also have more in common with co-operating state and local agencies involved in this type of effort than does the Department of Labor. The strengthened participation of the Employment and Manpower Services in joint planning and eventual determination of allocations of effort to serve employment and manpower objectives is, of course, highly desirable. The certification by the Bureau of Employment Security of areas where high and persistent levels of unemployment exists, and which are, therefore, eligible for public works assistance, does not exhaust the contribution which can be made by the Department of Labor agencies.

If the *preventive* aspect of public works initiation is to be strengthened, the Employment and Manpower Services will have an even bigger role to play. But the function providing the informational basis for their contribution already lies within the Department of Labor, namely, their function to collect and distribute information on facts and trends in labor supply and demand, and other labor market factors and processes. Their effective contribution to using public works as a measure for the prevention of probable unemployment, however, will call for a considerable improvement in the type of statistics which have prognostic value as to probable increases and decreases in job openings in the short run and in particular labor markets.

The controlling fact which argues for the eventual authoritative direction and initiation of public works and other forms of job-creating efforts as prevention-of-unemployment measures within a single employment and manpower agency is that timing is the essence of their effectiveness. The lead time between the indications of probable unemployment and its actual occurrence is a matter of a few months or even weeks. Decisions must be made quickly and boldly by an agency whose efforts are evaluated in terms of their objective to prevent, not merely to provide remedies for, unemployment.

One other function, the provision of housing needed to make possible a desirable movement of labor, appears to us to fall into the same category as the above functions from the point of view of objections to transferring them to the Department of Labor. That is, these housing functions are those which appropriately, and probably most effectively, are performed where they are now located, but with a strengthened participation by the Employment and Manpower Services in the decision as to their timing and location in the light of desirable movements of labor.

Incidentally, the considerations which point in the direction of the above conclusion with respect to the assignment of the demand-for-labor-producing functions seem to us, at the present time, to be equally compelling whether we are speaking of the transfer of these functions to the Department of Labor or to an independent labor market agency, at least as far as the United States is concerned.

What principle can be suggested, then, as a premise for a practical decision with respect to the immediate transfer of these functions, all but the last of which involve an amplification of the demand for labor, to a federal employment and manpower agency, independent or departmental, thus incorporating both supply and demand functions within the same agency? The principles suggested for immediate application by the above discussion are *first*, that the Employment and Manpower Services be assigned full responsibility and authority, under whatever comprehensive unit of organization they are placed, for policy and operations connected with the development and movement of the *supply* of labor and for organizing the labor market in such a way that, under any given conditions of labor demand, the existing manpower resources are developed to and employed at their maximum productive potential. *Second*, that their contribution to *demand* functions, i.e., to the creation and amplification of employment possibilities *incidental to their fulfillment of the above responsibility*, and their stimulus, advice, and assistance to, and support of, community industrial development, etc. (of the type referred to in Chaps. 2, 3, and 6) be recognized as a legitimate and significant aspect of their activities with respect to the more effective functioning of the labor market, and that their efforts be supported by adequate resources for effective expansion of such activities. *Third*, that the liaison arrangements between the employment and manpower agency or agencies in the Department of Labor dealing with supply aspects of the labor market and the agencies in other departments dealing with its demand aspects be strengthened by providing authoritative representation of the former in not only general policy, but in allocation decisions of the latter until such time as it becomes feasible to establish an independent agency integrating or co-ordinating policy and operations with respect to both the supply and the demand aspects of an active and positive labor market program. The reverse representation is equally important.

Practicability must necessarily be a compelling consideration at the moment. But the essential and necessary reciprocity of the supply and demand operations in the labor market is clear. The nation's economic health is a function not only of the effectiveness of each set of operations, but of the effectiveness of their mutually contributory relationship to each other in the full light of their interdependence.

Transfer of Supply Functions

The last two types of functions which at the moment lie outside the jurisdiction of the Department of Labor are geared to the supply problems in the labor market. The most significant of these activities are those having to do with the actual conduct of vocational education and retraining courses, and rehabilitation efforts. At present these are located, as far as federal activities are concerned, in the Department of Health, Education, and Welfare. Such activities are significant supply elements in an over-all employment and manpower program. At the moment they must be related to those parts of the over-all program carried on in the Department of Labor through a large number of interagency agreements and financial and functional arrangements. These measures are complicated to operate and lead to frequent wasteful conflicts.

The political, bureaucratic, vested interest and other practical problems facing any move to transfer of vocational education and the labor-demand-creating tasks are, as we have seen, present in this case also. The transfer of training presents problems of its own, and the problem of the variety of state and local organizational and taxing arrangements for the conduct of vocational education is even greater than in the case of the labor-demand-creating functions. The patterns by which vocational education is related to general education are varied, not only with respect to organization, but also with respect to the principles and convictions held locally (where primary responsibility for secondary education rests) about their appropriate relation and about the nature of education itself. Indeed, the transfer of federal functions related to vocational education and training from one federal department to another, in order to integrate this type of activity with other employment and manpower activities, is, in many ways, a superficial issue. The basic issue is the reformation of vocational education and training itself in the light of the nation's economic and manpower needs at the present and in the future.

The ultimate authority to institute such reforms lies with thousands of local school boards over the country, although their initiative and vision of need can be, and are, stimulated to a limited degree by conditions for financial aid and professional supervision provided for vocational as well as general education from state and national sources.

It is not probable, however, in the foreseeable future, if ever, in a matter as important as this to the residents of over 8000 local communities, that these residents will be in sufficient agreement on the relation of vocational to general education or on the purposes of education to make possible the implementation of any national policy comprehending the whole field of vocational education.

Theoretically and practically, of course, general as well as vocational education is the very foundation of what can be achieved in the employment and manpower area. Our own impression, however, is that no federal or state department is going to make much progress in firming up those foundations by attempting to promote a frontal effort at the reconstruction of the whole vocational educational system rooted in the customs and traditional preconceptions in thousands of local communities.

Yet certain possibilities are beginning to appear for stimulating movement in this direction, and the mandate for amplifying such stimulus is already possessed by the Department of Labor (as well as by the Department of Health, Education, and Welfare). What are these possibilities?

First is the rapidly extending co-operation which the managers of the Employment Service have established and are establishing with school boards in local communities, providing high school youth with group and individual vocational and occupational counseling, testing, and initial placement. These Employment Service efforts are concerned not only with high school graduates, but with school leavers as well, and, in many cases, the application of effort from the ninth grade on is the subject of experimentation. Here is the opportunity, in connection with the contacts incidental to this going youth counseling, testing, and employment effort, to bring to the attention of local school officials and school boards, as well as to state authorities, the modifications in their provisions for general and vocational education needed to make those provisions consistent with and adaptable to the preparation required by youth for finding a productive and satisfying place within the changing job pattern in the United States.

This is being done by the managers and staffs of the Employment Service in a number of states and communities with notable results. This stimulus can be amplified on condition that those who provide the financial and staff resources for the Employment Service recognize the usefulness to the employment and manpower function of this activity and provide the required resources, resources enabling the Employment Service (a) to employ managers of sufficient stature to have such influence with school authorities, (b) to engage in the kind of labor market research needed to place in the hands of the managers and their deputies the facts essential to making their suggestions for vocational education realistic and sound, and (c) to devote the required time to this important long-range effort, the results of which may not appear in the current year's report.

Another opportunity for Employment Service personnel to stimulate a reconstruction of the communities' vocational education facilities grows out of the fact that Employment Office managers and their deputies universally participate, usually as key figures, in community redevelopment and industrial expansion efforts. Among the critical factors involved in the planning for and implementing such redevelopment and expansion are the provisions in the community for vocational education and training. In connection with the deliberations and action of representative community bodies engaged in such projects, the opportunity is available for the manager of the Employment Office to "educate" the members of such bodies as to the changing demands on the facilities for vocational education of the industrial and business system locally and nationally.

The retraining responsibilities laid upon the Department of Labor by the Area Redevelopment, the Manpower Development and Training, and the Trade Expansion Acts also present an unparalleled opportunity for the Department of Labor agencies, the Office of Manpower, Automation, and Training, the Employment Service, and the Bureau of Apprenticeship and Training, not merely to advise and stimulate others in the setting up of occupational training arrangements, but themselves to evolve new approaches to the performance of functions in this area of vocational and occupational education and training. Although the Department of Labor agencies must enter into arrangements with the Development of Health, Education, and Welfare and state and local education authorities for the actual instruction given in training and retraining courses, their authority in the determination of the kinds and scope of the courses required, the evaluation of their results, and the possibility of promoting in-plant training with supplementary classroom instruction provide a good deal of room for experimentation in developing the kinds of vocational and occupational training and retraining which will undergird the Employment and Manpower Services in the performance of their mission.

Testimony from the field indicates that the functional relationships of the Employment Service and the Office of Automation, Manpower, and Training, with local and state educational authorities and with the Office of Education in Health, Education, and Welfare are leading to mutual benefits, and that the experience is widening the understanding by the educational authorities of the realities of vocational and occupational demands on educational facilities. The necessary co-operative arrangements have not proved impossible, at least within the scale of operations provided for by current legislation, and there is long-range advantage in the broadening and sharpening of the concepts of vocational education in general resulting from this required collaboration between the existing educational and the existing employment and manpower administrators.

The position can be reasonably supported, therefore, that, with respect to the institutional vocational education and training aspects of an active labor market policy and practice, the present period of experimental effort, involving collaborative organizational assignments, can advantageously be continued. As experience develops new approaches to, new content for, new standards for evaluation of, and new possibilities for the integration of the total complex of vocational, occupational, and apprenticeship training, resources and processes can be made. The institutional and in-plant facilities and staff, and the efforts related to both youth and adults can be better coordinated. And, as the question of the relation of vocational to general education becomes clarified, the situation may change.

The logic of the place and role of vocational training efforts in the total national effort for the development and employment of the nation's manpower resources at their maximum quantitative and qualitative potential will continue to reassert the desirability of the inclusion of responsibility for these efforts in the functions of a unified and integrated employment and manpower agency, whether that takes the form of an independent agency or of one lodged in the Department of Labor.

Finally, although agencies for rehabilitation of the physically and mentally handicapped quite obviously provide services which make available manpower resources which would otherwise be unavailable as contributors to the nation's economic productivity and health, there are two considerations which argue against their inclusion in the Department of Labor. The first is that they are so predominantly identified with a social service, and even a relief, emphasis that they becloud the economic service image we have seen is so necessary for promoting the widespread inclination to utilize the Employment and Manpower Services on the part of workers and employers. This widespread use, providing the services to a clientele representing adequately the great variety of skills and jobs required for effective contribution of the services to the nation's economic strength and growth, we have seen, is essential to providing effective service to any particular group of clients, including, of course, the handicapped.

It is not suggested that the Employment and Manpower Services close their doors to the handicapped with respect to counseling, testing, placement, and retraining. It is suggested only that the process of their rehabilitation in order to qualify them to be successfully served by the indicated services be arranged for and conducted by agencies specifically qualified to do that. This is, in essence, the second consideration leading to the conclusion that a rehabilitation division fits uneasily and not very logically into the functional framework of the labor-market-oriented Employment and Manpower Services. Such a division would lean heavily for the great share of its activities on medical and psychiatric therapeutic services.

LIAISON FUNCTIONS

It would be shortsighted to abdicate the position that, eventually, the· authority to initiate and maintain not only the labor supply functions, but also the labor-demand-creating functions involved in an active labor market policy should reside in a unified and integrated employment and manpower agency. The practical political and jurisdictional problems at the moment, however, make unreasonable a blitzkrieg approach to the single agency objective.

One step is possible, however, toward facilitating the kind of coordinated attack on the employment and manpower problems which is consistent with the reciprocal contributions of each of the agencies to the others and with their interdependency for achieving results as participants in implementing an active labor market policy and program. It has been suggested that this might be in the form of the establishment of authoritative liaison relations in which high-level representatives from each of the departments involved take part in the deliberations of the others in the formation of policy and major operational decisions which affect and are affected by the decisions and actions in any of the departments in the area of employment, manpower, and labor market affairs.

There would be advantage in adding to the negotiating responsibilities of these representatives a collective responsibility for the overseeing of, analysis of relations between, and making proposals for the better integration of, the total range of Employment and Manpower Services performed in their several departments and agencies. Their cooperation might be implemented through their membership on an interdepartmental and agency co-ordinating council.

INTEGRATION WITHIN THE
DEPARTMENT OF LABOR

Chapter Nine   With respect to an immediate approach to the
development of a more nearly integrated policy
and operation of the Employment and Manpower Services, then, we
are, aside from the suggestion for authoritative liaison arrangements
among the several departments, concerned with those services already
assigned to the Department of Labor. A large majority of those services, as we have seen, is lodged there in any case. As far as the organization of the Secretary of Labor's office is concerned, the totality of
those tasks was until recently the appropriate concern of the Assistant
Secretary for Employment and Manpower. Since that office was vacant
for a considerable time in 1962 of a permanent appointee, there was
an understandable confusion as to who was directing and co-ordinating
what.

A recent order of the Secretary has been issued, designed to re-
organize the allocation of policy and operational responsibilities for
Departmental efforts in the employment and manpower field under
the Under Secretary as Manpower Administrator. The preparation of

179

this order and the consideration of the most appropriate and effective distribution of tasks was the subject of careful and thoughtful analysis and appraisal within the Department. As is the case in every bureaucratic reorganization, there were matters of internal history and relationships to be considered as well as of logical adaptation to the nature of the objective problem to be dealt with.

It is too early to evaluate the adequacy of this specific attempt at co-ordination of employment and manpower activities within the Department of Labor. But it may be safely predicted that the considerations below will have a bearing on the degree to which the assignment of functions results in more satisfactory end results.

The degree of success of the effort of the Manpower Administrator to develop a focused and integrated performance of the total range of services under his direction will be influenced especially by the clarity of the concept of the central mission of the services around which their objectives and tasks can be integrated, and a decision as to which of those services is considered to be the key and core service in the operation of all of them. *For it is those involved in the activities of that key area who can, from their experience, best furnish the clue to the practical shaping of the total program.* When that question is answered, there are the further alternative possibilities of (a) assigning to that key operation (say placement or training) the responsibility for integrating all manpower and employment functions around its ultimate mission, (b) gearing planning and policy to the accomplishment of that key operations mission, or (c) attempting some new over-all approach to the formulation of programs and their implementation.

We can quickly dismiss from the potentially key activities those in several areas in which Department of Labor agencies at the moment have only, or primarily, an advisory or stimulating involvement: creation of demand for labor, preventive measures, rehabilitation, vocational education, and advice to and co-operation with other agencies. Also, we can dismiss those areas of activities which are primarily supporting services to main line activities: research, forecasting, and information; employer services; financial benefits; and education of the public. That leaves the *placement and placement-related tasks and training* as those areas which are most directly and intimately involved in carrying out the central mission of the Employment and Manpower Services. These activities are the responsibility of the Employment Service and of the Office of Manpower, Automation, and Training, respectively. Training, although it holds the public eye at the moment, is appropriately considered as a prelude to placement.

If it is not, it can scarcely be considered as integrated with an over-all employment and manpower program.

Up to the passage of the Manpower Development and Training Act of 1962, the Bureau of Employment Security and the state Employment Security Systems had the policy and operating responsibilities, not only for the placement and placement-related functions area, but for the "supporting service" areas as well, that is, responsibility for much of research and information, employer services, benefits, advice to and co-operation with other government agencies. Moreover, they were the ones carrying the heaviest load among all state and local agencies in the co-operative efforts for: increasing the demand for labor, industrial development, preparation for emergency mobilization, and retraining of the unemployed. Moreover, whatever authoritative co-ordination of these numerous activities was carried out was done by the Bureau of Employment Security.

After the passage of the Manpower Development and Training Act, the Office of Manpower, Automation, and Training was established with responsibilities (but not with exclusive responsibilities) for reporting and distributing information about short- and long-range labor force, labor market, and economic conditions affecting employment; for developing plans to meet unemployment and underemployment; and for carrying out the mandate of the training features of the Area Redevelopment and Manpower Development and Training Acts. In addition, this office was supposed to appraise and co-ordinate the several manpower activities of the Department. In view of the fact that the Bureau of Employment Security had previously carried out most of the activities performed by the Department of Labor in these areas, confusion of jurisdiction was bound to arise. That confusion has never been completely removed.

The focus of our concern here is not to criticize this former allocation of functions, but to explore alternatives for creating the central directing and co-ordinating functions for the numerous employment and manpower activities which are the responsibility of the Department of Labor. That function logically centers in the office of an Under Secretary or Assistant Secretary for Manpower and Employment. We have said that in the interest of effective results, and in the face of the peculiarities of the indirect kind of authority which must be exercised by federal administrators in the present state of federal-state-local division of labor, policy, planning, and operations are inseparable. Any result-getting policy must, therefore, be established consistently with operating realities and in close consultation with those who are operationally face-to-face with those realities.

We were, therefore, questioning what area of activities provides its administrators with the clearest clue to a workable over-all policy in integrating the several activities. That area, we suggest, is that of placement and placement-related activities carried out at the moment by the Employment Service within the Bureau of Employment Security.

THE KEY ROLE OF THE EMPLOYMENT SERVICE

There is no functional area whose end objective is so closely related to the objective of the whole set of employment and manpower activities, and whose continuous work reveals more the hard, cold facts of life to which policy, plans, direction and co-ordination must be adjusted as the Employment Service. An indication of the relationship of this area of functions to the others will disclose the reason for this. The placement and placement-related activities carried on by the Employment Service (such as vocational counseling, testing, employer order-getting, and other contacts) have the following relationship to the other activities:

For Research, Forecasting, and Information

An important body of data in the United States about the present labor force and labor market conditions, and about probable short- and long-range future developments is supplied incidental to the routine operations. Also contacts are made through placement and order-getting activities which enable the effective gathering of data concerning matters of critical importance for vocational education, occupational training and retraining, the progress and consequence of automation, and for anticipation of the occurrence and growth of labor surpluses and shortages. If the responsibility for serving other agencies and even the President himself with such information is located anywhere else than in the Bureau of Employment Security, the occupant of the position will have to depend on that Bureau to supply much of the basic data on which those reports are based.

In that task the Bureau of Employment Security, and the Employment Service in particular, has accumulated a considerable amount of experience, as indicated by an examination of the type and volume of research done, the type and volume of data furnished to the Bureau of Labor Statistics, the Office of Manpower, Automation, and Training, the Council of Economic Advisors, Congressional committees and other government agencies, and the manpower and labor market data gathered and made available at the local, state, and national level for the benefit of private and public agencies.

FOR TRAINING AND RETRAINING

Consider for a moment the requirements for effective results in a retraining program and the degree to which the local managers of the Employment Offices are the only experienced full-time people available for meeting these requirements in the localities where training is to take place. The requirements and what is involved in meeting them are as follows:

1. *Selection of the type of training* most needed and for what skills, and with greatest possibility for meeting local or wider demands. This involves:
   a. Possession of readily accessible labor demand information locally and beyond.
   b. Access to sources of information about labor demand.
   c. Knowledge of occupational potential available among the unemployed and the underemployed in the community.
   d. Knowledge of the kind of training facilities available.
2. *Selection of trainees.* This involves:
   a. Available roster of candidates.
   b. Knowledge of their experience and aptitudes.
   c. Possession of facilities for testing and appraisal.
   d. Experience in spotting probable occupational capacity.
   e. Experience in spotting probable acceptability to employers.
3. *Motivation of potential trainees.* This involves:
   a. Experience in sensing motivation and amplifying it.
   b. Access to those to be motivated.
   c. Facilities for and experience in counseling.
   d. Knowledge of present and prospective demand to give substance to motivation.
4. *Responsibility for follow-through.* Experience in local training efforts and area redevelopment has shown that some responsible local agent must focus the numerous voluntary and paid contributions made and keep the associated teachers, in-

stitutional arrangers, etc. operating effectively. Even though conduct of the courses is delegated to vocational education authorities, the courses do not organize themselves. Organizing involves:

a. A co-ordinating, stimulating, watchdog, record-keeping agent with a full-time job related to the training process. This has usually been the manager (or his deputy) of the local Employment Office.

5. *Effective placement of trainees.* This involves:
a. Facilities for placement.
b. Experience in placement.

6. *Assuring community support,* countering local objections, and integrating conflicting interests. This involves:
a. Knowledge of and experience with the local people in unions, management, education, and politics.
b. Knowledge of the play of local forces.
c. Continuous on-the-job residence where the training is taking place.

Training and retraining courses, once approved, provided with funds, and set in motion, do not run themselves.

FOR EMPLOYER SERVICES

The contacts leading to these services are a normal and necessary part of the placement process, and have been developed in all major offices of the Employment Service, not only in order to amplify the reservoir of job orders from employers but to assist employers in the maximum and effective use of their manpower.

FOR EFFORTS TO CREATE A DEMAND FOR LABOR

The administrators of the placement activities are the only ones in possession of the labor force and labor market data without which community industrial development and in-migration of enterprise must fly blind. And if more is needed than is available, they are in the best possible position to get it. The managers and administrators of the local, state, regional, and national offices of the Employment Service have contributed this necessary element to industrial and community development projects within their areas of operation, and in a number of cases these managers have been the stimulators and promoters of such projects.

FOR PREVENTIVE MEASURES

The placement administrators are already performing many tasks of a preventive nature. They are in the position to obtain the prognostic information absolutely essential for any expanded preventive measures.

FOR REHABILITATION

The placement services, particularly counseling, are the processes through which many cases needing rehabilitation are spotted; it is, therefore, a natural referral agency. After rehabilitation has qualified handicapped workers for available work, the placement services are again used.

FOR BENEFITS

If these are expanded to include allowances to facilitate training and the movement of labor, they are closely related administratively to unemployment insurance. The important contributions of the placement services to unemployment insurance is well known.

Moreover, it is clear that these activities in these several areas are reciprocally essential to an effective performance of the placement job of the Employment Service. It is also frequently forgotten that, with the exception of unemployment insurance, the Employment Service itself took the initiative in instituting these services in order to do a better job of placement and to obtain the maximum utilization of the nation's manpower. Indeed, the campaign for an integrated set of Employment and Manpower Services and their development in the above areas as well as in the placement and placement-related fields (counseling, testing, inter-labor-market clearance) and in the development of aids (such as the *Dictionary of Occupational Titles* and the General Aptitude Testing Battery) have been largely carried on by the Employment Service. It will be recalled that of the total employment and manpower tasks carried on in the Department of Labor, 15 of the 19 carried on with indirect authority, and seven of the eight carried on with direct authority are responsibilities, predominantly or wholly, of the Employment Service. And in the absence of efforts at the national level to provide integration and co-ordination of the total number of manpower and employment functions, the Employment Service has been the chief instrument of integration. The effort has been accompanied by the attempt to define and highlight as an integrating focus of all the services included, the concept of the Employment Service as a *manpower* service, and the 1900 Employment Service offices as the manpower centers of their communities.

In addition to the central importance of the placement activities to all the others, and of their reciprocal importance to placement, it is not difficult to assign as an end object of all the Employment and Manpower Services, lacking any more adequate concept of mission, a satisfactory placement of workers in jobs. In the first and last analysis it could be argued that this is what the totality of services is all about. And it is the biggest single element in the objective of the Employment Service.

Certainly it is the Employment Service which is the key and core service in a total set of Employment and Manpower Services. Those involved in this Service from federal, through regional, through state, to local offices are not only the ones who are performing the central and critical function, but also those who have their fingers on the pulse of the performance of all other functions. They operate at the heart of the whole set, not only of the supply, but of the demand-creating aspects of an active labor market policy and practice. This is true in the United States, and it is true in every industrial country with whose Employment and Manpower Services we are familiar.

The conclusion to which we come on the basis of these observations is that the totality of employment and manpower functions within the Department of Labor must be administered by an Under or Assistant Secretary of Labor with responsibility for objectives, policy, planning, and operational co-ordination focused there. In the light of the indirect kind of authority exercised by the federal government and of the dynamic pattern of federal-state relations through which the job must be done, the recommendations to him for integrated over-all policy and plans must provide for the close collaboration and consensus development among the Office of Manpower, Automation, and Training, the Bureau of Labor Statistics, the Bureau of Apprenticeship Training, and, especially, of the Bureau of Employment Security, which has the best developed and practical contacts through the states with the local offices and their managers and the longest experience with the operational problems involved. We cannot emphasize too strongly that central policy and plans, however logical and desirable, are not likely to resemble end results in a federal-state-local relation such as we have unless the operating people have contributed their experience and been motivated voluntarily to back them with their acceptance and willing performance. A condition of achieving this is either punishment for failure to comply, or involvement of the operators through representation in the recommendation of the policy and plans.

Particularly important within the Bureau of Employment Security, both as a provider of the great majority of the services involved and as the chief agency which has developed the closest approach to a concept and to the operation of an integrated set of services, integrated around the idea of a total manpower effort, is the Employment Service.

Between the alternatives of first, an over-all Labor Department administration in which the Employment Service plays a very large and most significant role, and second, one in which the complete responsibility for an over-all program is lodged in the Employment Service, we would defend the first. The primary reason is that there are areas of effort (e.g., vocational education, training, retraining, rehabilitation, creation of a demand for labor, preventive measures against unemployment, and financial benefits) whose objectives and operational pattern, although related to and supported by the Employment Service, do not completely coincide with those of the Employment Service.

In the allocation of responsibility for policy and operations, the division of labor can be arranged in a number of ways. However, consideration should be given to the operational necessity for all aspects of the program by whatever bureau administered to depend on ultimate performance in the local offices supervised (although indirectly through the states) by the Bureau of Employment Security.

Evaluation of consistency of separate bureau and office objectives, policy, and plans with over-all objectives, policy, and plans must, of course, rest at the top. Evaluation of performance in the separate areas of performance might well be made the responsibility of a review and evaluation office independent of the individual operating bureaus and offices.

THE NEED FOR LOCAL
INTEGRATION AND LEADERSHIP

The final issue is whether, with respect to integrated Employment and Manpower Services, central policy and plans, as modified in operations, can be implemented effectively unless responsibility for that implementation and carry-through is pinpointed in a single office under a single manager in a particular labor market. This is the point at which the job is done, and where the end results are produced that determine how well the mission has been performed. This is where policy and plans come to life, blossom into performance, and yield good or bad results with respect to the integrated employment and manpower mission we have been talking about.

Our own conviction is that there is no other way. There must be an over-all manager of Employment and Manpower Services in each labor market, responsible for continuous, on-the-job management of an integrated program if there is to be any bringing out into life of an integrated mission and policy. In labor markets large enough to require it, he should have deputies responsible for the particular areas of activity. If that is the case, what are the alternatives for achieving such a focus of local responsibility?

We assume that, under our federal-state structure, no one is going to propose the establishment of a new branch office of the federal Department of Labor in each locality. It would, of course, be possible to set up local offices for training, for research, for administering the Trade Expansion Act, for the Bureau of Apprenticeship Training, and for employer services, as well as the present Bureau of Employment Security offices. But this would defeat the very object we are seeking, an integrated and co-ordinated organization of Employment and Manpower Services at the local as well as the national level. Besides, the operations involved in each of these are so interrelated that, whatever is done about physical location of the offices, the management of the functions performed has to be focused if we would avoid duplication, waste, and confusion. Whatever degree of overlapping jurisdictions in responsibility for employment and manpower functions exists at the federal level, it cannot be duplicated at the ultimate place, the local labor market, where performance takes place, if the achievement of end results is what counts.

The other alternative is to accomplish the desired result by utilizing the existing or amplified facilities of the 1900 Employment Offices and their managers, where they are up to the job, or their replacements if they are not up to the job.

There is a host of practical problems connected with implementing this suggestion. But the relationship of local, through state, to federal Employment and Manpower Services is already established on this basis in the performance of those tasks which are, at present, under the umbrella of the Bureau of Employment Security. And, as we have seen, those tasks constitute the largest share of those which are the responsibility of the Department of Labor. It should not be impossible to arrange procedurally that the additional tasks be the operational responsibility locally of the employment and manpower manager, as stimulated, guided, aided, and supervised by the Bureau of Employment Security, within policies enunciated by the Under or Assistant Secretary for Employment and Manpower upon the consensual recommendation of the directors of the Bureau of Employment Security, Office of Manpower, Automation and Training, and the Bureau of Labor Statistics. The logical and most effective approach to achieving, at the local level, an integrated set of Employment and Manpower Services is to make the present Employment Offices the community employment and manpower centers, and to allocate to their managers the responsibility for implementing national and local policy and programs, and for co-ordinating and integrating, in that area, all aspects of such programs.

SUMMARY

The issues raised in Chaps. 7, 8, and 9 are two aspects of the same problem, the establishment for the Employment and Manpower Services of a status as initiators and leaders, in their own right, for creating in the labor market the stimulus to and the conditions of economic health, strength, and growth. In the last two chapters we considered that the greatest obstacle to this was the lack of an authoritative integration of those services, a lack of unified objectives, direction, and co-ordination.

Examination of the allocation of functions in the total employment and manpower field indicates four conditions affecting any attempt to integrate them:

1. A dispersion among over twenty federal offices and bureaus in six departments, four independent agencies, the Executive Office of the President, and in eight Presidential committees, of responsibility for the 31 major tasks requiring performance in this field.
2. A dispersion among five bureaus and offices within the Department of Labor of responsibility for the tasks in which the Department of Labor has a role to play.
3. An organizational policy and operational relation between the federal agencies and the state-local agencies in which the predominant type of authority of the former is of the indirect variety.

4. The dependence of all services for their ultimate performance at the local labor market level on the managers and staffs of the 1900 Employment Offices indirectly supervised by Bureau of Employment Security.

The last two conditions are critically important for any attempt to integrate the services, even those which are the primary responsibility of the Department of Labor, and to bring them to focus in a co-ordinated impact on the problems of development and maximum utilization of the nation's manpower, and of facilitating genuinely free movement of workers within the labor market. They are equally important as determinants of where the controlling authority for policy and operations can most appropriately and effectively be placed.

The adaptation to this condition by concentrating all of the services under the jurisdiction of a national labor market board and directly subordinate regional or state and local boards was regarded as impractical at this time. The logic, but not the immediate practicability, of transferring functions of demand-for-labor-creating services and of vocational education, training, and rehabilitation to the Department of Labor from the Department of Health, Education, and Welfare and other departments was defended.

Nevertheless, the position was not abdicated that eventually, not only logic, but desirability and necessity would require the concentration in, and direction by, a unified and integrated agency, inside or outside the Department of Labor, of all Employment and Manpower Services, relative to both supply and creation-of-demand operations, essential for the maintenance of an active labor market policy and program. As an immediate approach to the problem, the assignment from the several departments involved of high-level representatives to perform a liaison function, involving authoritative participation in policy formation and major operational· decisions relative to employment and manpower affairs in which the departments had reciprocal functions to perform and were interdependent for the effectiveness of that performance, was suggested.

All of these are, of course, alternatives to the suggestion made that, under the over-all supervision, policy directions, and planning of an Under Secretary or Assistant Secretary of Labor for Employment and Manpower, the policy and operations with respect to all of the varieties of functions, carried on by the Department of Labor, be geared to making effective the placement and placement-related functions performed by the Employment Service in the Bureau of Economic Security, and the training function carried out operationally by the Office of Manpower, Automation, and Training and the Bureau of Employment Security in cooperation with the Department of Health, Education, and Welfare. In other words, those who administer this group of activities should be given the status of contributing to policy for and operations of all the services, rather than the status of administrators of service agencies to a variety of other programs.

The justification for this rests on the following observations:

1. The placement and training functions (particularly the first), broadly defined, are the only functions whose effective outcome is approximately identical with, rather than merely contributory to, the ultimate objective of all the services established to develop and employ the nation's manpower at the level of its highest quantitative and qualitative potential.

2. The administrators of the Employment Service are the only ones who have participated in and, therefore, have experience with, the development and operation of all the other services. They have either initiated or participated in the development of these other services as necessary and desirable efforts in the attempt to make more effective the bringing of men and jobs together for maximum utilization of our manpower resources. This may not be a perfect clue to the principle of co-ordination, but it is a practicable and defensible one. If policy established by the Under Secretary or Assistant Secretary for Employment and Manpower is to lead to effective results, it must in the first instance be clearly related to the necessities of operations for those services whose operational objective is to bring men and jobs together in a way which utilizes their skills at the highest level and avoids any waste of our manpower resources. And those with the greatest amount of experience in these operations, i.e., the administrators of the Bureau of Employment Security, particularly the Employment Service, must have a large and influential voice in establishing these policies.

3. Even if the several services are federalized, the successful integration of policy and operations for all of them (whatever central principle for co-ordination is used as a guide) will stand or fall with the capacity of the federal administrators to establish working policy and operational relationships with the state and local agencies. The relationship which the Em-

ployment Service and the Bureau of Employment Security have established with such state and local agencies over the years, as a product of trial and error, is not perfect, but it is a working one in which men have experience and which state and local people have accepted. Any alternative to strengthening the position and status of the Employment Service and the Bureau of Employment Security as an influential partner in the initiation of policy and development for all the Employment and Manpower Services will have to wrestle with the problem of establishing a pattern of federal-state relations which the ultimate performers in the states and local areas have a confidence in, and an acceptance of, equal to that which they have in the present pattern.

4. Aside from the establishment in every labor market of a local office of the U.S. Department of Labor, or of the several employment and manpower operations of the Department, the only alternative is to make the present (or better qualified replacements for) managers of the Employment Offices the co-ordinators at the local operating level of the integrated Employment and Manpower Services desired and promoted at the federal and state levels; that is, to make the local employment exchanges the local employment and manpower centers, and their managers the local Employment and Manpower Services manager.

ROADS TO INTEGRATION

Chapter Ten This book has been focused primarily on policy premises with respect to the mission, operational field, and status of the Employment and Manpower Services and the establishment and implementing of an active and positive comprehensive but integrated labor market program. The organizational and administrative problems involved have received only incidental and chiefly illustrative mention.

The question may well be raised, however, as to whether an integrated policy and program for the Employment and Manpower Services is possible under the present organizational and administrative arrangement.

FEDERALIZATION?

It will immediately occur to some that the federalization of the major areas of activity: placement and placement-related functions, research and information, training and retraining, unemployment insurance and other benefits, would simplify this process of integration whether the integrating agency is within the Department of Labor or established as an independent agency. Many who have watched with a concerned and critical eye the development of public activity in this area have long been staunch advocates of such a move. We believe that eventually the increasing necessity for marshaling our economic forces in response to the compelling necessity for national economic strength and growth in the face of challenges to the economy of the nation as a whole will not only argue for, but make imperative, that move.

The opportunity to review the operations of the services, not only at the center but at the grass roots, here and abroad, and to observe the requirements for effective end performance in the communities, where manpower development and employment becomes, not a program, but a living activated productive reality, has raised, however, certain doubts as to whether federalization is likely to accomplish, at this time, what its advocates hope for.

The case for federalization which has been heavily persuasive with those of us who have favored it, rests basically on the belief that (1) *uniformity* in the excellence of performance and in end results is difficult to achieve under a federal-state system; (2) the *objectives and standards* believed to be consistent with the nation's needs and essential to those end results will not be adopted and acted upon expeditiously if central authority is weak; (3) whatever may be true of particular local situations, the *initiative and leadership* required to meet the nation's needs and to promote over-all and well-co-ordinated progress cannot come from diffused centers of initiation and responsibility; and (4) it would be easier under such a federalized arrangement to promote the kind of developments in the services the advocates of federalization and reform believe desirable.

There is much evidence that these reasons are essentially sound. The question remains as to whether and to what extent federalization can be expected, at the present time, to provide a net improvement in the situation until certain other developments have taken place.

We are not thinking here of the possibilities of improvement in each of the services separately. (Actually, most advocates of federalization are concerned with the federalization of the particular services, particularly of Unemployment Insurance and the Employment Service.) But the issue arises in the present instance with reference to the integration of all of them as integral parts of an over-all employment and manpower program and agency. We have barely begun the process of conceiving of and organizing for an integrated program of services at the federal level. We are much closer to it at the local level. We could very easily compound the difficulties of the eventual achievement of a country-wide integrated employment and manpower program by moving to federalize part by part the placement, the training, the financial benefits, and the research aspects of the program. We are not ready, either in concept or organization, to achieve the operation of an integrated national organization of all the Employment and Manpower Services, to say nothing of its federalization. For that which is to be integrated is not simply the activities centering in Washington, but those *and* the activities carried on throughout the whole country. The centralization of authority implied in federalization is not necessarily synonymous with functional integration, although it is one method of trying to achieve that objective. Given the authority to do so, a centralized administration would still have to do the job, in collaboration with a field staff of state and local people. It may be well to consider whether we have the groundwork laid in prerequisites and experience for such a task.

The co-ordinated program and administration now being effectuated in the Department of Labor will, for example, have to wrestle with a very important feature of federal-state relations, the variety of sources of funds for the programs to be co-ordinated. The power to set standards, to achieve uniformity, and to exert leadership, which resides in the control over funds, is very great. Certainly the financial relations involved are a key factor in all interactions between the federal and the state and local agencies, whether those latter agencies are staffed by federal or by state and local employees. Parts of the total program are supported entirely by federal funds, parts (at least in the future) by matching funds, and a large part by that child of financing expediency related to the financing of unemployment insurance benefits and the administration of unemployment insurance and the Employment Service. The financial resources in this case, ostensibly flowing from a federal payroll tax on employers, are in reality regarded (as far as benefits are concerned) as coming from several state funds, and in the perception of many employers from *their* funds, a perception derived from the implications of experience rating. Moreover, aside from the latter financial resources, the federal contributions to certain services, particularly to retraining, arise from appropriations related to the implementing of several acts of Congress of limited duration. In the light of the inevitably critical role played by financial allocations in federal-state relations, it would seem reasonable to assume that the achievement of a more integrated and effective total employment and manpower program via the method of federalization could well be vitiated by the variety and complexity of federal-state financial relations involved at present in its implementation. Certainly it should be recognized that the focus and systemization of the sources of funds furnish an important area of adjustment that will need to be worked out and agreed upon before the focus and systematization of programs can produce satisfactory results.

However, the prerequisites for advantageous results from a federalized system are not limited to systematic and appropriate financial arrangements conducive to those results.

It will not be necessary to repeat here the need for local initiative, enthusiasm, and know-how in dealing with the particular labor market characteristics and industrial, business, political, social, and power structure features of particular states and communities, set forth in Chap. 5. It is no criticism of federal politically appointed officials, whose term of office is limited at best to the time span of a single administration, to say that it is unlikely that they can become sufficiently familiar with that variety and complexity of local circumstances to take them into account in formulating and effectuating their general over-all policies and programs. This is a basic reason for the importance of participation in policy and plan formation of the permanent operating chiefs of the services, who have a better chance and longer time to acquire that familiarity, as suggested earlier in a foregoing chapter. Those who make a strong point of this reason for a nonfederalized system, however, might well question whether the frequent political change of state officials of the services guarantees much better precise and adequate acquaintance with state and local pecularities.

In the operation of services which touch so closely the life and interests of people in thousands of local communities, the adaptability of policy and practice to the local variables named above is a matter of crucial importance. One of the advantages of the present federal-state system is that federal authorities must gear their policies and practice to those local variables as presented and emphasized by state and local administrators. That experience can be exasperating at times, and the temptation is to assign the cause for it to the "stubborness" and "provincialism" of state and local administrators. But it can also be advantageous to federal authorities. The variables themselves are the ultimate cause, the variables and the perception local people have of the opportunities and constraints they present in implementing any policy, federal, state, or local at the grass roots. The federal administrators can use all the understanding of those variables and perceptions they can get, and are now forced to get, in order to operate a federal-state system. Such factors will not "go away" by the simple expedient of federalization of the services.

The major factor which calls into question the desirability of federalization of the Employment and Manpower Services, at this time, however, is that which stimulated the writing of this book. There is not an effective working consensus, on the part of influential people in Congress, in the federal departments involved, among the representatives of pressure groups at the national level, and certainly not among legislators, officials, and pressure-group spokesmen in the states, as to the major policy premises for development and operation of the services.

The issue is not basically stated as the advantages or disadvantages of integration through federalization until a prior question is answered. That question is, "Integration and federalization of *what*, for the achievement of *what central mission*, within what *operational field?*"

This is not to say that there are no firm convictions on these matters, but only that the convictions do not shape up into the approximation to a consensus which provides a sound set of guideposts giving direction to the development and operation of the services. Until there is a clearer agreement and sense of direction as to what the Employment and Manpower Services are expected to accomplish and become, it is untimely to deal with the question of whether a federal or a federal-state system would come closer to meeting that expectancy.

GREATER INTEGRATION WITHOUT FEDERALIZATION

There are, however, ways in which the present organizational and administrative relations between the federal, the state, and local agencies can be strengthened, the operation of the services can be brought closer to the meeting of national as well as state and local labor market needs, and the leadership and guidance of the federal agencies can be vitalized. Some of these ways can be briefly mentioned.

WIDENING THE POLICY HORIZONS

An obvious requirement for making progress toward a national positive integrated labor market policy and program is that there shall be a greater focusing and a heightened visibility of the Employment and Manpower Services as a national effort and as co-ordinated, not only among themselves, but with the other important economic agencies of the federal government as well. This will require a broadening of the basis for recommendations as to policy, planning, and programs beyond the Department of Labor, even with respect to those functions assigned primarily to that Department.

One step in this direction has already been suggested in Chap. 8, namely, the provision of authoritative high-level reciprocal liaison representation in the policy and program deliberations of each department and agency carrying on labor-market-relevant functions and of the other departments charged with aspects of such functions. Furthermore, it was suggested that these liaison representatives might form an interdepartmental and interagency council with responsibility for studying and recommending steps looking toward the greater integration of these activities.

Beyond this step, which is related basically to the Employment and Manpower Services themselves, there is need for greater administrative

interaction and stronger operating liaison relations of those services
with the formulators of policy and the planners of programs with
respect, for example, to the fiscal, monetary, procurement, agricultural,
and trade areas. In a sense, this is presumably provided for in part
through the interaction of Cabinet members with each other. Another
arrangement contributing to this objective is the ad hoc group conferences called by members of Congress for a preliminary exploring of
objectives, issues, and guidelines for economically oriented legislation
in which they are interested. A considerable amount of interaction also
takes place among the legislative liaison officials in the several departments and the Senators and Representatives and their legislative assistants concerned with legislation in this field.

What is visualized here, however, is a body which could have more
detailed and continuous overseeing of the interdependencies and possibilities for mutually beneficial and horizon-broadening interaction
among all those departments and agencies determining policy and
programs directed to maintaining and increasing the nation's economic
strength and growth. Possibly the objective could be advanced through
a Secretariat arrangement related to the Council of Economic Advisors.

As the significance of the labor force and labor market elements in
the operating strength and growth of the economy becomes more
clearly recognized, it may be possible to return to what, we understand,
was an original intention, that one of the Council of Economic Advisors should have a primary and specific, rather than only a secondary
and general, grounding in the economics of the employment and manpower area.

There are two advisory groups whose potential for broadening the
basis of recommendations as to policy, planning, and programs looking
toward an integrated system may be considered, although both are related to one agency, the Bureau of Employment Security, within the
Department of Labor. The first is the Interstate Conference composed
of Employment Security state officials, those administrators through
whose efforts the present federal-state systems of Unemployment Insurance and the Employment Service are operated in the field.

This body has no statutory authority, but it does have political
power residing in the influence it can bring to bear on the Senators
and Representatives from the several states. Its original function in the
early days of the Social Security Board was to facilitate the realization
of a hope strongly held by many advocates of the federal-state system,
that each state would be an experimental laboratory in which experience useful to all the states would be accumulated and brought to
their attention.

It is in connection with this original function that its chief potential for the kind of service we are discussing is to be found. Through its technical committees on operating problems, the conference provides a definite, formally organized medium through which state and local problems and interests can be brought forcefully to the attention of federal administrators, a service the importance of which has been emphasized throughout our discussion. For the horizons of an integrated employment and manpower program need to be widened, not only with respect to the requirements of national affairs, but with respect to those of its adaptability to local circumstances. The record of recommendations made by this conference's technical committees over the years reveals a number of valuable contributions of this nature. Since the work performed at the local community level, moreover, is the closest we have come to an integrated employment and manpower program, much could also be learned from experience of this group as to the kind of co-ordination at the national level which will support and strengthen that at the local level.

Insofar as our present interest in progress toward an integrated but comprehensive positive labor market policy and program is concerned, however, the conference has made understandably limited contributions. The limitation resides partly in the fact that the subject has not had the urgency formerly that it is coming to have today, partly in the fact that there have been very real and numerous administrative and operating problems to which their attention was quite properly directed. An even more important reason, however, is that a major concern has been to protect the rights and interests of the states, and that these rights and interests have been predominantly oriented toward Unemployment Insurance. Since we are in no way officially connected with the Department of Labor or the Bureau of Employment Security, we may perhaps be permitted an "outsider's" privilege to observe that the additional legislative and pressure-group-oriented activities of the conference have contributed more to the state and local freedom of action with respect to the operation of Unemployment Insurance and Employment Service than to progress toward a well-integrated and co-ordinated operation of all the Employment and Manpower Services on a country-wide basis.

The Federal Advisory Council, a statutory body, has also made very limited contributions to this latter objective. That is probably to be expected, since it was not the basic problem on which their advice was sought. The mandate given them in the Wagner-Peyser Act is broad enough to cover such an issue, however. The agenda for and reports from their meetings indicate many recommendations with respect to the Employment Service and Unemployment Insurance, considered primarily as separate operations. The focus of concern has been mostly on what might be called operational and organizational policy with respect to the specific services rather than on basic policy with respect to the co-ordinated relation of these two aspects of the Employment and Manpower Services with all others, and with the more general economic policies formulated and implemented by agencies other than the Bureau of Economic Security.

There is no reason, of course, why the experience and intelligence of these competent representatives of labor, management, and the public on the Federal Advisory Council and that of the state administrators organized in the Interstate Conference should not be focused upon this latter type of issue.

STRENGTHENING INDIRECT CONTROLS

There are always possibilities for strengthening the usefulness, and hence the persuasiveness, of the indirect controls exercised by federal authorities in relation to the states. A growing proficiency in the exercise of these indirect controls is important, for the same sort of methods will have to provide opportunity for persuading many subunits to engage in an internally consistent and well-co-ordinated labor market program, whether the staff and agencies involved are all federal or part federal and part state and local.

Examples of such efforts to strengthen the indirect influence of the federal agencies are as follows: more specific indication of which policies are "musts" (rather than merely recommended) as criteria for the receipt of federal funds, and improved reporting providing a basis for ascertaining whether these criteria have been met; the broadening and continued improvement of federal technical and staff assistance to state and local administrators; the greater systemization and specification of research and forecasting results so that they are operationally meaningful and useful at all levels, from federal to local; these are all examples of such moves.

Of particular importance, partly because they relate in our judgment to the weakest link in the whole roster of federal-state relations, are the standards and procedures for evaluation. It is not merely that the effectiveness of controls is no greater than the adequacy and preciseness of evaluation standards and procedures, but that the process of evaluation provides an opportunity for guidance and for the discovery of ways in which all programs can be improved and better co-ordinated. In connection with our present interest in an integrated active labor market policy and program, evaluation needs to be made, not only of the way in which the operations of each type of service are performed, but of the way in which, and effectiveness with which, they are co-ordinated and woven together into a well-integrated attack on the total economic needs of the labor market and the labor force, and of the degree to which they are contributing to the solution of national labor market and labor force problems.

Closely related to the problems of evaluation is the problem of the formula on the basis of which allocations of funds to the states are made. This formula leads managers and administrators to place heavy emphasis on "building a record" with respect to those work-load results which can be quantatively measured, such as number of placements made. There is nothing wrong in itself with an emphasis on increasing the number of placements. But this aspect of the work of the services is not the whole, particularly in consideration of the concept of mission and operational field we have been discussing. Certainly the effectiveness of the total performance can not be measured by reference to this kind of result alone. Although the measurements are being refined by assigning different "time value" weights to work loads of varying difficulty, the fact still remains that much of the legitimate and valuable activity necessary to the carrying out of an employment and manpower program, particularly those which are designed to produce advantageous labor force and labor market conditions in the future beyond the closing date for annual reports, is not measurable or appraisable in such terms, which pertain at best to a limited area of the total operations. Moreover, there is something anomalous about allocating funds on the basis of last year's performance instead of on next year's probable needs and proposals for meeting them. And the performance of and requirements of staff and time and money for the major managerial task of continuous analysis of total labor market needs, the adaptation and development of the services to meet those needs, the participation with other agencies in a united attack on the problems, and the co-ordination and weaving together of all community and state and federal efforts at the local level, which produces the very foundation for an integrated labor market program, are not measured at all by such a formula.

This matter of evaluation and allocation formula is under intensive study in the Bureau of Employment Security at the present time. The concern needs to be broadened to all aspects of resource allocation for all the Employment and Manpower Services.

The power to evaluate is a large part of the power to guide, control, and integrate. Within the framework of the present federal-state relations a real potential for progress toward an effective labor market policy and program on a national scale lies in the improvement of the standards, and procedures for that evaluation.

Whether the administrator of the Employment and Manpower Services is an officer of the Department of Labor or the chief of an independent labor market board, his contribution to such progress can be effectively undergirded by the formulation and implementation of such evaluation standards and procedures. And the job will probably be most effectively done and contribute most if carried on by an agency independent of any one of the subdivisions of the several services.

SUMMARY

Progress toward integration of the Employment and Manpower Services and toward their operation and development in accord with an active and positive labor market policy and program need not await the federalization of those services. Indeed, there are problems connected with the latter move which raise a question as to its desirability at this time. These problems have to do with the lack of experience with a co-ordinated approach to the whole labor market problem at the federal level; with the multiple source of funds for operating different parts of the program; with the maintenance of adaptability in program; with the stimulus of initiative, enthusiasm, and of the utilization of know-how, at the local and state levels; and with the lack of consensus as to the appropriate mission and operational field for the Employment and Manpower Services.

Even within the framework of the present federal-state organization and administration there are a number of possibilities of moving closer to such an objective. Widening of the liaison interactions with other agencies, both those performing related employment and manpower tasks, and those concerned with other economic resources and processes, is one step. Focusing the attention of the Interstate Conference and the National Advisory Council on the issues of policy and integration of the services broader than the specific administrative and substantive problem which are their normal concern is another. A number of instruments for indirect controls possessed by the federal agencies can be strengthened. And, most important, the process of and standards for evaluation can become powerful means for developing state and local services which are consistent with and contributory to an over-all well-integrated national labor market policy and practice.

A POSITIVE
LABOR MARKET POLICY

Chapter Eleven The phrase and reality of "a positive labor market policy" is of recent origin as compared with the phrase and reality of "employment and manpower activities and agencies." When, in the several countries, particular and separate employment and manpower services are being introduced, there is widespread debate over the reasons for their adoption, and counterreasons against their adoption. These reasons are centered normally on the specific advantages or disadvantages these specific programs are expected to produce, and the specific costs related to their operations. Thereafter, the debate normally has to do with practical modifications to meet new problems faced by each of the varied individual activities, such as the employment service, including international recruitment and movement of labor, labor market research, unemployment and mobility benefits, vocational education and training, retraining for the unemployed, rehabilitation for the handicapped, development of new sources of manpower, selective efforts ,to increase job opportunities in the face of structural and seasonal changes in the economy in particular areas, allocation of public funds for construction, procurement, and other measures to prevent or alleviate unemployment, services to employers, etc. But the reasons pro and con for particular individual public services are not necessarily related to reasons for an over-all labor market policy, positive or otherwise.

It is only recently that the concept of the *co-ordination* and *integration* of all these services by reference to *a positive labor market policy* has become a subject of serious discussion. The situation, therefore, is that some few nations, e.g., Sweden and France, have found compelling reasons for an active attempt to develop a consistent policy and practice with respect to the integrating of all Employment and Manpower Services and Agencies. Other nations, e.g., the United States, have barely begun to think about the need for an over-all positive policy with respect to those services and agencies.

CHARACTERISTICS OF AN ACTIVE AND POSITIVE LABOR MARKET EFFORT

A nation which had provided for all the public activities named above would, of course, be considered to have the elements of a labor market program. But most industrial nations have provided for a large portion of these services, and certainly not all of them can be said to have an active and positive labor market policy. A positive labor market policy implies that, at the very heart of the nation's efforts to make more productive, effective, and just the operation of the economy and society, there is an agency or agencies which have the knowledge, the will, and the power to direct the dynamic development and the employment of the nation's manpower toward its maximum conribution to these ends and toward maximum self-realization in work for individuals involved. It implies that the administrators of those agencies are not just carrying out bureaucratic duties laid upon them to administer a set of partial programs having to do with the welfare of workers, developed to meet specific needs at particular places where, and at times when, that need becomes highly aggravated. It implies that they know why they are doing what they do, and understand the relevance of their tasks to over-all national and social goals. It implies that their operational decisions are based on stable premises and not on the shifting pressures and demands of time, circumstance, different groups, and individuals. It implies that they visualize the significant and critical place of manpower resources among the nation's total resources, and that they are concerned to analyze the nature, condition, needs, and quality of those manpower resources and the efficiency and effectiveness of their productive relationships with the other resources. It implies that they are alert to the opportunities and problems revealed by such analyses that can promote or retard the nation's economic and social health, and that they *take the initiative* in prescribing the measures that will turn these problems into opportunities for increased economic and social strength and growth. It implies that these administrators have created through their efforts so widespread a recognition of the significance and contribution of their role that their voice is heeded in the making of every major decision having to do with the structure and dynamics of the nation's economic life.

WHY AN ACTIVE AND POSITIVE POLICY?

What reasons can be advanced for the desirability, even the necessity, of this sort of positive labor market policy and practice?

First, that type of policy is required to *anticipate* and provide adaptation to the industrial and occupational changes taking place in the labor market. Among these, some of the most important are the decay of certain industries, the short-range and possible long-range effects of automation, the changing patterns of defense production, the market shifts accompanying national trade policy, and the imbalances in the volume and quality of manpower requirements likely to result from the decline of some, and the expansion of other, sectors of the economy.

Second, that type of policy is needed to bring into sharp focus and high visibility the impact of private employment and manpower decisions of workers and employers on the public interest in over-all economic stability and growth, and to stimulate their taking that public interest into account in their private decisions.

Third, no other kind of a policy, and practice consistent with it, will produce in the mind of Congressmen and legislators, public officials, pressure groups, workers, and employers an image of a dynamic, effective, well-organized, and useful set of services which will encourage their widespread use and support. That image is created largely by what the services do, not simply by the publicity they hand out.

Fourth, no simple performance by the services, as hewers of wood and drawers of water for other economic or social welfare projects, initiated by other private or public agencies, is consistent with the significance of manpower and labor market factors in economic life. Those who are charged with facilitating the development and employment of the nation's manpower resources can as legitimately be expected to provide active initiative, leadership, planning, and direction in that area as those charged with serving the public interest in the monetary, fiscal, investment, production, and trade areas.

Fifth, no other kind of policy and practice will enable the manpower resources and the operations of the labor market to be taken into full account when decisions are made and action is taken with respect to other economic problems, relevant, for example, to fiscal policy and the processes of the money, product, investment, and trade markets.

The interaction and reciprocal impact of the resources and processes involved in these areas and those in the labor market has been amply documented throughout this book. Particularly important are the following:

1. The selective application of labor market operations at particular times and places to avoid the consequences of the economy-wide impact of monetary and fiscal moves in places where their stimulating or braking effects are not required or desirable from the point of view of over-all economic stability.

2. The provision for development and transfer of manpower to take care of labor shortages without the necessity for the potentially inflationary effects of relying entirely upon wage differentials sufficient to counteract all the disutilities to workers of such development or movement.

3. The provision, through adequate labor market services, of experiences for people which reduce their fears handicapping the carrying through of productivity-stimulating technological improvement and economic-growth-promoting shifts in product, in production, and in trade arrangements, etc.

4. The bringing into the foreground of public, particularly legislative, consciousness of a positive approach to unemployed manpower resources more conducive to economic health and growth than the relief approach. For example, the transformation of underutilized to fully utilized manpower, the transformation of idle to active labor reserves, the transformation of redundant to available workers.

5. The making more flexible and responsive to need of the labor-mobility-and-movement "expansion joint" in the economy through market-wide clearance procedures, and the reduction of obstacles to free choice of movement to available jobs. To those who are inclined to think in terms of economic theory, this aspect of an active and positive labor market

policy and program may be characterized as restoring to the labor market, by government action, the approximation to 'perfection' assumed in laissez-faire political economy, but made unattainable because of the inequalities in the possession of knowledge, opportunity, and financial resources produced by the operation of a laissez-faire economy.

6. Finally, such an active labor market policy is essential in order to provide society with a sound economic foundation for the achievement of a just and satisfying life by its individual members and for the building of institutions and values compatible with the development and survival of a free society.

SOCIAL WELFARE BASED ON ECONOMIC HEALTH

We have stressed, throughout, the importance of an active and positive labor market policy and practice to the development of a healthy and growing economy. In concluding this set of reasons, it is well to remind ourselves again that there is no basic conflict between such an objective and the goal of achieving individual and social well-being in all aspects of living. On the contrary, the contributions of an active and positive labor market policy to such a welfare-goal achievement are significant and basic. But the contributions legitimately expected of a labor market policy are derived from, and follow from, the economic results of such a policy and its implementation. Those results by no means provide all of the economic foundations on which the good life is built. But it is the objective of the implementers of an active and positive labor market policy that the economic results of their effort shall be so woven together with the results of economic effort in other areas, private and public, local and national, that those foundations are secure, and that on those foundations individuals through their own efforts and initiative can maximize their own welfare.

Labor market services are economic services. They increase the economic opportunities of individuals by preparing them for work, counseling them, and aiding them in locating the work in which they can make their maximum productive contribution and have the satisfaction of using their highest productive capacities and skills. They increase the knowledge of economic facts and trends so that employment choices made by workers and employers, and manpower development choices made by private and public agencies, institutions, and individuals are more likely to lead to full employment at the most productive and satisfying work now and in the future. They contribute in many ways, and can contribute more, in particular localities and for particular employers, to stabilizing and expanding the industrial operations from which employment opportunities arise. They provide the public administrative mechanism through which the labor force required by a changing and growing economy can be developed quantitatively and qualitatively, and be made available at the time and place it is needed. They provide those economic benefits which reduce the obstacles to the movement of workers to those occupational, industrial, and geographical areas where employment opportunities are available. They provide those economic benefits between periods of employment and during preparation for new employment, which not only help solve the maintenance problems of unemployed workers but provide a degree of protection against the deterioration of their skills and morale essential to a continuation of their most productive work.

In a world in which work in gainful employment and the rewards therefrom are such dominant building stones in the foundation for all of living, the Employment and Manpower Services, by striving to increase the effectiveness of labor force development and the employment process in the labor market, amplify the chances for the welfare of individuals in all aspects of living.

Such a contribution to individual welfare results from the operation of each separate one of the Employment and Manpower Services we have discussed. But it is amplified when these separate services are woven together in an integrated service in which each is supported by the others and the whole effort is directed toward a well-defined mission by reference to which not only their co-ordinated operation, but their co-ordinated development, can be charted. And when the operations and development are vitalized by an active and positive labor market policy which clarifies the roles and stimulates the activation of the Employment and Manpower Service *as an integral reciprocal part of the totality of public economic efforts in all markets*, their contribution is still more amplified.

SERVICE TO A FREE SOCIETY

In the presentation of the need for, the problems of, and the benefits from an active and positive labor market policy and program, we have understandably focused our attention primarily upon the impact of that policy and program upon the actors in our economic system and upon the health of the system itself. There are reasons enough for developing and maintaining such a policy and program when it is viewed from that point of view alone.

The significance to our free society of that effort would be incompletely presented, however, if we did not recognize the key role which the free movement of labor in the labor market has played, and can continue to play in the creation and survival of that free society.

In promoting and making more possible and probable the opportunity for freedom of movement in work, the Employment and Manpower Services satisfy more than the economic interests of the nation and the aspirations for economic and social well-being of millions of its individual people. The results which flow from that basic freedom have a mighty impact on the kinds of noneconomic institutions we have, on the psychology and habits of individuals, and even on the development or decay of the central values that individuals in our culture seek to realize through those institutions.

Consider, for example, the contribution of free choice of movement by workers to the development of the typical familial, political, religious, educational, and other institutions characterizing Western society. Had these institutions developed to satisfy the life needs of a working population whose movement was severely controlled, had their particular forms not been subject to acceptance or rejection, and to critical and creative efforts of men and women whose opportunity for place and type of livelihood was subject to individual choice, the support provided by these institutions for the general freedoms of the individual would have been far less vital.

Faith in and reliance on the individual, so central to the development of our economic, social, and political life, could not have outlived its brave declaration unless individuals could choose, to a high degree, as employees and employers, those with whom they would associate themselves in work. Whatever may be true of the few who inherit a superior social and economic status, the achievement of an increasingly satisfactory status by the many through their own efforts is geared to the freedom with which they choose the place for and type of "making a living."

Had the Marxists given appropriate attention to the human initiative, inventiveness, and adaptive skill unleashed by the freedom of movement of workers, they would have been less confident of the "internal decay" of a bourgeois business civilization. Had they taken due account of the normal reaction of individuals to an economic system which promised them an individual status toward which they could move by making free choices as to how and where they would make a living, the Marxists would not have been so puzzled by the "dumbness" of workers who resist placing their complete confidence in the "class struggle."

In the final analysis, it is probably the preservation and amplification of this freedom, so clearly influenced by the effectiveness or ineffectiveness of the public Employment and Manpower Services, and so basic to all our other freedoms, which not only justifies, but makes imperative, that those services be guided by an active and positive labor market policy and program.

INDEX

Index

About the Author

E. WIGHT BAKKE, Sterling Professor of Economics and Director of the Labor and Management Center, Yale University, received his B.A. degree from Northwestern University and Ph.D. degree from Yale. He brings to the writing of this book thirty-three years of observation of, and participation in, the development of employment and manpower services in the United States and Europe. Dr. Bakke began his research career in 1931 with his ground-breaking study of unemployment insurance and the employment exchange system in Great Britain. He has been the author of a number of books on unemployment, the labor market, and industrial relations subjects.

This book is set in Baskerville, a face designed and cut by John Baskerville of Worcestershire, England, about 1750. Although not in general use until the 1920's, this extremely graceful and highly legible face today enjoys a deserved popularity. The body type is complemented by the use of Square Gothic for the chapter titles and the headings in the front and end matter.

DATE DUE